·S·E·E·K·

ALSO BY DENIS JOHNSON

Fiction:

The Name of the World
Already Dead
Jesus' Son
Resuscitation of a Hanged Man
Fiskadoro
The Stars at Noon
Angels

Poetry:

*The Throne of the Third Heaven of the Nations Millennium
    General Assembly*
The Veil
The Incognito Lounge
Inner Weather
The Man Among the Seals

·S·E·E·K·

REPORTS FROM THE EDGES OF
AMERICA & BEYOND

DENIS JOHNSON

HarperCollins*Publishers*

HarperCollins books may be purchased for educational, business, or sales promotional use. For information, please write: Special Markets Department, HarperCollins Publishers Inc., 10 East 53rd Street, New York, NY 10022.

The author thanks the National Millennium Survey collection of the College of Santa Fe for permission to reprint "Hippies."

The excerpt on page 31 is reproduced courtesy of *Omni* magazine, Vol. 16, Issue 1, "Finding God in the Three-Pound Universe: The Neuroscience of Transcendence."

FIRST EDITION

Designed by The Book Design Group / Matt Perry Ratto

Library of Congress Cataloging-in-Publication Data is available upon request.

ISBN 0-06-018736-0

00 01 02 03 04 ❖/RRD 10 9 8 7 6 5 4 3 2 1

While editing these pieces, it's been brought home to me how enormously indebted I am to Will Blythe, begetter and editor of several of them; and to my wife, Cindy Lee Johnson.

This volume I dedicate, with thanks, to Cindy and Will.

CONTENTS

The Civil War in Hell   1

Hippies   17

Down Hard Six Times   37

Bikers for Jesus   53

Three Deserts   75
—Hospitality and Revenge   77
—Distance, Light, and Dreams   85
—Dispatch from World War III   94

The Militia in Me   101

Run, Rudolph, Run   119

The Lowest Bar in Montana   135

An Anarchist's Guide to Somalia   143

Jungle Bells, Jungle Bells   171

The Small Boys' Unit   179

·S·E·E·K·

THE CIVIL WAR IN HELL

It's late September and the Liberian civil war has been stalled, at its very climax, for nearly three weeks. The various factions simmer under heavy West African clouds. Charles Taylor and his rebels are over here; they control most of the country and the northern part of the capital, Monrovia—the part where the radio station is, and many nights Taylor harangues his corner of the universe with speeches about who he's killed and who he's going to kill, expectorating figures with a casual generosity that gets him known as a liar, referring to himself as "the President of this nation" and to his archrival as "the late Prince Johnson." Meanwhile Prince Johnson, very much alive, holds most of the capital. Johnson's titles are Field Marshal, Brigadier General, and Acting President of Liberia; "Prince" is just his name. Johnson's men eliminated the president two weeks ago, and they've been roaming the city ever since, exterminating the dead president's soldiers, piling their bodies on the streets—as many as two hundred one night—or scattering them along the beaches. *They*, the president's decimated Armed Forces of Liberia, occupy a no-man's-land between Taylor's and Johnson's checkpoints, more or less in the middle of the city, a gutted landscape of unrelieved starvation where the dwindling group robs and loots and burns and the skeletal citizens wander, dying of cholera and hunger. In Johnson's sector are stationed about a thousand troops from the ECOWAS—Economic Community of West African States—a sixteen-nation group that has sent this peacekeeping force to Monrovia with instructions, basically, not to do anything. The ECOWAS forces enjoy a strange alliance with Prince Johnson. Everybody thought they'd arrest him; instead the ECOWAS troops stood by while Johnson's men shot and kidnapped the president, Samuel K. Doe, the first time he set foot outside the executive mansion after several weeks of lying low, and they ducked for cover while Johnson's rebels searched out and killed sixty-four of Doe's bodyguards, hunting from room to room of the ECOWAS headquarters. Meanwhile, two U.S. ships wait offshore with a force of Marines, exasperating everyone by merely *floating* and *floating* while the corpses mount . . . because nobody wants either of the rebels to rule the land, and the only people capable of installing an interim government of reasonable types are the American Marines, for two reasons absurdly obvious to all Liberians: first, because they're Americans, and second, because they're *Marines*. Liberians don't want another coup like the one in 1980, when Samuel K. Doe, then an army officer, took over and executed the cabinet before TV cameras on the beach. The firing squad was drunk and was obliged, in some cases, to reload and shoot again from closer range.

Doe was of the Krahn, the most rural and deprived of Liberia's tribes, looked down on as uncivilized and often accused of savagery and cannibalism. Suddenly the Krahn were running the place. Doe ruled in a way generally agreed to have been both stupid and cruel. He lasted ten years. Halfway along, Doe weathered a coup attempt. General Quiwonkpa, its leader, was divided into pieces and the pieces were paraded around town, and then, in order to assume the strength of this bold pretender and in front of reliable witnesses, Doe's men ate him. Now, five years later, Doe has fallen at the hands of Prince Johnson. According to Johnson, Doe "died of his wounds."

The first American settlers arrived in Liberia in the 1820s, sponsored by the American Colonization Society, which was founded by

President Washington's nephew Bushrod Washington. They were freed American slaves returning to the continent of their origins. In 1847 they founded an independent nation and began more or less legitimately governing the Gio and the Mano and the Krahn. The Americo-Liberians, as the colonists' descendants were called, held sway until 1980 and Doe. As most Liberians see it, their history is wedded to America's. The U.S. enjoys an almost mystical veneration in the region. Liberians don't know that most Americans couldn't guess on which of the seven continents they actually reside, that images of their war have rarely been shown on U.S. television, that their troubles have scarcely been mentioned on U.S. radio. They can't understand why the Americans won't send in troops, or call for an interim government, or offer to host peace talks. They don't understand that among Americans they have no constituency, that even among black congressmen they have few advocates. They don't know why the Americans are making them wait.

West Africa is the land where God came to learn to wait. And then wait a little longer. The Nigerian freighter *River Oli* has waited eight days now to leave the port of Freetown in Sierra Leone, waited to bring five hundred ECOWAS troops and two hundred tons of rice and canned food to Monrovia. Waited for the rice to come. For the fuel to be found for the ship. For the decision to be made as to who would pay for the fuel. For the slings to be located with which to load the rice. For the man to be found, the man who had the key to the room where the slings were kept. For the decision to be made whether or not to break down the door because the man who had the key couldn't seem to find it. For the door to be forced. For the rice to be loaded. For the soldiers to get on board. For the judgment to be reached that everything was at last in order. For the several prostitutes and two Freetown policewomen to disembark with fond reluctance in the early hours, straightening their wide black belts. The *River Oli* leaves twelve days after its scheduled day of departure, eight and a half days after its sworn and emphatically ordered day of departure, four days after there's anybody left in West Africa who actually believes in its departure. The Ghanaian troops aboard sing *Abool-ya, abool-ya*—"loaf of bread"—as night falls and the moon rises and the schools of flying fish scatter like buckshot before the bow.

The freighter takes two days to land at Freeport, Monrovia's waterfront. For his own reasons and against the advice of his mates, the captain chooses to dismiss the port's pilot. He's going to dock the vessel himself. He plows it into the pier, gouging a wedge many yards deep and causing a forty-foot concrete span to buckle as if it were a drawbridge.

Smoke rises out of the town's scorched buildings. From somewhere among them sporadic gunfire reaches the ears of the Ghanaian soldiers on deck, and with a single sound, like that of an anvil falling, five hundred Israeli G-3 rifles lock and load. The men descend the gangplank to their peace-keeping duties as the afternoon rain begins. The ECOWAS forces start unloading the two hundred tons of relief food.

It isn't nearly enough. Nobody knows how many are left in the city, but certainly it's upward of forty thousand people. For ten weeks Monrovia has been cut off from any source of supply. Gasoline runs between twelve and twenty dollars a gallon, U.S., but you can buy two gallons for eight cups of rice. In the detention centers the imprisoned Krahn—tribesmen of the dead president—have had nothing to eat for a month, and sometimes if one manages to cook up a bowl of broth another will knock it out of his hands in terrified spite. Women move up and down the streets holding comatose infants to their empty breasts. "It makes you weep," a Ghanaian military doctor confides. "Sometimes I cry," the ECOWAS press officer agrees. Their cheeks scored with ritual scars, they don't look like men given easily to soft sentiment. A Monrovian who's just seen Prince Johnson drive by says, "I was the closest to him. He pointed. We couldn't hear what he says. But we know he has love and compassion for us." The man hasn't eaten for eight days himself. "If I try to walk my eyes will turn around and I'll fall." People will eat anything, and here and there a figure pauses by the street, vomiting out something that didn't work as food. Cans of Pestall bug poison lie scattered in the gutter, hacked open, the contents swallowed down by ravenous Monrovians who couldn't read the labels.

The rebels began their campaign last December, coming in from exile through the Ivory Coast to the north and east. Johnson broke away from Taylor not long afterward, either as a result of disputes over strategy—according to Johnson—or because Taylor—so Taylor claims—sentenced Johnson to death for murdering his own men. In any event the guerrilla war meandered and muddled along southward through the rain toward the capital and was never really expected to arrive. But suddenly, at the end of June, they were here. Taylor's bunch shut down the airport. Johnson closed in from the other edge of town, seized the capital, and isolated the president in his mansion and most of the president's army in the space of a few blocks downtown. The ECOWAS troops arrived. The citizens began to leave. Most of the British diplomats went home. All of the French departed. A half dozen of the U.S. foreign service remained, and the Marines set up machine-gun positions around the embassy. The electricity went off in Monrovia. The water stopped running. The food ran out. The civil war turned nauseatingly murderous. An atmosphere of happy horror dominated the hours as Taylor's men, dressed in looted wedding gowns and shower caps, battled with the army for the mansion. The shower caps were for the rain. The wedding dresses were without explanation. Meanwhile, Johnson's troops, wearing red berets and women's hairpieces liberated from the wigmakers, raced through the streets in hot-wired Mercedes Benzes, spraying bullets. The people living around the British embassy grew bold enough to ask Johnson's rebels not to dump the corpses of their victims on the beach there because of the stink. The rebels said sure, okay. There are miles of beaches in Liberia.

Even the Lebanese were getting out, hoping to get back to Beirut. Most of the refugees left on foot, moving out of the capital into Taylor's territory and marching west along Liberia's finest highway toward Sierra Leone, streaming along like a crowd after a football match. In general this is a five-day hike over fairly level terrain, but it was fraught with difficulty because Taylor's rebels—boys from the Gio and Mano tribes, most of them between the ages of eleven and fifteen, armed with AK-47s and M-16s—had dedicated themselves to separating out and killing anyone from the Krahn or Mandingo tribes, also those from the president's army or the former government. Thirty-eight miles out, in the town of Klay, refugees encountered the first checkpoint. "Do you smell that smell?" the rebels asked, speaking of the stench of putrefaction on the breeze. "You'd better know who you are," they said, "or you're going where that smell is coming from." Anybody who didn't speak the right dialect, anybody who looked too prosperous or well fed was shot, beheaded, or set on fire with fuel oil. Some of them were drowned in the Mano River. Refugees arrived in Sierra Leone telling of checkpoints fenced around with posts and the posts topped with severed heads. The voodoo rumors began: Taylor's men were invulnerable to bullets, they shot each other just to scratch each other's backs; before each battle Taylor's men slaughtered a young woman and drank her blood and ate her heart; Taylor's men could turn into snakes and elephants, could stretch or shrink their arms and legs at will, could make themselves invisible. The raping and slaughter of this conflict were no more awful than those of other civil wars, but a certain sickly inference seemed to draw itself out of them: Insofar as they were attached by the threads of superstition to the exercise of certain dark powers, these atrocities became inscrutable.

And now, on September 28, the rice and the canned goods, the reinforcements and the ammunition, also a few tons of cooking oil and a handful of European journalists, have arrived on the *River Oli*. The new folks can scarcely take in what they're seeing of Monrovia. Nothing works, nothing is for sale, everything's falling down, it's over for this place. The main street, U.N. Drive, lies ankle-deep in water and trash. Throngs mill up and down it destroying walls and fences and searching through buildings voraciously, but there's nothing left to loot. The ECOWAS soldiers fire continually in the air above the crowds, driving them back from the waterfront. DOE— MOTHER PUSSY, the graffiti reads, ESCAPE/WE WANT RICE and GOD SAVE

LIBERIA and PEACE NO WAR. No surface is without its share of bullet holes. The drive is lined with burned structures and littered with twisted wrecks. A jackknifed semitruck blocks two of the four lanes crosswise, a streetlamp from the median crushed under it like a frond. The car dealerships' huge windows open jaggedly onto empty showrooms where families camp now, keeping out of the rain. Surprisingly, the dogs look healthy. Nobody eats the dogs, the journalists learn, because they feed on human corpses. The people are starving, but the dogs have put on weight.

The safest area to sleep in is Mamba Point, the district with the embassies. Johnson's men prowl the streets there, and the sound of gunfire is more or less constant, but a jujuesque sort of diplomatic immunity seems to pervade for a couple of square blocks, and people like to believe they're protected here. Nevertheless, the rattling of weaponry sounds too close too often—and yet it's impossible to say from *where* this gunfire is coming. Noncombatants ply between the buildings cautiously: Am I walking in a fatal direction? What's the weather like ahead? The beach down the hill still stinks of death, though most of the corpses have been covered with sand and marked with driftwood. There's a little bit of commerce, perhaps, with the British and American embassies, which get supplies by helicopter. Everybody's hungry in Mamba Point, but nobody's dead yet from starvation. The wet season is passing; still it rains enough to keep the barrels half full.

Field Marshal Prince Johnson—Brigadier General, Acting President of Liberia, and Commander in Chief of the Independent National Patriotic Front of Liberia (INPFL)—wages, as part of his revolutionary struggle, a haphazard, sometimes enigmatic public relations campaign. In late August he entertained ten Nigerian newsmen brought in by ECOWAS, taking them around his sector of Monrovia on a forty-five-minute tour during which he shot into a car containing a European couple, killing the man and wounding the wife, who was dragged off by Johnson's soldiers and has not been heard from since; he also executed a looter by firing his side arm point-blank into the person's face. Today, September 29, Prince

Johnson takes the step of actually bringing reporters to his head-quarters, inviting a couple of American journalists and a French TV crew, recent passengers on the *River Oli.*

The Field Marshal's base lies on the capital's outskirts in the res-idential compound of the Bong Iron Ore Mining Company: down U.N. Drive past Freeport; past the BMW dealership, now housing an ECOWAS platoon; past the Liberian Nail Factory and the Faith Healing Temple of Jesus Christ and Liberian Marble and Terrazzo Tile, Incorporated—all smashed, burned, looted, with some of Johnson's rebels on a second-story balcony tossing bottles of Star Beer down on the pavement below; past alternating ECOWAS and INPFL checkpoints, where Ghanaian troops inspect the vehicles, or Johnson's boys, brunette or blond or redheaded, peer out from behind their artificial bangs and stick the barrels of their rifles inside the cars; down a dirt lane and through the Caldwell Coffee Farm and past the one-room New Life Mission Church and School. Then the dozen or so buildings of the Bong Mining compound begin. The hub of Johnson's operation is a concrete hospitality building surrounded by gunnery teams, aimless troops, tents, and cars. The structure, no larger than the average American home, seems to float on a sea of vehicles, mostly Mercedes sedans with their hoods raised. From out over the fields comes the crack of gunfire—it's said that the INPFL executes several Liberians every day—and, from the building, the muffled whomp of amplified music.

Inside, Field Marshal Johnson holds one of his morning concerts. The large main room is full of troops wearing red berets, and in the center of the throng stands Prince Johnson, gripping an acoustic gui-tar and singing "Rivers of Babylon" a Creole-reggae version of Psalm 137. He's backed by other guerrillas on conga, two electric guitars, and a rinky-dink electric organ. They're good. They could easily make a living in some Los Angeles nightclub. *And there we wept,* Johnson sings, *when we remembered Zion.* The crowd encir-cling him sways and claps the rhythm, chorusing in five-part har-mony, their AKs swinging and the gas masks bouncing on their thighs and their bandoliers winking under the strong lights of

Johnson's own video crew, which is filming this occasion. Johnson doesn't stop when the visitors enter, but he smiles and nods vigorously and shuffles like Michael Jackson and goes down on one knee like Elvis Presley; the troops roar. He's a fair-sized man, about six feet tall, well built, with an incongruously high tenor voice and a shouting-blues singing style. His cap isn't red; it's camouflage, like his fatigues. On his breast he bears a Distinguished Service Cross, a scorpion cast in silver, and a green-and-gold sheriff's badge. He tickles the troops with another quick step. He wears yellow, high-topped, lizard-skin shoes.

The camp runs on generators and the room is air-conditioned, but it's hot with bodies and muggy with the sweat of partying teenage warriors. The field marshal mops his face as he moves behind his massive wooden desk. The musical instruments are pushed back to make room for folding chairs. The two American journalists sit together across the desk from Johnson. He's got a large gavel, but he doesn't use it; instead, a young press officer invites them to proceed, and there begins an interview, or press conference, that really, at first, differs in no way from the usual kind. Johnson seems to have the answers prepared to a number of questions regarding his views, goals, and conduct. Replying to those for which he's not prepared, he affects coyness: "That story remains to be told," or "There we cannot comment." When he answers at length, he tends to lapse into Creole. When pressed on a point, he seems to feel he's not being understood; he provides more and more elaborate and elementary explanations—he explains the difference between war and cease-fire, between soldiers and politicians, between an acting president and an elected one. Uniformed women circulate with white wire baskets full of twelve-ounce cans of Budweiser; Prince Johnson dips his cigar in one of the numerous ashtrays advertising Kool cigarettes. Behind him on the wall hang two portraits of Jesus and one small pen-and-ink drawing of Yasir Arafat. In the middle of the room stands a two-foot-tall wooden lion on which people have parked a couple of wads of pink chewing gum. He's offended when his guests ask where the beer comes

from. "You think we looted this? Would you ask George Bush where
he got the things in his office?" He gives each of the American journalists a T-shirt printed with the slogans WE WANT PRINCE FOR PEACE
and GLORY BE TO GOD ON HIGH PEACE UNTO LIBERIA and BRAVO INPFL.
"Charles Taylor kill my mother and my father. He kill my uncle, my
sister, and my daughter," he says, "but that's not the point. The point
of our difference is a difference in strategy. Taylor wants to wage a
war of nerves. I want to fight with bullets." He calls Charles Taylor
"immature." He says nobody's out for revenge, but the Krahn, the
president's tribe, "have to be pursued." He talks about the late president. "His body was lying in the Island Clinic for almost a month.
Just yesterday we had to bury him because he was smelling." The
body, he says, is buried "somewhere." He insists that Doe died of the
wounds he received during his capture. Doe was not executed. He
was merely interrogated. What did he ask Doe? Johnson's eyes show
a little confusion. "I asked him about the Liberian people's money. I
asked him so many things. Yes," he says, "I cut off his ears and made
him eat them."

The journalists believe they haven't heard him right. Made him
eat *what?*

"I have a videotape of this interrogation," Johnson says suddenly. "Would you like to see it?"

The folding chairs are repositioned just outside, on the patio,
where the TV is. Johnson's troops crowd in front of the set. The
Budweiser goes around again. For a few minutes Johnson stands
nearby, watching the videotape, beaming broadly, but then he's
called away to confer with Varney, his lifelong deputy.

On the screen, Samuel K. Doe, president of Liberia, sits on a floor
in his underpants, his shirt open, his hands tied behind his back, his
bleeding legs stretched out before him, bound tightly at the ankles.
He's been shot in the right knee, and his left thigh is badly gashed,
apparently by a second bullet. A flabby balding man, he blinks fran-
tically at the lights and the camera and the sweat running into his
eyes, and tries desperately and above all to *smile:* Yes, there's a war
on, a terrible misunderstanding, yes, we've been killing one another,

but let's try to find grounds now for *pleasantness*. He moves his head this way and that as his captors poke at him with rifles. "I have something to say," he keeps repeating. "Say it! Say it!" the crowd around him cries, but they don't let him say it, whatever it is.

"What have you done with the Liberian people's money?" It's Prince Johnson talking, and the camera pulls back to show him seated behind a table. Instead of medals, he now wears two grenades on his chest. He's got a Budweiser before him. "Where is it? Where's the money?" his followers cry.

"If you loosen my bonds," the president insists, blinking and smiling, "I can talk to you. I'm in pain, I'm in a lot of pain," he says.

They pour beer on his head and tear his shirt off. "What?" he keeps saying, trying to understand the questions, searching the faces around him, looking up, down, from side to side, "What? Excuse me. What?"

"I will kill you," Johnson tells him loudly. The boys yank the president around to face his captor. "I want to say something," Doe repeats. "If two men fight, and one wins—" He's shouted down by the crowd. "I plead—you see me," he says. "Please loosen me. You can tie my feet, but my hands swell up." He leans over and blows on his legs. He seems to be trying to cool his wounds.

"I might spare you, but don't fuck with me," Johnson tells him. Johnson wears a gold watch on his wrist. He fools with it while he glares at the president on the floor. A woman wipes Johnson's face with a cloth. Behind him, the pictures of Jesus, and the one of Arafat. This interrogation takes place, in fact, in the room where he's just conducted his press conference and his concert of reggae hymns. The president is stretched out on the floor where guitars and amplifiers now stand. On the screen, the field marshal pops another Bud.

"We are all one," Doe pleads. A boy puts a pistol against his head. Swirling voices accuse him of murder and corruption. "Let me tell you something," he gasps, "whatever happened was ordained by God." "Cut the man's ears off," Johnson orders, and two boys hold the screaming president while another saws his left ear off with a field knife and tosses it into his lap. "I say cut the man's ear!" Johnson says. Doe struggles wildly, howling, as they take off the second ear. The boy with the pistol rests his foot on the president's bowed neck.

Suddenly the power dies. The generators cease, the TV screen goes blank. The insects whir all over the compound, and then the throb of the generators masks the jungle sounds as they come on again. But the TV isn't working.

A man comes forward and fiddles with the wall socket and then with the extension cord. He calls another man, who repeats the process, and together they go off and come back with yet another cord. But nothing seems to help. The television is not working. It must be the wall socket. The journalists' driver is anxious to leave. "You can't stay here past one o'clock," he tells the journalists, "because then everybody's drunk and anything can happen." But the journalists want to stay.

A longer electric cord is found. Then various lamps and equipment have to be rearranged before a socket can be freed. After twenty minutes, the TV screen lights up.

At that very moment an adjutant appears and yanks the cassette from the video player. "Come out front," he orders.

Out front Field Marshal Johnson is addressing fifty or sixty of his troops. "You go rape," he cries, "I go kill you!" *Yes sir!* "You go loot, I go kill you!" *Yes sir!* "You go steal, I go kill you! You fuck, I go fuck you!" *Yes sir! Yes sir! Yes sir!* He grows unexpectedly eloquent, exhorting them to endure, to accept the task, "to be willing to risk life so that your name will be written in history. . . .

"Bye-bye," he says, and walks off abruptly, smiling. The concert resumes inside. *Oh, how I love Jesus,* the rebels sing, *because he first loved me . . .*

What, the journalists ask Johnson—leaning close to his ear as he strums and sings—what about the tape? Are we going to see the rest of the tape?

Now another press conference begins. Johnson sits at the same desk from behind which he interrogated President Doe. "We think it's not the time to show the remainder of the tape," he declares.

His press officer wants to know, "What are you going to say in your articles about the field marshal?" Delicately the journalists try to indicate that whatever they may say, it's going to look bad that the rest of the tape wasn't shown. There've been rumors that more of the president was missing than just his ears. "We didn't cut off his genitals," Johnson insists. "We didn't shoot him. I kept him in the bathroom tied up. He cried the whole night, calling my attention to loosen him. But he is a trained military man. Those tactics don't work with him. At three-thirty in the morning he died." And in fact it's already been confirmed by Max Hill, a doctor at the Island Clinic where the corpse was brought, that Doe died either of his leg wounds or of fright. He wasn't executed. "There's nothing more on the tape," the press officer insists. "Just a few more questions we asked him."

Still, the journalists say—still. We should see the whole thing.

Johnson rises, leaves the room. "We'll see the rest," the press officer announces.

The tape cuts quickly to a point several hours later in the interrogation. Doe is naked now except for a codpiece of wet rag, earless, still bound as before, sitting out by a river. He keeps losing consciousness, his head drooping forward onto his bloody chest. "If you loosen my bonds," he keeps saying, "if you loosen my bonds." "We can untie your elbows," an adjutant tells him, "but we won't untie your hands." At this point in the interrogation, Prince Johnson does not appear to be present.

"What did you do with the Liberian people's money?" they keep asking him. "I'm in pain, I'm in pain," the president replies. "What did you do to the economy?" they repeat.

"Please, wipe my face," he says, and a young rebel swipes at his face and neck with a cloth. The adjutant is outraged. "Why did you wipe him?" he asks. "I don't know," the boy says. "Why did you do it?" the adjutant says. "I'm sorry," the boy says. He seems helpless to call to mind the murders and depravity that have brought the president to such ruin. "What you wipe the man face for?" the adjutant demands. But the adjutant, too, seems to sense that this person, stripped of his heirs and his office and his clothes, relieved of his pride, and even of parts of his body, has been reduced to a nameless and innocent essence, and is no longer the criminal Samuel K. Doe. The president loses consciousness and they pour water over his head from a bucket and he wakes to plead again: "If you spare me, I'll tell you everything . . ."

By now it is well into the afternoon. Lunch is served in plastic bowls, which the journalists hold in their hands with a certain wariness.

That night there isn't any rain. The dry season is near. Soon the water will be gone and the situation will be truly desperate. It can only be a matter of days before ECOWAS moves against Charles Taylor. It's hard to predict Prince Johnson's fate, but if sanity returns to Liberia he can hardly be expected to survive unless he flees.

It's dark now, and there's no break in the racket of weaponry. A small cease-fire is over. In Mamba Point, the journalists stay out of the way of bullets in a flat without power or water, like every other flat, but well appointed, a luxury apartment abandoned by U.S. embassy staff. On their portable shortwaves the journalists listen to the world news services: Everywhere on earth the people are at war, or preparing for war, or trying to extricate themselves from war—civil war, tribal war, even, in the Middle East, at long last, World War III; border disputes, factional clashes, punitive strikes, holy campaigns; and these must be photographed, catalogued, monitored, brought to light, but there isn't space in the papers to tell about them all, not even half of them. Liberia doesn't get much radio time. Just the same, the journalists huddle at their small sets, hoping for news of this African war as if it came from some distant region and had some source other than themselves. The question is: Where is Liberia? Does anyone out there care?

HIPPIES

It felt like the International had one last trip left in it. Two shocks had blown and the frame was cracked and quite a bit of the electrical system had gone dark. This thing's from 1970 and it's been a while since it went on a ride. But you could feel that last trip coming. And Joey said these people he knew from Austin intended to pick him up in Long Beach on their way to the Rainbow Gathering in the national forest over in north-central Oregon. The Gathering of the Tribes it used to be called, tens of thousands of hippies in the woods, seven days of Peace and Love. Four hundred miles to over there where it is—a distance the International could surely make and even possibly manage to retrace back home. You could feel that one last trip coming.

Peace and Love! This tall skinny mean guy in Iowa City in the seventies had a poster on his wall of a peace sign, the upside-down Y symbolizing peace, which he'd altered with a Magic Marker into a lopsided swastika, and he'd added words so that the Peace-and-Love slogan beneath it read PEACE OF THE ACTION/LOVE OF MONEY. I never forgot it. . . . I who have had so much of peace and so much of love, I have never really believed in either one.

*   *   *

The Magical Mystery Message to see the Rainbow was coming from a
couple of directions, wasn't just coming from Joey and the teenage past.
All spring Mike O, a friend of mine from North Idaho, had been both-
ering me I should go. Mike O, a regular Mr. Natural: Barefoot Mike,
Underground Mike, one of the originals, close to sixty years old now;
his white hair hasn't been cut or combed since youth and his white
beard looks inhabited. How did we all get so old? Sitting around laughing at old people probably caused it.

How long since I'd seen Joey? We'd taken our first acid trip together,
Carter B and him and me and Bobby Z. Hadn't seen Carter in nearly
thirty years. Joey since—wow, since '74. That summer I was with
Miss X. Bobby Z and Joey came to see us on the second floor where
we lived in this place like a box of heat. They owed me a disruption—
Joey did anyway, because Bobby and I had invaded him two years
before, when he'd been living on the side of this mountain in
Hollywood and studying to be, or actually working as, some kind of
hairdresser. "What do you want?" I said when I answered the door.
"You're not gonna stay here." The place had only one room to sleep
in, and a kitchen the size of a bathroom, a bathroom the size of a clos-
et. There weren't any closets.

Miss X and I were always fighting. Every time a knock came on
the door we had to stop screaming and collect our wits.

"We're economizing on space," I said when I saw who it was this
time.

"Obviously," Bobby said.

Joey had his guitar case leaning up against him and his arm
draped around it like a little sibling. Miss X stood behind me breathing hard with the mascara streaking her cheeks, radiant with tears
and anger and her wet eyelashes like starbursts.

In short, three weeks or two weeks or one week later I made loud
vague accusations in a scene, basically the result of the August heat,
that ended with Bobby Z and Joey heading north for Minnesota,
taking Miss X.

I was stabbing through the window screen with a pair of scissors as they headed down the back stairs, and I didn't see Bobby again until he was sick on his deathbed five years ago in Virginia, and Joey never since.

It's funny, but Joey called me from Huntington Beach just last night—two years after this trip to the hippies I'm describing—just to say hello, partly, and partly because his band broke up and he's just started AA and begun a program of meds for his depression and needs a place to lay back, because he's homeless. He mentioned he'd heard from Carter B. Carter said he's got hepatitis C and thinks I probably have it, too, because he must have picked it up way back during the era we were sharing needles when we were kids. I feel all right. I don't feel sick. But it's funny. Thirty years go by, and the moves we made just keep bringing this old stuff rolling over us.

The International throws a tire down in the Tri-City area of Hanford, Washington. It's so hot on the tarmac I get confused in my head and forget to put the nuts back on when I change the flat, and the loose rim tears up the wheel a good bit before I figure out what's happening and pull over, and I have to roll the thing in front of me a half mile to a garage and get the whole business straightened out. But the truck still works when all is said and done. After I'm in the mountains I start getting glad I agreed to go. Our vehicles, our hamlets and commerce miniaturized in the shadow of these mountains . . . RU FREE—Minnesota plates on a VW bus in the one-street town of Mitchell not far from the beginning of the Ochoco National Forest. Five youngsters all around twenty years old and a dog, gassing up.

The eastern end of the Ochoco Forest seems quiet enough, a showcase for the public administration of nature, having narrow roads of unblemished blacktop with level campsites scattered sparsely alongside them. The Rainbow Gathering's website has provided a map leading out toward the wilder part of the mountain and down a dirt road toward a cloud of dust where hundreds of pickups and vans and tiny beat-up cars have parked at the direction of a bunch of wild-looking toothless young pirates with a hand-held radio under a plastic awning and a dirty illegible flag. Even down here, where people wait for the shuttle-vans that take them up the mountain to the gathering or where they shoulder their frame backpacks and start up the hill on foot, all dressed up in the ashes of their most beautiful clothes, in their long skirts and tie-dyed T-shirts, just like the hippies of thirty years ago, even down here there's a feeling of anarchy Third-World style, the pole and tarp lean-to, the people with shiny eyes, the lying around, the walking around, the sudden flaring madness, only this is celebratory and happy madness rather than angry or violent. The shuttle-van climbs up past further checkpoints where serious authoritative hippies make sure nobody's just driving up out of laziness to park all over the mountain and get in each other's way. Past the first camp—the A-Camp, the only place where alcohol is permitted, although this segregation has been accomplished voluntarily and nobody would think of enforcing it. Past other camps of teepees, dome tents, shacks of twigs and plastic tarp to where the WELCOME HOME sign stands at the head of the footpath. The path heads into the series of clearings and copses where a whole lot of hippies, nobody can accurately count how many, have come to celebrate themselves, mostly, right now, by walking around and around, up and down the trails, past the kitchens set up under homemade awnings and canvas roofs, food centers staffed by those who want to give to those who need to take. Mike O has instructed me to equip myself with a big enamelware cup, a spoon, and a sleeping bag—to come as a taker, and be confident I won't need more. No money changes hands here, at least that's the idea, everything is done by bartering. But I've brought a couple hundred dollars in my pocket because Joey and I might look for mushrooms and seek some sort of spiritual union together through exotic chemicals like in the old days, and I don't care what they say, I've never seen anybody trade dope for anything except sex or cash.

You hear wildly varying figures, eleven different guesses for everything— 4,000 feet elevation, 6,700 elevation, 8,000 elevation. Claims of anywhere from 10,000 to 50,000, as far as attendance. But let's say ten thousand or more hippies touring along the paths here in the American wilderness just as we did up and down Telegraph Ave. in

Berzerkely almost thirty years ago. Yes! They're still at it!—still moving and searching, still probing along the thoroughfares for quick friends and high times, weather-burned and dusty and gaunt, the older ones now in their fifties and a whole new batch in their teens and twenties, still with their backpacks, bare feet, tangled hair, their sophomoric philosophizing, their glittery eyes, their dogs named Bummer and Bandit and Roach and Kilo and Dark Star. And as they pass each other they say, "*Lov*ing you!"—*Lov*ing you! It serves for anything, greeting and parting and passing, like "aloha," and might burst from a person at any time as if driven by a case of Tourette's, apropos of absolutely jack. Everybody keeps saying it.

Scattered over about one square mile of Indian Prairie in the Ochoco National Forest we have the pole-and-awning kitchens and camps of various tribes and families and impromptu more or less hobo clans: Elvis Kitchen, 12-step Kitchen, Funky Granola, Avalon, Greenwich Village. The billboard map near the WELCOME entrance lists and vaguely locates the groups who wish to be located and who have notified someone among the oozing anarchic strata from the Elders down to the children as to where they'd be:

Aloha
Bear Fish
Bliss Rehydration Station
Brew Ha-ha
Cannabis confusion cafe
Carnivores cafe
Cybercamp
Faerie Camp
Eternal Book Assembly
Madam Frog's Dinkytown Teahouse
Northwest Tribe
Ohana Tribe
Ohmklahoma
Shama Lama Ding Dong
Rainbow Solar Bubble

Deaf Tribe

Jesus Kitchen

Ida No & Eye Don Kare

Free Family

Sacred Head Church

BC Tribe

Twelve Tribes [w/ Star of David]

Thank You Camp

Camp Discordia

. . . and the infamous "A-Camp," the only region whose temporary residents have agreed that among them alcohol shall be one of the chemicals of happiness.

> *Alcohol: Near the parking area there is a place called "A-Camp." Rainbow says "We love the alcoholic, but not the alcohol." Personalities change on alcohol (and hard drugs). Sometimes people can't control themselves as well. Therefore you are respectfully asked to leave the alcohol in A-Camp when you hike in to the main gathering space.*

—so says the Unoffical Rainbow Website. The whole region commandeered by the Rainbow tribes, as always without benefit of permits from the U.S. Forest Service, parking and all, covers about four square miles. The givers, the ones who hand out food and take care of things to the extent they're taken care of, the putters-up of portable toilets and showers and medical stations and crude signs like the directory and map or the small billboard illustrating how germs get from dogshit to flies to foodstuff and then to human fingers and mouths, along with advisos to interrupt this process by keeping your hands clean, these who make it all possible arrived and started erecting their camps a week or so before the general celebrants showed up, the takers, the bunch of us who just materialize and stash our stuff under a bush and hold out our blue enamelware cups for hot cereal offered every noon by, for instance, the orange-garbed

bald-headed Hare Krishnas, who ladle out three to four thousand
such lunches every day of the party.

Joey and I have planned to meet up at the camp of the Ohana
tribe, a nomad family of twenty or more who caravan around North
America living only in government-owned forests like the Ochoco. I
don't find Joey right off and have no real explanation for my presence among them, but the young teenagers who seem to make up the
most of the Ohana don't care where I put up my tent and don't seem
to hold it against me that I look like somebody from a TV news
team, olive shorts, khaki shirt, baseball hat, and jogging shoes. Hey.
Even socks. On the other hand nobody seems inclined to talk with
me, either. At a glance they see there's no sense asking me for reefer.
Ohana means something in Hawaiian, they tell me. Peace. Or Love.
They're not sure.

I've located Joey. He looks the same, only older, just as sad or perhaps more so, having lived thirty years longer now and found more
to be sad about.

Joey and I sit out front of my tent in the dirt while he tunes up.
He's played professionally for decades, and he doesn't do it just for
fun very often anymore. But just to oblige me . . . We sing a few of
the old ones while the teenage Ohanans get a fire going about six feet
away and start good-naturedly hassling whoever wanders past for
drugs.

It's the second of July and anybody's who's coming is probably
here. The woods aren't quiet. You can hear the general murmur of
thousands as in a large stadium, just a bit muted by the forest. The
sky turns red and the day dies and Joey has to put away his guitar
thanks to competition: Drums start up all around, they call from far
and near and not quite anywhere in the forest, they give a sense of
its deeps and distances and they sound like thoughts it's thinking.

We stumble through the night amongst them: the drums, the
drums, the drums. All through the forest, pockets of a hundred, two
hundred dancers gather around separate groups of ten or twenty
maniac percussionists with congas and bongos and tambourines and

every other kind of thing to whang on loudly, and the rhythm rises up from all directions into the darkness of space, until the galactic cluster at the center of Andromeda trembles. The yellow strobing light of bonfires and the shadows of the dancers on the smoke. Naked men with their penises bouncing and topless women shaking their beautiful breasts. Every so often when the mood gets them a cry goes up and a hundred voices rise in a collective howling that really just completely banishes gravity for a moment and dies away.

We hear it rained quite heavily two nights ago, but this night is all stars and stillness, the smoke of fires going straight up in the orange light, and the ground isn't particularly uncomfortable, but just the same camping out always feels wrong to me—to sleep outdoors feels desperate, broke, and lonely—brings back those nights under a billboard on Wilshire where Joey and Carter and I found a bush to hide us, panhandler punks moving up and down the West Coast drunk on wine and dreaming of somewhere else, brings back those nights in a bag in the hills above Telegraph Avenue when I literally—literally, because I tried—could not get arrested, couldn't land a vagrancy charge and a bed and a roof and three meals of jail food. In my tent on the earth of the Ochoco Forest I don't sleep right. Neither does Joey. By next day noon we're already talking about finding a motel. The morning's too hot and the party's bumping off to a bad start, we keep running into many more people looking for dope than people who look stoned, and the Krishnas run out of gruel twenty minutes after they start serving. Joey and I join what they call the Circle, about a thousand people sitting in a pack on the ground—no standing up, please—getting fed with one ladleful each of spiceless veggie broth, courtesy, we believe, of the Rainbow Elders.

Once upon a time in the cataclysmic future, according to Rainbow lore, which filters down to us from the ancient Hopi and the Navajo through the cloudy intuitions of people who get high a lot, once upon a time in the future "when the earth is ravaged and the animals are dying," says the unofficial Rainbow Internet website, claiming to quote an Old Native American Prophecy, "a new tribe of people shall come unto the earth from many colors, classes, creeds, and who by their actions and deeds shall make the earth green again. They will be known as the warriors of the Rainbow." I see hardly any blacks, hardly any Indians from either continent, but it's astonishing to see so many youngsters on the cusp of twenty, as if perhaps some segment of the sixties population stopped growing up.

The Rainbow Family, consisting apparently of anybody who wants to be in it, not only have a myth but also have a creed, expressed succinctly way back when by Ralph Waldo Emerson in his essay "Self-Reliance": *Do Your Thing;* and with great reluctance they've allowed to evolve out of the cherished disorganization of these gatherings a sort of structure and an optional authority, that is, an unenforced authority, which defaults to the givers, the ones who actually make possible things like this gathering and many other smaller ones around the country every year since the first one in 1972; and the givers defer to the tribal Elders, whoever they are.

An online exchange of letters headed "God can be found in LSD" winds up urging that those participating in these experiments in spontaneous community-building only

- Be self-reliant
- Be respectful
- Keep the Peace
- Clean up after yourself

and that anything else going on is nobody's business unless someone's getting hurt. "In that event, our system of PeaceKeeping (we call it 'Shanti Senta,' not 'Security') kicks in, and the unsafe situation is dealt with." Speaking as a congenital skeptic, I have to admit that no such situation occurs all weekend, as far as I can learn. And nobody can tell me what Shanti Senta means, either.

I go walking in the woods with Mike O, who's spent the last few days under a tiny awning dispensing information about the Course in Miracles, a heretic sort of gnostic brand of Christian thinking that doesn't recognize the existence of evil and whose sacred text is mostly in iambic pentameter. He's a grizzled old guy, wiry and hairy, lives in the Idaho mountains in an underground house he dug out with a shovel, never wears shoes between April and October. He stops a time or two to smoke some grass out of a pipe, a couple of times also to share a toke with passersby, because Mike is a genuinely unselfish and benevolent hippie, and after that he has to stop once in a while and rest his butt on a log, because he's dizzy. We pass a gorgeous woman completely naked but covered with black mud. She's been rolling in a mudhole with her friends. I guess I'm staring because she says, "Like what you see?"

"In a day full of erotic visions, you're the most erotic vision of all," I tell her. To me it's a poem, but she just thinks I'm fucked.

Somehow these flower people sense I'm not quite there. They see me. And I think I see them back: In a four-square-mile swatch of the Ochoco Forest the misadventures of a whole generation continue. Here in this bunch of 10,000 to 50,000 people somehow unable to count themselves I see my generation epitomized: a Peter Pan generation nannied by matronly Wendys like Bill and Hillary Clinton, our politics a confusion of Red and Green beneath the black flag of Anarchy; cross-eyed and well-meaning, self-righteous, self-satisfied; close-minded, hypocritical, intolerant—*Lov*ing you!—*Sieg Heil!*

Joey and I have discovered that if we identify ourselves as medical people ferrying supplies, the Unofficals at the checkpoints let us pass and we don't have to bother with distant parking and the wait for one of the shuttle brigade of VW vans and such, and in the comfort of an automobile, Joey's pretty good Volvo, we can come and go as we please. Coming back up from a burger run in town, we pick up this guy hitching. He says he's staying in the A-Camp. "I'm not the big juice-head," he says, "but at least those folks understand I like cash American currency for what I'm selling."

"And what's for sale?"

"'shrooms. Twenty-five an eighth."

I don't ask an eighth of what, just—"How much to get the two of us high?"

"Oh, an eighth should do you real nice if you haven't been eating them as a steady thing and like built a tolerance. Twenty-five bucks will send you both around and back, guaranteed."

And this is why certain people shouldn't mess with these substances: "Better give me a hundred bucks' worth," I say.

It makes me sort of depressed to report that as we accomplish the exchange this man actually says, "Far out, dude."

We now possess this Baggie full of gnarled dried vegetation that definitely looks to be some sort of fungus. Back at my tent I dig out my canteen and prepare to split the stuff, whatever it is, with Joey while he finds his own canteen so we can wash it down quick. And here is why I can't permit myself even to try and coexist with these substances: I said I'd split it, but I only gave him about a quarter. Less than a quarter. Yeah. I never quite became a hippie. And I'll never stop being a junkie.

For a half hour or so we sat on the earth between our two tents and watched the folks go by. In a copse of trees just uphill from us the Ohana group had started a drum-circle and were slowly hypnotizing themselves with mad rhythm. Joey revealed he did, in fact, eat these things once in a while and probably had a tolerance. He wasn't sensing much effect.

"Oh," I said.

In a few minutes he said, "Yeah, I'm definitely not getting off."

I could only reply by saying, "Off."

I was sitting on the ground with my back against a tree. My limbs and torso had filled up with a molten psychedelic lead and I couldn't move. Objects became pimpled like cactuses. Ornately and methodically and intricately pimpled. Everything looked crafted, an inarticulate intention worked at every surface.

People walked by along the trail. Each carried a deeply private shameful secret, no, a joke they couldn't tell anyone, yes, their heads raged almost unbearably with consciousness and their souls carried their bodies along.

"Those are some serious drums."

Anything you say sounds like the understatement of the century.

But to get hyperbolic at all would be to hint dreadfully at the truth that no hyperbole whatsoever is possible—that is, it's hopelessly impossible to exaggerate the unprecedented impact of those drums. And the sinister, amused, helpless, defeated, worshipful, ecstatic, awed, snide, reeling, happy, criminal, resigned, insinuating tone of the message of those drums. Above all we don't wish to make the grave error of hinting at the truth of those drums and then, perhaps, give way to panic. Panic at the ultimateness—panic at the fact that in those drums, and with those drums, and before those drums, and above all *because* of those drums, the world is ending. *That* one is one we don't want to touch—the apocalypse all around us. These concepts are wound up inside the word "serious" like the rubber bands packed explosively inside a golf ball.

"Yeah, they sure are," Joey says.

Who? What? Oh, my God, he's talking about the drums! Very nearly acknowledging the unspeakable! He's a mischievous bastard and my best friend and the only other person in the universe.

*Lov*ing you!

According to the psychiatrists who have embarked together on a molecular exploration of what they like to call "the three-pound universe"—that is, the human brain—what's happening right now is all about serotonin — 5-hydroxytryptamine, or 5-HT for short, "the Mr. Big of neurotransmitters," the chemical that regulates the flow of information through the neural system.

I read this article in *Omni* called "The Neuroscience of Transcendence" that explains the whole thing. Having ingested the hallucinogen psilocybin, quite a bit more than my share, I've stimulated the serotonin receptors and disrupted the brain's delicate balancing act in cycling normal input messages from the exterior world— adding special effects.

At the same time, the messages outward to the motor cortex of the brain are disrupted by the same flood of sacred potent molecules, bombarding key serotonin receptors and sending signals *unprovoked by any external stimulus*. What's happening *in here* seems to come from *out there*. The subjective quality underlying all of experience at last reveals that it belongs to everything. The mind inside becomes the mind all around.

> *Serotonin and the hallucinogens that act as serotonin ago-*
> *nists—like LSD, mescaline, DMT, and psilocybin—also trav-*
> *el to the thalamus, a relay station for all sensory data heading*
> *for the cortex. There, conscious rationalizings, philosophiz-*
> *ings, and interpretations of imagery occur. The cortex of the*
> *brain now attaches meaning to the visions that bubble up*
> *from the limbic lobe—of burning bushes or feelings of float-*
> *ing union with nature. The flow of images is scripted and edit-*
> *ed into a whole new kind of show.*

EXACTLY!

YES! Bugs Bunny with a double-barreled twelve-gauge shoots you in the head with a miracle.

I watched helplessly as two beings encountered each other on the trail. Two figures really hard to credit with actuality. But they weren't hallucinatory, just very formally and exotically got up as if for some sort of ceremony, covered in black designs and ornamental silver. They greeted each other and transacted. It was brief and wordless with many secret gestures, the most sinister transaction I've ever witnessed, the most private, the most deeply none of my business. Initiates of the utterly inscrutable. My eyesight too geometrically patterned to allow them faces. They had myths instead of heads.

That is very definitely *it* for *me*. I crawl into my tent. It's four feet away but somehow a little bit farther off than the end of time. It's dark and closed and I'm safe from what's out there but not from what's in *here*—the impending cataclysm, the imploding immenseness, the jocular enormity.

It's been somewhere between twenty-five minutes and twenty-five thousand years since I ate the mushrooms, and already we have the results of this experiment. The question was, now that a quarter century has passed since my last such chemical experience, now that my soul is awake, and I've grown from a criminal hedonist into a citizen of life with a belief in eternity, will a psychedelic journey help me spiritually? And the answer is yes; I believe such is possible; thanks; now how do you turn this stuff off?

Because what if the world ends, and Jesus comes down in a cloud, and I'm wrapped in a lowgrade fireball all messed up on chemicals? Is the world ending? God looms outside the playroom. The revelation and the end of toys. The horrible possibility that *I might have to deal with something.*

And the drums, the drums, the drums. Fifty thousand journeys to the moon and back in every beat.

Four hours later I succeed in operating the zipper on my sleeping bag: tantamount to conquering Everest. I got in and held on.

Me and this sleeping bag! People we are going places now!

After several hours I crawled out into the universe and took up my rightful position in outer space, lodged against the surface of this planet. It wasn't raining rain, it was only raining starlight.

This musician friend of Joey's from Austin, this guy named Jimmy G, sits down beside me with a magic-mushroom guitar and serenades me with his compositions until almost dawn. He's about fifty maybe, white-haired, very skinny, with a variety of faint colors washing over him ceaselessly. It's incomprehensible to me that a genius of this caliber, whose rhymes say everything there is to say and whose tunes sound sweeter and sadder and wilder and happier and more melodic than any others in history, should just live in Austin like a person, writing his songs. Songs about getting our hearts right, loving each other, getting along in peace, sharing the wealth, caring for our mother planet.

By then, all over the world, the drums have stopped. Teenage Ohanans in the tent across the trail make tea on a campfire without uttering a word amongst them. Nobody talks anywhere in the Ochoco Forest; it's a time of meditation. Today is the Fourth of July, the focal hour of the Rainbow Family's gathering. Despite all the partying, this is *the day of the party.* The idea is to enter a silence at dawn and meditate till noon. Then get real happy.

Joey and I walk around watching folks start the day without talking. The strange silence broken only by two dogs barking and one naked man raving as if drunk, really raving, feinting and charging at people like a bull, stumbling right through the fire-pit down by the Bartering Circle.

Noon sharp, the howling starts. The wild keening of human hippies emulating wolves. Minutes later, the drums. In the big meadow where the Circle gathers for meals everybody jumps up dancing, some naked, some dressed in clothes, others wearing mud. The sun burns on them as the crowd becomes a mob the size of a football field. A guy pours Gatorade from a jug into people's upturned open mouths, another sprinkles the throng with a hose from a backpack full of water, like an exterminator's outfit—he's a sweatbuster. Higher and higher! I crash under a bush.

Just before sunset I wake up and get back among the Circle and encounter a definite palpable downturn in the vibes. There's not enough food and not enough drugs. The party has scattered among the various camps, the drum-circle that must have included a hundred or so wild percussionists mutters back and forth to itself from just a couple places hidden in the woods.

As the sunset reddens the west, black thunderheads form in the south: a lull, a dead spot, a return of the morning's silence as the Rainbow Family watches a squall gathering, bunching itself together in the southern half of an otherwise clear ceiling.

Then a rainbow drops down through the pale sky.

The sight of it, a perfect multicolored quarter-circle, calls up a round of howling from everywhere at once that grows and doesn't stop, and the drumming starts from every direction. Then it's a double rainbow, and then a triple, and the drums and howls can't be compared to anything I've ever heard, it's a Rainbow Sign from Above— *Lov*ing you!—then a monster light show with the thunderheads gone crimson in the opposing sunset, the three rainbows, and now forked lightning and profound, invincible thunder, every crooked white veiny bolt and giant peal answered by a wild ten-thousand-voiced ululation—a conversation with the Spirit of All at the Divine Fourth of July Show! Far fuckin out! The Great Mother-Father Spirit Goddess Dude is a hippie!

And this is why a certain type mustn't mess with magic potions: I'm thinking, all through this spectacle, that I should have saved a couple buttons for today, I should be *high* to *dig* this. Forgetting how I dug the starlight last night by zooming around somebody's immense black mind in my sleeping bag and almost never witnessing the sky.

But after the rainbows and the storm the night comes down and we get just a little flashback: I close my eyes and remember that first ride on White Owsley's acid, remember surfacing behind a steering wheel behind which I'd apparently been sitting for some hours, trying to figure out what to do with it; and there was Joey, and Carter B and Bobby Z, the four of us coming back to the barest fringes of Earth, a place we'd never afterward be able to take quite so seriously because we'd seen it obliterated, finding each other in this place now—none of us having ever taken acid before or even really talked to anybody about it, four teenage beatnik aspirants returned from an absurd odyssey for which none of us had been the slightest bit prepared and which we felt we'd just barely survived—remember watching Joey and Carter disappear into an apartment building and remember heading with Bobby, somehow *traveling* through streets like rivers behind this *steering wheel*—five hundred mikes of White Owsley's!—remember steering magnificently through Alexandria, Virginia, in a gigantic teacup that once had been a Chevrolet under streetlights with heads like glittering brittle dandelions, remember letting it park itself and remember floating into a building and down the halls of the Fort Ward Towers Apartments, down the complicated curvature of the halls, and finding, at the end of the palatial mazes, finding—Mom! Mom in her robe and slippers! Her curlers from Mars! Mom from another species! Mom who said It's five in the morning! I nearly called the police! WHERE have you BEEN and remember turning to Bobby Z, who's dead of AIDS, at his funeral I threw dirt onto his coffin while his sister, my old highschool sweetheart, keened and screamed, turned to Bobby Z and said, Where have we been?—and the question astonished and baffled and shocked him too, and we both said, Where have we been? WHERE HAVE WE BEEN?

Bobby them drums are riding themselves up to the very limit and right on through like it was nothing. Where where where have we been?

Where did we go?

DOWN HARD SIX TIMES

In July in the subarctic, night-flying presents no problem. The nights don't get dark. It's long past supper in Anchorage when prospector Richard Busk bolts two extra seats into his de Havilland Beaver airplane and loads up for a flight to his mining claims in the Bonanza Hills of south-central Alaska.

Busk is building a small house out there, so he's carrying lumber for the window headers, half-inch plywood for the walls, and a new tire for one of his all-terrain vehicles; also two absurd newlyweds out of North Idaho.

Not that his passengers are odd-looking: What makes them absurd is the fact that panning for gold in the Alaskan wilderness strikes them as a good idea for a honeymoon. Both have short brown hair, both wear blue jeans—Moon One and Moon Two. They've brought some gold-panning equipment—pans and picks and little tweezers—and even a gasoline-powered portable dredge (it weighs about ninety pounds; they'll find out it's not so portable) and intend, quite insanely, to return home from the Alaskan wilderness with gold from which to fashion their wedding rings.

*　　*　　*

The newlyweds haven't found Alaska so easy. Everything here seems to operate according to Murphy's Law. They've already seen more than a few cock-ups on this run. They've already had their jeep towed down from a mountaintop at the end of the Nabesna Road east of Anchorage, where they'd camped beside it for two days in the rain, worshipping its dead battery (Moon One had left the key turned in the ignition) before walking out. The new missus had written in her journal:

> *July 12: For two nights we've been stuck up on a mountain near an abandoned mine. I'm scared, nearly crying for fear. DJ left me to go for help. I wish I were home with my children. This is a very frightening place. I'm worried about avalanches.*

But things are looking up now. They've made it this far and left the turncoat car behind, and now they're in this plane with this prospector, heading north across Cook Inlet and along its green marshy shore for a dozen miles, then striking out west through a few smudges of low clouds toward, and apparently up against, but then, happily, *over* the Blockade Mountains, frothy with snow, white and blue with shadowy drifts at 9:30 P.M., a good three, almost four hours before the sunset.

As far as they can see—over a hundred miles at this altitude—there's nothing to witness but the peaks standing up amid the true and natural loneliness of the planet Earth. There's nothing happening here that hasn't been happening for eons—the rise and fall of mountains, the falling and melting of snow, the interminable downward migration of glaciers through arroyos. Nothing happening but the circling of the wind and the seasons and the waters, the lives of animals and plants, granite and lava and sand. And gold—the enormous, dirty-blue, intricately jagged ice fields slinking down through the valleys, grinding the gold out of the quartz, pumping the Tlikahila River full of runoff, full of *gold nuggets* and *gold dust* and *flakes of gold.* And it's happening all over—how many square miles of wilderness? Two hundred thousand? Five hundred thousand? A half-million square miles of gold!

There must be plenty of the stuff in the Bonanza Hills. It's just a question of continuing to fly along in this somewhat antiquated single-prop Beaver. Busk himself doesn't know how old the aircraft is, but he bought it more than five years ago in Ottawa, Canada. It's a bare-bones bush machine without any ornament except a squiggly Cree Indian inscription painted on the side. Busk hasn't yet found anybody to decipher it for him. The honeymooners think it's a rickety-looking crate, but they've been assured—by Richard Busk, as a matter of fact—that there's not one thing to worry about. The engine, a Pratt & Whitney radial, was rebuilt less than a year ago and hasn't flown more than a hundred hours since then—87.6 hours, to be exact. It's true—but not serious—that a little oil weeps through an O-ring onto the right-hand exhaust outlet, and this makes for a little stream of smoke out behind the cowling (which is patched with aluminum squares of three different colors: silver, red, and blue); although Moon One wonders if he isn't correct in remembering that it was in fact something along those lines—some sort of O-ring problem?—that caused the space-shuttle *Challenger* to blow up in the middle of the sky . . .

These two *cheechakos*—newcomers—have come here with the same dream as everybody else: of finding a welcome in this inhospitable terrain, of being blessed to prosper in this land that has mistreated so many people just like themselves—eaten them or starved them, abandoned them and frozen them, broken their bones and left them paralyzed a hundred miles from help, drowned them or buried them alive, attacked them and clawed them to death.

Originally they had planned to rendezvous here with a prospector friend of theirs from Montana, somebody who'd show them the way to the gold. But they couldn't find their friend anywhere in Anchorage, and were starting to feel as if maybe somewhere along the Alaska Highway they'd lost even Alaska itself. Maybe they'd mis-placed Alaska in the vicinity of Tok, a truckstop-like community they came to after crossing the border and traveling thirty miles of empty highway. Suddenly, in every direction, they saw things landing and taking off, crossing the horizon with supplies for some vast enterprise. The state bills itself as the "Last Frontier"—and certainly they'd got out past the shopping malls and beyond the grasp of fast-food chains, but they couldn't escape the clear sense that the nation's Last Frontier is being chewed up fast by the nation's Last Pioneers. The roaring eighteen-wheelers and hovering choppers and the propeller planes rising and descending sent out the rumble of commerce at a basic level—the two cheechakos felt the oil companies plundering the ground under their feet, and the backwoods outfitters sucking up the solitude around them and using wondrous inventions, especially the airplane, to shrink the wilderness to a journey of a few hops. The whole sunshot, continually daylit endeavor had a feeling of Vietnam to it.

But then, in Anchorage, where they searched the funky airstrips for somebody, anybody, to get them out to a gold claim, they found Richard Busk, hopeful proponent of a New America, leading member of the America First Party, dreamer of the Big Dream—the dream of gold, freedom, self-sufficiency. A man at a charter flying service told them about Busk— "a colorful character. He's famous."

And when they found him, Busk seemed in fact the ghost of the first American pioneer—tall and slim and slow, with a clear gaze and a busted-up face. In his pocket he had photos of himself standing next to a kill he'd made recently, with a single arrow, near his cabin in the Bonanza Hills: a big, dead creature sort of like an elephant, only with fur. "That's twelve hundred pounds of brown bear there," he said. "He stretched out ten feet wide from paw to paw." How do you kill something like that with one arrow? "I hit him in the lung and he ran a few hundred feet and went down. They bleed out quick," he said. He'd set up shop temporarily in a booth in an Anchorage restaurant frequented by Alaska oldtimers. This booth was over a hundred miles from his mining operation, but a lot of rural folks had come in from the hills this summer to campaign for presidential candidate and ex–Green-Beret hero Col. Bo Gritz. They hoped he'd lead them in forming a New America for people like themselves who live, as they described it, "on the cutting edge of freedom." They meant to do their best for Gritz, though generally they had no use for politicians or bureaucrats. Busk himself refuses to pay taxes on the money he makes.

Richard Busk was like nobody the honeymooners had ever met before, but instantly they trusted him, and they were overjoyed when he offered to spend two or three days showing them how to prospect in the Bonanza Hills. Even if some of his ideas sounded, okay, *extreme,* Busk himself tended to put a person at ease by his open and natural manner and his clear and candid speech. He seemed well-acquainted with just about everybody who wandered in. He'd been out here since the early seventies, and it stood to reason he'd be one of the region's familiar figures.

The summer sun has managed to bare the peaks and they stand up gray and black, in places slightly green with a little vegetable stubble. The little Beaver passes along with an illusory slowness between two ranges, carrying Richard Busk and his two cheechakos toward the Bonanza Hills.

At one point the engine with only 86.7 hours on it hacks and gurgles violently and then produces one half-second of breathtaking, cathedral-like silence before Busk manages to yank it back to life again. Then it starts making varied intermittent completely unidentifiable percussive noises, which come and go under the engine's general roar, submerging and popping up again, sort of in the manner of spooks on a haunted-house amusement ride, but much, much more alarming.

Busk had some trouble in this same Beaver about four years back, coming from Bristol Bay across the tundra country with a load of salmon. This very same engine, with only 170 hours on it after a rebuild, just kind of locked up inexplicably, and the propeller quit turning. What had happened was that the nose-ring had been put on cockeyed, and eventually, suddenly, finally—very finally—the whole assembly went bad. Putting the plane down in that region of unbroken flatness was easy; but Busk spent two weeks getting a new engine out to it and flying the thing back. These things happen once in a while.

As a matter of fact, the bush pilot who flew him out that time dumped his own plane on Busk's airstrip as they landed—came in at a forty-five degree sideways slant and corkscrewed across the runway. Once in a while your luck tends to run like that.

Now, for instance. Right now the famous Richard Busk tries to keep the engine's rpms steady, figuring any sudden change might stall it out, and he keeps his head against the right-hand window, looking for a decent place to dump this thing. There's nothing down there but the raging Tlikahila River, jagged glaciers, metallic-looking stretches of marsh, and hundreds of thousands of spruce sticking up like punjistakes.

Moon One has his notebook in his lap and scrawls, for anybody who might someday find it in seventy-five zillion empty acres of Alaska, perhaps in a grizzly bear's stomach: "Oil making sunburst pattern all over right windshield—gray smoke coming up out of the floor." Moon Two tries to catch his eye and he smiles, winks, shrugs. She seems relieved. He writes: "random clattering and thundering noises . . ." but can't write any more because it's too dark inside the plane: Black oil, spraying from the cowling, completely covers the windshield. Smoke streams out behind them through a quarter-mile of sky.

Meanwhile Busk whirls around in his seat and strains backward to get hold of a gallon jug of oil with one hand, holding the controls with the other. His pistol falls into Moon Two's lap, and she tries politely to hand it back, but he's busy dumping the gallon down a spout that juts up from the floor between the front seats. His face looks funny, and his lips move at the mike of his radio set, repeating two syllables that might be "faygay" or "payday" but probably must be "Mayday! Mayday! Mayday!"

It's raining as they execute a smoky forced landing in Port Alsworth, a community made up of a hangar and an airstrip and a few buildings on the edge of Lake Clark—seventy miles short of their destination in the Bonanza Hills.

The 'mooners doubt now they'll ever get there. Or anywhere else. Maybe they'll just stay here all their lives, maybe for all eternity, just standing like statues with the famous Richard Busk beside his Beaver looking at the oil fanning out behind the cowling and dripping down off the fuselage. Only a drop left on the dipstick's tip—Busk figures the engine had been losing about a quart per minute and would have seized up bad in another five or ten and they'd have had to dump down into a half-thawed marsh.

They eat fifteen-dollar cheeseburgers in the two-table café and spend that night in a hundred-dollar room—two bunkbeds, no bath, ten yards to the outhouse. They're all just glad to be breathing. Richard Busk sits on the edge of one of the lower bunks, wired from the recent ride. The honeymooners listen to him talk while the twilit midnight turns just a little bluer but fails to get dark.

"I've been down six times—down hard—and it does take it out of you. It puts stress on you," Richard tells them, in case they didn't know.

Moon One thinks: Wait a *minute*. Six times?

"Well, more than that, if you count the soft ones like this."

Glenn Alsworth, who despite his youthful appearance seems to own everything around here, including Lake Clark Air Service, whose airstrip they'd landed on, had greeted them after their miraculous arrival: "What's the famous Richard Busk up to now?"

They're not from around here and they have no idea that this guy is *the* Richard Busk—the *famous* Richard Busk. Not the famous prospector—the famous *pilot*. Famous for *crashing*.

—Famous for plunging downward repeatedly into this unforgiving landscape with its vengeful climate and its gigantic loneliness, famous for descending suddenly, inexplicably, and *always with a freshly rebuilt engine,* swiftly and silently out of the clouds; famous for banging across the ground delivering up landing gear, windshields, guy wires, stabilizers, other bits and pieces of flying machines, also, here and there, a few of his teeth. Apparently the same strange Power that keeps him alive through these scrapes has determined that Richard Busk doesn't belong in the sky, because he just keeps falling out of it.

This same Power has let the honeymooning cheechakos down pretty easy. They might have experienced something like the time Richard Busk, after sheep-hunting in the Wrangell Mountains, landed his Piper PA-12 on a glacier up at 5,700 feet, picked up his sheep, flew off the cliff, got up air speed, and headed out, only to have the engine quit. "But I was sure we had gas," he explains to the couple now in the undark Alaskan darkness. It turned out that at some point honeybees had come in through vents in the fuel system and clogged the lines. He'd sailed powerless through a twisting canyon and capsized the Piper in the boulder-strewn Nazena Creek. He crawled out and subsisted, he says, "on four raisins a day," until the day a chopper found him. He shakes his head. "These times put stress on you."

A few years ago he landed a plane upside down, after cartwheeling it hundreds of feet. He was trying to outrace a storm on his way to Port Moler, but a "burble" tripped him up in the middle of the air—a wind shear just suddenly flipped him over. Richard went through the windshield and left the plane in pieces behind him.

Heading out of King Salmon late one evening, into a twenty-five-knot wind with the day's last load of fish, in the first Beaver he'd owned, he suddenly found himself going for no possible reason *straight* up and had to get his nose down and land on the twilit beach full of boats and anchors and gear, executing a ninety-degree turn on landing—and managed to do it all, pulling up eight feet short of a thirty-foot embankment. He'd hit a rock on takeoff, is what he'd done, and destroyed his tail assembly.

All these rigs he's crash-landed have to be retrieved from their strange wilderness perches, from the tundra wastes, from sandbars and beaches and mountain peaks. There's the whole business of hauling them out of gullies or rivers or holes, turning them rightside up, banging them back together, turning a crash site into a runway in order to get them airborne again. One, after an unscheduled sea landing, had to be towed through the town of Naknek—down the main street between the phone poles and past the stores—to a pond and sunk there in order to wash off the corrosive salt water.

These cheechakos! They didn't know! This is the famous *Richard Busk*. He's the father of six boys and two girls, with another due next fall—"but," he admits, "I've had more plane wrecks than children."

Everybody else around here knew. They're all asleep now while the honeymooners listen and learn. Everybody else around here—a few pilots and mechanics, the Alsworth family and their domestic employees—they all sleep the sleep of people who don't get jammed up like this, who *don't get stranded in Alaska* and who *don't mess up planes*. The newlyweds can't sleep, not until the adrenaline fades. There's nothing to do but listen to Richard's hair-raising tales, and the sound of the rain.

It's raining hard two days later when Glenn Alsworth, their new pilot, lands his Cessna on a mesa in the Bonanza Hills and puts out the Idaho newlyweds and their gear. "I'll pick you up in nine days," he tells them. "Write it *down*, write it *down*," Moon One begs. He and Moon Two are all by themselves today. Richard Busk waits back in Port Alsworth ministering to his defunct Beaver. He's not worried about these cheechakos. They'll figure things out. He's drawn a map for them on a table napkin, and given his best advice: "The secret of the whole thing is: don't panic."

As the plane lifts away from them into the black thunderheads, Moon One actually *feels* himself getting tinier and tinier and finally disappearing. While his good wife sobs, he makes a polite attempt to get their bearings, standing in the downpour with the handmade map that shows them the way to the trail head, and to a four-wheeler ATV. The paper dissolves in his hands. He has a USGS map of the general region, but it's not as if it would *tell* where they *are*.

The 'mooners can't find the trail in this messy weather, but they can spy the cabins and machines scattered around like little toys about a quarter mile below them, down by the creek. Moon One sorts through their gear, loads a knapsack with what he hopes and believes may be the essentials of survival, and, with no comprehension of how deceiving sizes and distances can be in country of such openness, he leads Moon Two over the mesa's edge and down through the brush, both of them soaked and chilled, anything loose about them flapping crazily in the wind, and they stumble, fall, roll in the mud, right themselves repeatedly, working their way down the quarter mile, which turns out to be more like two miles, until, she weeping, he smiling and exhorting good cheer but also, quite often, swearing wildly, they break out of the scrub onto the bank of the creek, which turns out, now, to be a raging river.

It's been raining like this off and on for a couple weeks in the region, and even under the current deluge and the thudding wind, the baffled honeymooners make out the crash and steady explosion of Synneva and Bonanza Creeks, now maelstroms, chewing through the valley at thirty miles an hour, dragging boulders and vegetation. But they can see the cabin, right there across the water. There's nothing to do but find the shallowest spot, and plunge through. This day Alaska is kind to them, doesn't drown them, doesn't mangle them too badly. They crawl to the cabin and unbolt the door.

Moon Two drips and shivers. Her husband sits her down in a chair. He's got to build a fire. But first he'd better make a speech. He takes her hands in his and promises: "Whatever happens in life, after we get out of here we'll never, never set foot inside Alaska again." Fortunately the rattling of her teeth prevents her from sharing her thoughts. He tries to think of something else to say. "Never," he repeats. She probably knows he's lying. He has certainly once again screwed everything up, but, oh well, she can't divorce him out in the wilderness—

The wilderness! Alaska!

Checking the soggy USGS map, Moon One draws a circle about one hundred miles across—he's in that circle, she's in that circle. There's nobody else in that circle. He determines their position to be at least seventy miles from that of the nearest other person.

He stands in the doorway, dripping the pure Alaskan rain slightly above the temperature of snow, surveys the distance they've come down the hillside—which was, it's obvious from this perspective, actually a cliff. The only new part left of the New World! He steps to a woodpile and begins busting up wet spruce with an ax. The Last Frontier!—*his* last, if he doesn't get it together.

The next day, during a break in the rain, they survey the mining operation: the cabin, its outhouse ravaged by bears; three sheds; two stories of a proposed three-story dwelling, plus a dilapidated canvas quonset hut owned by another miner, and a really nice new sixteen-by-sixteen spruce log cabin, its outhouse still intact, owned by one of Richard's friends. Three or four people own claims out here— Richard sells them off for about $15,000 per forty acres. Moon One pictures himself as the owner of a mining claim, a crusty prospector living here surrounded by natural resources.

Or he could set off into this immense solitude, and stake his own claim. To do that he'd only have to find minerals on a piece of federally owned land, stake it out—twenty acres is the usual size for a one-person claim—and file with the district office of the Bureau of Land Management. After that he'd be responsible for doing a hundred dollars worth of labor on the claim per year—a couple days' panning will satisfy that requirement of the BLM—and pay twenty dollars cash per claim each year.

He crosses the river, finds the trail that was lost in the storm, and climbs it to the top, where Richard Busk keeps a four-wheeler. At the landing strip the new prospector loads up, and with his equipment swaying behind him he slithers down the muddy mountain astride this strange machine, but decides against trying to ford the fifty-foot-wide creek with it. He ferries his stuff across on his back, and he's ready now to get into the gold business.

According to what he's read, the Bonanza Hills are fraught with "granitic intrusions": slabs of granite pushing up from deep under, indicating that high heat and pressure have been involved in the region's formation—good for making veins of quartz that often carry gold.

In the area of the main creek channel, a geological survey team estimated this ground to hold about ten dollars in gold per cubic yard—a good half-billion dollars' worth of precious metal in just this one portion of Richard's claims.

Others have found gold here before him. The first cache in the Bonanza Hills was built in a tree next to Bonanza Creek in 1913 by two prospectors who made this same journey by river and on foot, carrying their equipment on their backs. The little treehouse is still there, but there's nothing in it. As for Richard Busk, everything he uses, including his two backhoes, is flown out by plane or helicopter. He needs as much automated help as he can ferry over, because his claims total about 15,000 acres. He bought the whole enterprise eleven years ago. He's definitely found gold here, but he hasn't told anybody how much, exactly. Enough to keep him in airplanes.

After a few days the rain quits. The 'mooners climb the opposite hill and take a good look at the seventy-mile radius of nothing they've landed in the middle of—hills of a pale olive tint rolling off over the edge of the world, and everywhere the wash of a soft unlocatable sort of violin music stringing itself along the scrub and low spruce as the wind travels over the landscape.

Over the next few days they find disturbingly sizable bear tracks, but never a visible bear. They make friends with a giant ground squirrel, feeding it daily and naming it Smithers, after a town they passed through in British Columbia back in the days, two weeks ago, when they didn't live alone in the wilderness half-expecting never to see civilization again. The spaces around them look infinite, but the world begins to feel small and friendly. Life steadies down to something basic and perpetual, taking its power from just a few elements—fire, water, food, sex, gold.

Because of its weight, gold, if it moves at all, moves downstream in as straight a line as possible, hugging the insides of the curves. Fierce floods might churn between the banks, nudging the flakes and nuggets along, but wherever the action slows, the gold stops.

At the confluence of Bonanza and Synneva Creeks, where a sharp curve makes a likely spot, Moon One sets up his Keene's "high-banker"—kind of a superpanner. He's got himself the portable combo model, with a three-horse Briggs & Stratton engine. One of these things costs about a grand, but that's a couple pennies next to the piles of gold you can slurp up with it from the depths of Alaska. Once you get it bolted together and running, which doesn't take *for-ever,* it stands about three feet tall and three feet long and cuts the work of panning by 95 percent. With its steel clamps and white hoses, all of it brand new and gleaming, antiseptic-looking even, the highbanker wouldn't look out of place in the arsenal of a brain-surgery team. But it sucks up anything it can get hold of on the creekbed, spraying and sluicing with a powerful racket that sounds hearty even alongside the roaring Bonanza Creek.

It has power and endurance but no brain. The operator's supposed to supply that; also the savvy without which no gold comes up from where it hides.

And gold does hide—gold seems to *know* somehow that every-body's out to capture it and melt it down and lock it up in places like Fort Knox—taking advantage of its relative heaviness, it burrows downward with a mysterious swiftness until it hits bedrock, where it hides in the cracks and crannies while tons of *other* stuff gets on top—stuff like the stuff Moon One is sucking out of the Bonanza Creek while he stands in leaky waders in its near-freezing high-speed water, numbing himself completely below the waist. The movement of gold is predictable, yet it's hard as hell to get at. Meanwhile, every little thing that shines—every wet pebble, each reflective bit of shale or quartz, every tiny beetle's wing—demands to be investigated with a certain trembling passion.

Moon One spends a couple of hours each day dredging for gold in Bonanza Creek, and then crouches by the stream with his pan for quite a bit longer, washing out the concentrated dirt down to noth-ing but black sand, and the black sand down to—nothing. No gold!

In a week or so, if Glenn Alsworth retrieves them, they'll be in a position to learn that Richard Busk made it back to civilization just fine. However, on landing at the Lake Hood Airfield in Anchorage, the pilot he was with came down too fast and too sharply and turned the plane up on its nose.

Sometimes they hear the tiny sound of a distant engine in the sky. Moon One likes to stand on the hill when that happens, screaming and waving his arms. Glenn Alsworth isn't due to pick them up yet; they spend a good deal of their time remembering Glenn, and hoping he remembers them.

No gold for the tenderfoot prospector. But he's having the experience of a lifetime, and given *enough* lifetime, he's sure he could dredge up a fortune. There's something about this swollen shining creek itself that *feels* like gold. And something in him feels tantalized and lustful watching all this voluptuous water rush along, smoothing the gold beneath it.

The newlyweds won't wear wedding rings—not made from Bonanza Hills gold anyhow—but they really don't need rings in this Eden. They spend days wandering through the solitude discovering things you can't spend, but can only keep inside. They find a certain peace and a certain magic, and to some extent they start the process of finding each other.

BIKERS FOR JESUS

On Thursday night Mark puts his Ford Econoline van on a small bluff overlooking the grounds of the Eagle Mountain retreat of the Reverend Kenneth Copeland and camps too close to a family who seem unable to keep their small children in line. The children's playing is an irritation of some magnitude to a man who's driven x-hundred miles from Missouri pierced in his spine with the very spear that killed Christ crucified. It's hard enough anyway to sleep with his marriage in flames back home, his wife turned against him and their six children baffled, and their pastor and the pastor's wife trying to convince him he's a disturbance to the congregation.

But as far back as he can remember Mark has felt the spirit of God in him, and he's not convinced that others feel it quite so strongly, study scripture quite so thoroughly, or find themselves quite so liberally gifted with discernment. He's suffering for it now, suffering the isolation of his gift, camped under a dome of stars on the grounds of this former Texas Air National Guard base, watching the sparks of scattered campfires and hearing the whacked guitar and lone hymnal wail of some cowboy believer. "Of those to whom much is given, much is asked." Last summer at the revival in Montreal, spiritual readers, several of them, and separately, approached to tell

Mark they could see the spear of Christ embedded in his back. It represents his sorrows.

Friday morning he turns out and surveys the campground below him, where still only a few dozen parties have found their places. In his inward self he greets his Maker and his Savior, and his Savior tells him to move his van down the hill and park it near another Ford van, a brand new shiny blue one, an airport rental, beside which a freelance writer from Idaho has set a ragged nylon tent and filled it with an air mattress and sleeping bag and then discovered he's locked the keys in the rental with the motor on.

As he usually seems to do when acting on the direct instructions of Jesus Christ, Mark starts presenting his message before the other has had much of a chance to study the messenger—a tiny intellectual-looking messenger with spectacles and a goatee and a careful and very earnest way of speaking that makes him sound doctorly, or scientific. He does, in fact, identify himself as a scientist by trade, but gets no more specific than that, and it's clear from two minutes' conversation that Mark's a Bible wonk, the spiritual parallel to a computer whiz, and might understandably impress his fellow churchmen as something of an exegetical hacker, less a saint than a shit-disturber, who surfs scripture and verse mainly with an eye to running his own program. Anyway his pastor thinks so, and Mark's wife refuses to submit anymore to the head of the household, and the pastor's wife supports her in her challenge, which has come to consist mainly of a general ugliness and a lot of hateful put-downs, and Mark has taken himself to various three-day spiritual revivals like this one here in the flat middle of Texas, seeking . . . he doesn't say, exactly. Solace. Confirmation. Healing.

And in the case of this, the Eagle Mountain Motorcycle Rally near Newark, forty miles from Dallas, it's important to Mark that he's seeking it, whatever it is, among men. He expects to find men in abundance here because this is, after all, a *motorcycle* rally, and plenty of both men and motorcycles have arrived already. The country air is full of exhaust and the sawing fuzztone of throttles twisted back and forth. Mark has brought along his Honda dirt bike, a 90cc job with one-fourth the mass of a highway hog, the kind of bike children can be seen piloting around the grounds right now slowly with their feet stuck out for balance, cutting brodies in the dirt around the trash barrels.

Not that anybody would kid him about his ride. Most of the arrivals aren't bikies, but even if some look like the roughest sort of chargers in every other way, still they wouldn't be the type to compare and criticize. These are serious Christians—like Mark's other neighbor, for instance, Beauford (pronounced Bewford) Knabe, formerly a dealer in bulk amphetamine for a bikie gang in southern Illinois and now a Harley mechanic several years clean, sober, and celibate, who tries, displaying absolutely no symptoms of derision, to help the Idaho man break into his vehicle with a coat hanger, but unsuccessfully. "Don't sweat it," Beauford says. He looks like an extra in a sixties Roger Corman drive-in film. "For certain we'll find us a reformed car thief in this bunch."

They can see, on a rise a half-mile distant, Kenneth Copeland's Eagle Mountain Church, which they won't be attending. Kenneth Copeland Ministries, a televangelical enterprise dedicated to saving souls on a massive scale, expects as many as ten thousand people this weekend, and the preaching will be done from an outdoor stage of the type whose development was perfected in the seventies, for rock festivals: this arrangement facing a paved runway turnaround set out with three hundred rows of folding chairs, the stage flanked on either side by two cinema-size video screens and two eighty-foot-long U.S. flags hanging down like tapestries from the PA system's uprights, the stage itself mounted with several sharply gleaming Harley-Davidson motorcycles. Along the pavement's western edge, some two dozen food vendors have set up kiosks, and behind the stage is an airy hangar large enough to accommodate cargo jets, now accommodating stalls and tables and vendors of such paraphernalia as T-shirts and crafts and books and tapes and sew-on insignia, both the religious kind and the motorcycle kind. Behind the food-vendors' stalls a plump, moustachioed, affable man offers hand-lettered scrolls inscribed with more than a hundred verses from the Old and

New Testaments depicting God's relation to man and twice as many verses depicting man's relation to God. "They're free," he says, standing beside his easel, handing away rolled-up copies right and left from two plastic buckets. "God told me to do this," he explains. There's no charge for the event itself either—you just turn up and find a spot. The firewood is there for the taking.

A Saginaw County sheriff's deputy cruises the lanes of this tent city for an hour or so. He finds nothing to stop for other than the Idaho man, who flags him down to beg for help with his locked vehicle.

All morning the attendees roll in steadily and arrange themselves in about thirty acres of trodden pasture sectioned off by chalk-line vehicular pathways. Knee-high signs along the paved drive into the grounds say CAMPING and point the way—otherwise no signs direct them. Although there's nobody around to prevent it, and in fact there's nothing to discourage it—no posted rules, no printed exhortations or prohibitions whatever—beer seems entirely absent. And hardly any of these people, from the Middle-American retired-NCO-looking motorhomers in their khakis, stretchpants, and baseball caps, to the slow hairy Bigfoot-type bikies in their gang colors and leather chaps, appears to smoke cigarettes. There's no psycho menace now in these riders, so many of whom have spent years in prison, and belonged there. Who murdered for pride, raped for amusement, stole and dealt and extorted and whored for money. Dope demons walk around the place clean, setting their tents and ballooning open their camper-trailers, lighting campfires and charcoal grills, letting down the tailgates of pickups with custom Harleys guyed down in the back.

Not too many of the ten thousand chairs have been filled on Friday afernoon when Gloria Copeland, a vaguely Dolly-Partonesque woman in white jeans and a black blouse, opens the weekend with a hymn and a prayer. In a friendly, no-nonsense manner, she states that this weekend's gathering has a special purpose, to minister to convicts. The evening sermons will be beamed by satellite into every prison in Texas. "It doesn't matter where you are, where you've been, or what you've done . . . God *loves* you." She's finished and off the stage before much of an audience has gathered. Then a number of singers follow, all backed by recorded music. Some of these seem to be ministry staff, young women, mainly, the imperfections of whose voices in praise and song go away forever out of the giant amplifiers—no mountains, no hills to echo off of—a kind of vast sweeping magnificent karaoke . . . But after a desultory start before the scattered audience, Isaac Petrie, a young black singer with the same phony taped orchestra and chorus behind him, breaks loose and lifts them out of their seats, the skins of their arms and necks dimpled with gooseflesh and the tears flowing down . . . Mark can't help himself, doesn't want to, he's sobbing, sobbing, sobbing. The young MC comes onto the stage clapping and shouting out verses from Isaiah, the uplifting, reassuring Isaiah, prophet of God's sweetest promises in an Israel gone to hell. "C'mon, put yourself there!" he cries, and they stand swaying with their hands upraised.

They've come home to God, and to America, their country—57-channel America, Airport Terminal America, Visa-MasterCard America, America with cameras at your tragedy, at your triumph. Even the bikies have come home to America, the one where you can ride flatout a long ways, run your own shop, mind your own business, be who you are. Like spears of wheat they sway with their hands up, only they're not being arrested, they're sanctified, members of a whole different gang—SONS OF GOD MOTORCYCLE CLUB, their colors read, TRIBE OF JUDAH; THE UN-CHAINED GANG/SWORDS OF JESUS CHRIST.

It's the cool, sunny second weekend in October, weekend of the full moon. The *USA Today* weather map shows a big blue high front girding the state of Texas and steering Hurricane Opal well away to the east. Not that anybody here was ever worried about a little thing like a hurricane.

There's no telling where it comes from, this impression of an emphatic okayness about the psyches of the regular-looking Middle Americans here, unless they were actually utterly lost somewhere and now they've come home. In the heart of someone who might have just stumbled onto this rally, the man from Idaho, let's say, fifteen years a Christian convert, but one of the airy, sophisticated kind, the whole business is a millstone—if he's going to Heaven, shouldn't he be more excited? Is he going to Heaven? In his questions, his doubts, his failure to submit unconditionally, hasn't he been nothing but a cruiser, a shopper? Impressed with the drama of his own conversion—but as drama, rather than conversion—was he ever really broken? And more important, was he ever really healed?

Out on Highway 287, which cuts northwest out of Fort Worth and through the town of Saginaw and then abrubtly, almost immediately, into a world half grass and half sky, a Kenneth Copeland Ministries billboard stands over the low empty prairie, the only thing higher than the horizon, looking like the remnant structure of some exalted race and visible from such a distance that its message is for a long time illegible to the approaching traveler; and then only the last and largest word resolves, and then it swings past: ONE WORD FROM GOD CAN CHANGE YOUR LIFE . . . FOREVER.

They don't mind being clear about the stakes. With rock-bottom Christians, it has ever been so. Large outdoor camp-revivals have been part of the American scene since late in the eighteenth century. Then, and also later, in the 1840s, it wasn't unheard of for twenty thousand frontier people to convene in tent cities in the middle of the wilderness to be saved from sin as the "earner" of death—to be saved, in other words, from dying. Despair, though it weighed on many souls, was at bottom a fear of Hell. Existential nausea was the plague of a mind ensnared by the Devil. Life was hard all over, life hardest in the American wilderness, but life wasn't the problem. Eternity was. At Eagle Mountain the stakes are the same as ever, but it's easy to sense that even beyond the technological differences—the vast distances easily covered to get to places like this, the tricked-out trailers, the showers, the toilets, the telecommunications—there now can be felt an altered emphasis on the Christian idea of spiritual rebirth itself. It's not just about Forever any more. Jesus has saved these souls from misery and meaninglessness, too, from the dope, the booze, the ripping and running, the chasing after. Saved them not just to be born again as the children of God and resurrected after death, but to be born again as America's sons and daughters—to be made brand-new right now, to start all over, to be reinvented, as is the right of every American.

When they were sinners they not only ignored the teachings of the Bible, but misinterpreted the rules of American striving. Rather than seek the bedrock values on which America's success is built, Bible-based values, they lusted after flesh and money and things that ran down empty. Some of these things they can still have—they are not anti-Bible, un-American things—but have them only by building on entirely new ground, and then have them extravagantly, burning gas and turning wheels and throwing away the mufflers and jacking up the amps. Kenneth Copeland teaches that poverty is a curse, and the testimonies in *Victory,* the Kenneth Copeland Ministries' monthly magazine, frequently concern themselves with the believers' glorious transit from rags to riches ("From Pennies to Prosperity"; "The ABCs of Abundance")—a transit Copeland himself has made, and not at all apologetically.

. . . Born again not only to Heaven, but also to this—a glittering stage hung with eighty-foot-tall American flags, decorated with Harleys. And Kenneth Copeland's son John Copeland, his baby in front of him and his wife in a U.S.-flag vest behind him, on a Harley.

This is a biker rally, but Copeland attracts all types. As well as a tent set up by the Motorcycle Church of Christ, there's one sheltering folks from the Cowboy Church. Men and women seem to be equally represented. A scattering of blacks—a family here, a couple there, young couple, old couple. A Christian black rap group performs, trucked in from L.A.

African Americans were better represented at the frontier camp meetings of the early nineteenth century, but their campsites and services were segregated from the white ones. Outdoor meetings had long since become the form of worship most inviting to the outcast and the spiritually reluctant. In England as early as 1739, John Wesley held outdoor meetings at which, according to one diarist, "thieves, prostitutes, fools, people of every class and numbers of poor who had never entered a place of worship assembled and became godly." It wasn't a lucrative business. In the United States, Methodist circuit riders were salaried from $80 a year in 1816 to $100 in 1840. A populist religious movement characterized by emotional fervor, rejection of abstract creeds and formal ritual, lay leadership, a message emphasizing simple virtues and pinned firmly to cited scriptural verses—this was what swept the crowds together in young America.

The thread of this history leads straight to glitter-and-glory televangelism, a development in modern communications regarded by most of the viewing public, it's safe to say, as a hideous sham. It's not evangelism that's suspect, it's TV. In its mass appeal, its broad focus, TV softens and dilutes and equivocates: Any face on that screen has got to be a liar's, and for viewers by and large the TV preacher is a figure bobbing up sometimes above the broadcast surf, outfitted in really bad taste, striking at the hearts of little old ladies and the confused parents of sexually awakening teens and dealing extensively, it would appear, in printed timetables for the death of Earth.

Kenneth Copeland Ministries, for all their willingness to engage the medium, keep firmly rooted in the two-centuries-old revival traditions, particularly in their focus on the wretch, the prodigal, the outcast. On Friday night Hal Barnes, a young black lay preacher, stands in the disorienting glare of floodlights, his voice booming out into a great darkness and speaking the language of the disinherited: "Whoever you are, whatever you've done, it doesn't matter." He himself was a zealous doper for many years but shouts now that the Lord "*pulled* me outa that bag, *rolled* me up in a robe of righteousness, *fired* me up with the Holy Spirit, and *smoked—me—up . . . Hit* me in the *main*line with holiness. . ." The Texas night around him roars and shouts "Praise the Lord!"—"Praise God!"—"Praise Him!" Those in the back are fully a quarter-mile from the stage, but can watch the action on the massive video screens.

Then a regular storm of welcome breaks and nearly flattens Kenneth Copeland as he strides aboard the stage—in casual dress, jeans and sportshirt and motorcycle boots. Not the big-haired sequinned mannequin of TV evangelism, but an earnest, gleeful, boyish guy, almost giddy—very much informed by his own humble beginnings. He does this a lot, this is his fifth rally in six months, he has two more scheduled in the next ten weeks, but he still looks stunned by all the surrounding show, which he himself has produced through decades of ceaseless striving—starting with rallies in shopping malls, attended sparsely by folks gathered up from house-to-house calls and mimeographed fliers pinned by wipers to the the windshields of cars baking in the Southern summer—but not solitary striving, he would insist; he never walked alone. His first word: "Ha-lay-*looo*-yah! *Praise* the Lord!"

He welcomes everyone and reminds them of the prison mission, and he and the audience count down the last twenty seconds until the broadcast begins, four!—three!—two!—*one!* And as the screams subside Copeland begs the prisoners watching now "in every corrections institution in the *state*" to cast away their pride and listen to the sermons and come to Jesus Christ. "We don't want anything from you," he tells them. "You give nothing. *These* people"—with a sweep of his arm out toward the dark vital mass of souls— "give of their substance: money. Money they worked hard for." Will an amount be named? Actual numbers spoken? "It doesn't matter where you are, where you've been, or what you've done. Jesus can heal you, Jesus can release you not just from sin, but from anything." And with an immense, imperial confidence he commands— "You're coming *outa* there!" And there can be no doubt of it. He's seen the dead rise up, the crippled man walk, he's seen captive after captive forgiven and freed. This guy isn't lying.

This is Kenneth Copeland's moment, but it is not his hour. He embraces and introduces an old friend and preaching buddy, Jerry Sevelle from Louisiana, a suave gray man who delivers a lecture on the dangers of tradition, of following Doctrine but ignoring Scripture, and also recalls the days when he and Ken Copeland preached in rags, traveling in wired-together vehicles that ran on prayer as much as gasoline, standing on boxes in malls and theater parking lots. Before that Sevelle had been a countrified hippie, a pothead Cajun, but the Lord had called him, and he'd outgrown his youthful wildness.

From these reveries Jerry Sevelle segues gracefully, but frankly, into talk of tithing. "God gives to me; I give to others—to my church, to various ministries and mission programs—and then God gives me tenfold, a hundredfold, a *thousand*fold what I've sown. The money I give is *seed* I'm planting. And I expect a harvest when the season is ripe." He backs this up with biblical verses— "You reap what you sow,"—"Seed time and harvest"—perhaps, again, the original emphasis has shifted, but this isn't just a fresh, larcenous reinterpretation of worn phrases: the Apostle Paul, too, aimed an appeal to the Corinthians for donations to the poor at exactly this hope of returns: "Now he that ministereth seed to the sower both minister bread for your food, and multiply your seed sown." "If I give you seed and you don't plant it," Sevelle points out, "it doesn't grow."

Like most lay preachers laboring without benefit of the endorsement, the authority, of an established denomination, Sevelle seeks both to entertain and edify, focusing steadily on twin points: the Bible and his own experience. Copeland, too, in his occasional chats with the audience, refers constantly to the Word and quotes the verse, never straying from it except into the realm of what he's personally done, personally witnessed. It's Copeland's show, but for the most part all weekend he acts as a kind of MC for speakers with wild and enviable memories of slam-bang conversion, ecstatic worship, sudden visions. The mature Christian, Copeland insists, can expect direct access to guidance. "So then God says to me," Copeland remarks in the midst of a little story, and stops. "Listen here. Don't you think I know when God's saying something to me? If I had a friend and I'd been talking to him ever *day*, for twenty-five *years*—wouldn't I know his voice if he called me on the phone?" "God sent me." "God told me." "Jesus said I should." The Holy Spirit directs minutely—moment by moment—down to left and right turns.

*   *   *

Mark's newest neighbors have built a campfire, and he sits with them in its warmth on this chilly night—an almost straight-looking couple from near the Gulf. Among the others who come and go in the firelight, warming their hands a minute and saying good evening and perhaps not much else, are two extensively tattooed volunteers who man the tent for the Motorcycle Church of Christ. One of them shows how he's had to have some details changed in his decorations: "This used to be a demonic thing," he says of a beautiful, complicated scene on his forearm. "I had it changed into this cross. This one, I had to have her breasts covered up. Otherwise of course I wouldn't've had any tats done, after I got saved, because it says in the Bible not to mark your body."

John, more or less the host of this gathering, still drinks beer in moderation, but Beauford, who has joined them in the firelight, hasn't touched a drop in over three years. "I was driving home from this guy's house one night and I saw this thing on the highway, just beside an overpass. Like a Christmas display. I kept going slower and slower, just looking at this thing—a cross about twenty-five feet tall with two angels kneeling down on either side of it. I stopped the car and I got out and I started walking toward this thing—it was Jesus on the cross. I couldn't believe how detailed it was, just perfectly lifelike, and when I got close enough I realized it wasn't a display. It was Jesus. It was two angels looking up at him. He was bloody and suffering and dying. And he raised his head . . . and he just looked at me. With such pain. With such suffering on his face. And I knew it was for me, all that pain.

"I don't know how many times before that he was watching over me, and I never realized it, driving around no-hands with my head on backwards, thinking, 'Man, I'm not high enough.' I was moving thirty pounds of meth at a time. I'd say, 'Man, I feel like splitting,' and an hour after I'm gone the narcotics squad busts in. I got a feeling to leave this clubhouse one night and just a while afterward a rival club came down and four people got killed in the firefight. It got so people would point me out and say, *I'm* leaving when *he* leaves.

"So after I saw the cross, I got down on my knees and prayed to get right, especially to quit drinking, because I'd gotten a DUI. And I quit. After about six months, I was cleaning up my yard one time, picking up sticks and trash, and I bent over and there's this old empty beer can. I tossed it in the bag and I thought, I'm really *proud* I don't have to drink no more, *proud* of what I've done. And man, this voice comes behind me, a real voice, louder than I'm talking now, not a mental voice. I didn't turn around to see who it was. I knew who it was. And he said, 'Beauford, you didn't do this. I *gave* you what you *asked* of me.'"

Beauford is moved by his own account; he wipes his eyes and draws a ragged breath. But he doesn't appear agitated, or drunk with religion—rather, genuinely gifted with inner peace. When he went in for evaluation after some months' probation on his DUI, he says, he told this story to the psychologist from beginning to end— "'and that's it,' I told her. 'That's what happened. I don't care what you think.'" She stared at him for some time, her hand on a stack of forms and tests she'd intended to administer. "Then after a while she said, 'You know what? I gotta get some coffee.' A few minutes later she came back in and said, 'Look. Just go home,' and tossed all that stuff in the trash."

"Praise the Lord," Mark says. "What was the evaluation?"

"She recommended me to get the probation lifted."

"I would, too," Mark says.

One Word From God Can Change Your Life. FOREVER. But God has apparently been willing to grant much more than a single word to the Tribe of Judah and the Church of the Highway and El Shaddai's Warriors. Accounts abound with messages, rescues, apparitions, unmistakable voices—and the bikes, the hurtling fever maniac drifter bikes, the bikes themselves, figure notably in the visionary moment and its beautiful story. "I went up to get healed one time," says Mike, a youthful, uncharacteristically frail biker, lifting up a malformed left thumb. "Right there. It don't bend right. The lady healing touched me on the neck and I turned around and was walking away and I didn't feel a thing. Then all of a sudden I felt this tingling rush from where she touched me, down through my big vein here right to my heart, and my heart was *glowing* inside. Well, that night I was riding home, and my headlamp went out. Poof. Just like that. So I tried this and I tried that—nothing. Got back on the bike, sitting there with my head hanging, and all of a sudden it's just bright as day out ahead of me—but the headlamp was still broken. I fired her up and rode along fine with this bright light ahead, no problem. And when I got to my home a voice spoke out just as clear as I'm speaking to you now. 'Mike, the reason I didn't heal your thumb is that I first had to heal your heart of its hardness. And the reason I gave you light was to let you know that no matter what, no matter what, I'll always show you the way in the darkness.'"

Saturday morning the Idaho man attends a "Healing School" run by Gloria Copeland from the same big stage. She's apparently a serious person, not interested in oratory, in entertainment. She starts right in with a prayer— "Thank you for the Blood. There is healing in the Blood. Power in the Blood! Jesus Christ! There is power in the Blood!" She moves on to cite passages from Gospel pertinent to this subject—the story of the woman who only had to touch the hem of Christ's garment to be healed, the Centurion who expected him just to "say the word" to accomplish his daughter's healing. She asks the gathering to bow their heads, close their eyes, ask for whatever healing they want. Those who feel the need of a human touch form three lines and come forward—some on crutches, some on wheels, some just limping—to the waiting hands of various staff.

Ushers come to the head of each row with buckets for donations. Kenneth Copeland steps onto the stage and leads a prayer of thanks: "Lord, we're enjoying each other, enjoying our bikes, enjoying the praise of God . . ." As the white buckets go wobbling along the rows from hand to hand a woman up front pitches over unconscious, and a bunch around her begin fanning her with their Bibles and hankies. "Whatever it is, God's more than enough. Help her there," Copeland says. "God is greater than whatever is disturbing her comfort." In a couple of minutes a medical tech slides along the rows, and still later Copeland says, "That lady who—I found out from her grandson she's a retired preacher, been preaching many years—she got a little too hot, is what it was—and, praise God, she *deserves* a little extry attention."

Next come testimonies of healing. A man who'd wheeled himself forward is standing now, talking excitedly into a microphone below the lip of the stage. Another guy has had his sight restored, and pitches away his bulky mechanical glasses and says, "I can read those signs way over there!" He points at the signboards above the kiosks 150 yards away—the man from Idaho can't make them out himself, in fact. "Steak Subs!" the blind man shouts. "Ready Spaghetti! Indian Fried Bread! Mudslide! Sanctified Swine Memphis BBQ! Texas Taters! Thirst No More Lemonade! Root Beer Floats! Chopped Beef Sandwiches!"

The Idaho man introduces himself to the nearest person in his row, a middle-aged black woman who turns out to be Nancy, from Chicago. "God is saying something," she says intensely as they shake hands, and won't let him go, staring into his eyes . . . "He says you've been seeking, and just go ahead, you're doing fine. He says you got a cross in your back, but that's healed. And He says be sure and take a pen and a notepad with you, so you can write things down."

The man turns away, but something about what she's said strikes him now—more than the coincidence of the pen and the pad and the seeking. "Excuse me," he says, returning to her. "Nancy, did you say something about my back?"

"You got a cross pinching your right back, down low. But it's gone now. He fixed it yesterday."

For four months the Idaho man has been undergoing weekly treatments for a pinched sciatic nerve in his lower right back. It hasn't occurred to him until this minute that it didn't bother him last night and hasn't bothered him all day. "I believe you're right," he tells Nancy.

"You didn't want to ask for healing," she says, "but He healed you anyway."

"Do these little incidents happen to you very often?"

"Every day."

Saturday night Kenneth Copeland chats informally on stage with Mike Barber, former National Football League pro and currently a lay minister evangelizing in Texas prisons. "I expect God enjoys football," Copeland says. "Probably not near as much as we do, 'cause He's playing in a much bigger game."

Barber tries to tell about his work in prisons. He isn't at all slick, but rather nervous and stumbling over his tongue. "And he who has the Son has the Spirit. And he who doesn't have the Son doesn't have the Spirit . . . doesn't say, 'I have the Spirit in my heart . . .'"

The night's principal speaker is Mac Gober, Texan, Vietnam veteran, former Navy Seal, former bouncer, still a biker; a big-bellied, bald-headed, really *piled-up*-looking man in jeans and gang colors. In his youth he ran with the Devil, ended up hiding in the mountains, wanted on attempted murder, his brothers bringing him supplies. Hit with the Light in a bathroom, in a bar. Though Hell is alluded to in these sermons, fierce images of it have given way to personal anecdotes of misdirection and misery: sin as its own punishment. Gober offers the weekend's only graphic of damnation: "I go scuba diving sometimes and when you get down past sixty feet the pressure is unbearable—right in your ears, right into your head—and when I read in here that if you lead one of these little ones astray it'll be for you just as if a stone were tied around your neck and you were cast into the depths of the sea—I know it's gonna be *bad*."

The problem is sin. Any problem, every problem, all problems. "There ain't no crime problem in this country. There's a *sin* problem. If you empty your heart of sin and fill it up with Jesus, you ain't gonna hurt *no—body*."

"Amen! Amen! Amen!"

"There ain't a racial problem around here—there's a *sin* problem. If sin is removed and you're filled up with Jesus—man, you'll *love—ever—body!*"

The audience goes crazy. The woman seated—now standing—in

front of the Idaho man is speaking, he guesses, in tongues, uttering a stream of miscellaneous syllables while her husband, of whose presence she seems oblivious, embraces and comforts her. On either side of the stage the colossal image of the preacher's colossal head stares soberly forward and a caption beneath it reads: MAC GOBER.

Gober speaks not just to the convicts watching—and Copeland has reported thousands saved by last night's broadcast—but also to the wavering and tempted and troubled Christians among the audience in front of him— "the backsludden" he calls them. "You gotta stay away from the places where temptation hangs around. Guys I'm working with say, 'Mac, I just can't keep away from the prostitutes.' 'Well,' I tell them, *'stay offa Fourth Avenue.'* "

He asks them all to bow their heads, "and you fellas, you fellas, too"—looking into the cameras, into the eyes of the criminals he can't see— "don't mind about that guy next to you, never mind about what he thinks, this is *you,* your *life,* your *soul.* Now close your eyes and I'm gonna give you three categories to consider. Don't nobody look up. Just raise your hand if you're in this category: 'If I died tonight, I'd go to Heaven.' Now the next group, eyes closed, raise your hand: 'If I died tonight, I'm not sure where I'd go.' Now the ones who think, 'If I died tonight, I've done something so bad— and I'm so far away—I'm so lost—I know I'd go to Hell.'" People are sobbing now, just a few here and there in the vast audience. "Now put your hand down and lift up your head. If you were in the last two categories, come forward now. Come down here close as you can get to the stage, right here." Fully a third of these thousands get up. The audience is a scarcely visible ocean on the western shore of which the vendors' stalls are lit and selling Mudslides and Snocones to the teenage sons and daughters of these penitents flowing forward to confess as a general group, repeating the words in unison after Mac Gober.

Sunday morning, before the afternoon baptisms that will be the Eagle Mountain Motorcycle Rally's ultimate event, a young woman from the Kenneth Copeland Ministries staff stands on the stage giving out the prizes. There's one for the Oldest Biker: "Olin? Does this say Olin? I can't read this. Olin, the oldest biker at the rally." Olin doesn't come forward because, as somebody in the crowd who knows him reports, "He's resting." The Farthest Biker's prize goes to two men who straddled their hogs here all the way up from Guatemala. The Longest Woman gets a prize too—she came 1,800 miles. A man whose colors read JESUS IS LORD/CHURCH OF THE HIGH- WAY lands the prize for Best-Looking Bike.

Kenneth Copeland comes out to honor the person with the Best Testimony. Entrants have turned in written stories the afternoon before. The staff have read and judged among them and been most impressed with Meg's. "Meg didn't know how she'd get here. Didn't have hardly two dimes to rub against each other. But she knew God was gonna get her here. She quit her job in August, in Alaska, and just started out. Whenever she got a little money, she'd stop and send a tithe, a good part of whatever little she had. And she ended up here with a *new* set of clothes, and a *thousand* dollars in her pocket—lit- erally *gave her way* all the way down here!"

Copeland leads a prayer of thanks: according to the registration forms the attendees have been encouraged, but not required, to fill out, the population of this tent city is 10,700. "We thank You, Lord, for soul-winning Gospel preaching . . . bikes . . . boats, airplanes, whatever we can get our hands on, Lord, to witness to You.

"I know you might not know this about me, but my grandfather on my mother's side was a Cherokee Indian," Kenneth Copeland suddenly reveals. "So I think I can look on two sides of the experi- ence of Native Americans, that's what I'm getting at. And I've had to reconcile those two sides, and *we* have got to reconcile those two sides—now I know we have some Natives here today. Come up here. Come up here." He brings the Natives forward, about eight of them, and calls now for some whites— "I mean *lily white* people, *you* know the kind I mean," and several men and women turn up at his feet below the stage, whether shame-faced or not at the purity of their heritage it's hard to tell, because their backs are turned to the audience. Copeland puts the two groups face-to-face and the whites repeat after Copeland: Forgive my forefathers for "the pain, the theft, the breaking of covenants." Then the Natives ask forgiveness from the white forefathers for "raiding their camps and bringing strife. The strife," Copeland now declares, "has ended!" Now speaking as a Cherokee, he tells the Natives, "The Old Ways got us in trouble. It wasn't the White Man—it was the witchcraft. But there's a New Way—not the Red Man's Way, not the White Man's Way—GOD'S WAY!"

The white buckets ride the rows. On the first day the Idaho man put ten dollars in, twenty dollars on the second day. This time it's a fifty.

These things accomplished, these truths preached, these prayers spoken, these testimonies heard, these prodigals welcomed, these tithes received, these prizes awarded, a thousand souls, more or less, hike in cutoff jeans, swimsuits, terrycloth robes down the runway, past Kenneth Copeland's small red jet airplane, and along a path for a mile to the east edge of Eagle Lake to be baptized. It's the weekend's most organized event: dozens of ushers, five lines of initiates divided by Day-Glo-orange traffic cones, repeated instructions of crowd control from a sound truck—belongings on the right, observers to the left—amplified music, announcements about lost children.

Mark and Beauford and their Idaho companion won't be getting wet today. Although Mac Gober, among other speakers, has assured everybody a little repetition can't damn you, they've each been baptized once already, and they sit about fifty meters from the action, beside a woman whose T-shirt says IF YOU CAN'T TAKE THE HEAT STAY OUTA HELL and two young cowboys both smoking away on cheroots, on a knoll where observers are repeatedly encouraged to take themselves. Many of those watching, almost all of them, hundreds of people, have crowded around the shore, both to get a closer view and to avoid the fire ants and pointy Texas devil-burrs in the vegetation. Just offshore fourteen men, most of them in gang colors, stand up to their waists in the steel-blue water beckoning, beckoning, as the lines of people break off on the watery ends and each person slogs for-

ward into the embrace of two or three or four of the Tribe of Judah
or the Swords of Christ and goes down backward and comes up joyful, redeemed, entirely new. On the lake's far side, which is not
owned by Kenneth Copeland Ministries, some people are fishing
from a small motorboat.

No estimate of this year's numbers has been offered, but last year
nine hundred people received the sacrament of Baptism on the rally's
final day. By midafternoon the men in the water must be chilled and
exhausted, but they're having the time of their lives, and even Mac
Gober stands in Eagle Lake with his arms open wide. "Now, just go
to the first available person, please," the PA insists. "God is no
respecter of persons, so don't hold things up by waiting to get baptized by one particular person or another particular person . . ." and
when the last has washed forward, fallen backward in their arms
and been immersed and come up clean and labored back ashore with
glittering eyes, the bikies get into a water fight. Another Lost Child
announcement—little boy about four in a T-shirt that says DAD'S BEST
FISHING BUDDY on it. "Wait a minute!" the big voice cries out over the
lake. "He's been found! He's been found! Praise the Lord!"

THREE DESERTS

HOSPITALITY AND REVENGE

The dogs hear the jets before they arrive overhead, so you get the dogs barking, the dogs yammering, every dog in the city of Kabul protesting the violence that approaches, then the shock waves of bomb blasts rubbing the windows, then the lights of the antiaircraft—some like red droplets whipped from a wand, others floating up like orange bubbles and bursting into smoky flares, and blinding, winking muzzle-bursts in the hills like a single light racing madly back and forth, and Stinger missiles rising on crimson tracers—all, for the first several seconds, in absolute silence; and then the distant knocking noises and little pops like ice cubes in a drink, no bigger than that, until nearer positions start up loudly enough to knock a person off a chair.

Tonight, with the moon to see by, the old faction sends the MIGs and SUs not long after nightfall and twice more before dawn, and after that they come two or three times daily.

After several days our faction, the faction surrounding us, who seized the city last month without, as has repeatedly been said, a shot being fired, stop throwing so much precious ordnance after the bombers, the invisible targets miles above.

Nobody likes the new faction. They don't seem much interested in self-promotion, public opinion, the propaganda war. And they don't seem particularly intrigued with military strategy. They have a poor reputation as warriors. Rather than Generals and Soldiers, they call themselves Masters and Students—Mullah and Taliban.

At press conferences they continually invoke the name of Allah. Claiming a number of recent victories, the Information Minister states that these triumphs come from Allah. Three children have been killed in the air raids, but by the grace and power of Allah many bombs have fallen into the sand without exploding.

The Hotel Inter-Continental looks out on everything from a central height, one of Kabul's most prominent structures, visible from almost any point in the city. A quiet building, half of it wrecked by shelling but the other half still hosting clients. Just now I'm the only guest at the Inter-Continental.

Some of the staff have moved into a couple of the other rooms, and we live here, my staff and I, in stealth: walking very softly in the halls, hardly ever raising our voices above a whisper, conforming ourselves to the great silence that fills the building, the silence of all the people who aren't here.

In the evening I sit on my balcony with a pocket shortwave receiver and watch the day fade and the moon rise. The new faction has outlawed all music, but they're not bothered if I play the jazz program on the BBC, because, as a Westerner, I'm past all punishment, I can't be saved, I'm going to Hell.

The moonrise starts in the hills like a conflagration, almost as fiery as the dawn, and it's understandable that one of the first Europeans to visit Afghanistan, a British East India Company agent named Pottinger, was asked by two Mullahs to settle a dispute for them as to whether the moon was actually also the sun. Understandable that he told them, yes, the moon is indeed the sun.

The elevators are stopped, but we have electricity four hours a day, also a few minutes of hot water in the morning or afternoon. The waiters in the restaurant are very much that—people who wait, hardly moving, and having almost nothing to say to each other— until I appear to ask what's available today. Eggs, bread, lamb. Green or black tea or bottled water. There's never anything else. I always tip them ten thousand of their money. I never eat in my room. I take each meal in the restaurant while they stand and wait. I don't think they mind. It seems to give them pleasure serving as my silent hosts. Among the Afghans, it's said, the two most important aspects of living are hospitality and revenge.

For two days the former president and his brother dangle by their necks, dead, from a red-and-white concrete platform in the capital's center, their eyes swollen shut, mouths and nostrils stuffed with cigarettes and paper money, their blood dripping onto the pavement beneath.

Najibullah was the secular man, with a suit and a haircut, fat, moustachioed, Marxist-educated and therefore neglectful, maybe scornful, of Islamic precepts. The Twentieth-Century Man, the Cold War Man, which meant, in this region, that he was Russia's man. When they pulled out in '89 they left him a large arsenal, and they kept him supplied against the numerous factions. But after the Soviets fell apart and quit sending aid, his reign lasted only another 115 days. In the end to keep himself alive Najibullah took refuge with his brother Shahpur at the U.N. Special Mission compound in downtown Kabul, where they lived for four years, until a few nights ago, when the Taliban took the city.

And what is this platform serving, now, as Najibullah's scaffold?

"This is the traffic policeman place," a passerby explains. "If an accidental driver will have some problem, he is going to solve it. And this is the blood of Najibullah, also his brother blood."

On the concrete wall behind them, a very fresh-looking billboard depicts a dark fist upraising a bright Kalashnikov rifle over Arabic script: THERE IS NO GOD BUT ALLAH AND MOHAMMED IS HIS PROPHET.

In two years they've managed to secure two-thirds of the country, and now they've taken the capital. Around them the dregs of Marxist aspirations burble in the capital, huge concrete buildings raised with Soviet aid money, some half finished, others partly destroyed by the war, and the beat-up cars, the Russian-made Volgas and Latas and Muskoviches limping past, churning out black soot. Along the street Afghans drive their small, staggering flocks of sheep, also Soviet-made tanks. Public conveyances labeled GOOD YOUR TRIP and WELCOME TO THE BUS. Vendors pushing carts of heaped flour or nuts or twisted, multiform firewood, others selling bread, fruit, petrol, lamb kabob, and, as winter comes, shawls and heavy clothing. But the institutions are dead, the schools, the courts, the university, all closed, and not one foreign embassy open. Very little survives beyond the words of the Prophet and the Koran's commandments.

The latest president, Rabanni, fled north three weeks ago, and now hardly anybody ever mentions him.

It was the secular Rabanni government, not the Taliban, who put up the poster of the fist-and-Kalashnikov for Allah that served as backdrop to Najibullah's putrefaction, but such attempts on the part of the Cold War Men to persuade the people of their faith in the Koran came too late. The Taliban leave no doubt as to who most sincerely and faithfully wield the guns in the name of God.

The night desk clerk Ahmed and a couple of his friends have taken it on themselves to keep me informed. They race around the city for me, this city whose telephone system has been destroyed, serving as my wires to the world, getting damage reports, reports of skirmishes, news about peace talks, edicts, press conferences.

Conversing almost always in whispers with people who speak only the most rudimentary English, I'm beginning to lose my own words, my tongue feels newly arrived or lost in my mouth, and the language of my thoughts is stilted and shy.

I know a few phrases in Pashto, and whenever some of the new faction come around I bow with my right hand to my heart and say, "*Sungayay, Talib*"—How are you, Student? Like all Afghans, they're quick to smile when smiled at. A lot of them smoke cigarettes, the sale of which has been banned but still continues.

In the evening a muezzin, one of the Taliban, sings the prayer call in the downstairs of the Inter-Continental. In the somber temporary light of the drugstore, a few of the staff and a couple of Students listen to Radio Taliban. They've closed the other radio stations and the TV station, struck down satellite receivers from the roofs, smashed TVs and VCRs in the street. They've made themselves infamous by banning music and intimidating the intellectuals and frightening the women into invisibility and silence.

The staff insist that the Taliban go unarmed into their hotel, and for the most part the Taliban comply, piling their worn rifles out front on a table by the revolving door and wandering up and down the stairs and halls. They're country folk, picked out easily by their grimy turbans and tangled beards, their ratty shawls and combat boots and Kalashnikovs. They've never seen a hotel before. They can't seem to land on a feeling, a response—aloof, or astonished, or amused? They could live here free at the Inter-Continental if they wanted to, but they don't want to. They just want to see it.

To get here I came by the Grand Trunk Road from the Pakistani border. Once in the Khyber Pass it's all dirt, and somehow even more all dirt on the Afghani side of the pass—except for the vast mountain ridge covered with snow, incredibly high and distant: the Hindu Kush floating in the northwestern sky. Signs at the border read WELCOME FOR THE RECONSTRUCTION OF DRUG FREE AFGHANISTAN, and in the first town, where two kids ride tiny burros, mounted backward, and ducks fight over fruit rinds in the roadside irrigation ditches, another sign goes by fast—the first line: AFGHANI AMPUTEE BICYCLISTS . . .

At first there's pavement, a few camels, big grain fields, shepherds and goatherds, then the small city of Jalalabad, crowded with commerce since the Taliban have opened up the roads, lurching, desperate commerce in this scarcely believable interim of peace and order.

After Jalalabad, almost nothing, the road completely worn out but trucks and passenger vans using it anyway, passing through a landscape with an ancient empty feel marked with dead tanks and capsized military carryalls, the hundred miles to Kabul traversed in six hours, for three dollars, in a van full of Afghani men all dressed in the same beige suit of baggy trousers and long shirt called shalwar kamez, all wearing turbans or skullcaps, in accordance with the recent edicts of the Taliban, all bearded, in accordance with the edicts . . . the not-quite-road paralleling the khaki Kabul River, beside occasional small encampments of patchwork nomad bivouacs, bent women sweeping away the stones to make smooth floors where the tents will go. Twice in higher country we stopped while the men aboard got out to kneel and pray alongside teetering cliffs . . . and then it's dark, the headlights limply fingering the rocks while the moon rises. We come over the edge of the broken bowl of silver smog Kabul lies at the bottom of, the city glimmering in patches where electricity still reaches from the dam way east of it. The shouts of dogs down there and the sheep crying like children. And the engines, the trucks, the small cars aspiring, contending.

The Taliban have stopped the others, the two factions of General Dostum and Commander Massoud, at a mountain pass twenty kilometers north of town.

The fighting can go on for a few weeks more, during what passes for autumn in this high desert: cool days washed in a flat, white light and chilly nights without dew or frost. Winter will prevent any advance and there'll be no change in their positions until spring brings new offensives, perhaps a victory and a defeat, perhaps a compromise.

The city lies in a desert basin ringed by jagged peaks—geologists call them "young mountains"—and the fighting goes on in a region almost entirely dirt and rock rubble. Up there both sides have destroyed the same small villages over and over.

Fighting, it's what they do, it's all they do, there's nothing else to do.

We picture the citizen of the new century as an Information Miner, equipped for negotiating the free markets and traveling through cyberspace. But in much of the world the Twenty-First-Century man has nothing but hunger and a gun and maybe a religion but no longer a political creed. "We have bread and prayers," the Taliban say, "we don't need anything else."

At the U.N. Special Mission compound in downtown Kabul everything is bright U.N. blue, even the plastic hoses irrigating the flower plots. The U.N. compound is set about with brick walls, barbed wire, spiked gates within spiked gates, and sandbag emplacements buttressing the buildings, just like the Red Cross compounds, the Save the Children compound, the abandoned embassy compounds, all the official compounds.

At the Kabul Zoo, the lion Marjan lives in a similar walled compound, exiled from his natural domain, blind and nearly toothless, attended by his mate.

Officially the Kabul Zoo's gates are closed, but great numbers of the young Students, the country boys charged with keeping order, feel compelled to keep order at the zoo. The huge boar gets the most attention, a couple of platoons staring at it for hours, although this boar does nothing but stand still. Eight Taliban watch four monkeys wrestle and leap from a hoop. The bald eagle stands on his perch in his cage without companions or audience. The three bears, one of them sick and staggering, attract no interest at all.

Once the Kabul Zoo housed ninety varieties of animals and got a thousand visitors a day, but in the era of fighting that followed the fall of the Soviets and then of Najibullah, the people stayed away, and the animals found themselves in a place more dangerous than any forest Tanks and entrenched guerrillas fired at each other out in the street. As the shelling went back and forth, the tigers, the llamas, the ostriches were carried away to paradise. The aviary ruptured and the birds flew free into the heavens from which the rockets rained. For ten days the elephant ran in circles screaming until shrapnel toppled her and she died.

The zoo sits in the artillery-ravaged swatch that cuts through the middle of Kabul, the no-man's-land of numerous battles: low mud-walled residences that from only a little distance look like ruins from antiquity, larger buildings deconstructed and unrecognizable, here and there a grave mound right in the street, at the roadside knee-high totems of piled rocks warning of the presence of land mines. In the danger zones Afghani sappers with plastic face shields and blue Kevlar vests squat in the dust, picking at rubble with chisels and brushes like archaeologists of instantaneous death. Red Cross men with aluminum medical kits the size of large suitcases wait beside orange stretchers.

Nobody lives in this part of the city anymore, but people pass through on public buses or on foot, the men in the beige shalwar kamez and the women in burka in accordance with the edicts—the women with no faces, without so much as eyes, shrouded, sheathed, in royal purple or gold or black. Taxis like the caricatures of taxis, all mashed up, barely moving. A dump truck swings past carrying Taliban clustered around an ack-ack gun, and its loudspeaker broadcasts a voice chanting in Pashto: "We don't need votes, we don't need cheers, we're fighting for Allah. . . ." Several hop off to join the others observing the zoo's survivors.

The lion Marjan and his nameless mate seem only marginally attractive to the Taliban. Two or three expressionless boys look down into the vacant lot where the lions live.

A couple of years back an Afghani warrior jumped down into the lions' compound to demonstrate his courage. But he got too close to the female, and Marjan avenged himself on all his captors by tearing the intruder to pieces.

The man's brother took revenge that night, tossed down into the pit a hand grenade whose blast tore away the left half of Marjan's head, yet failed to kill him.

Marjan originally came here from East Berlin. Now he's a true Afghan, having enjoyed such hospitality as can be made available under hardship and having tasted revenge, tasted it it from both sides, its sweet and bitter portions.

A French dentist repaired the lion's jaw to the degree that he can eat now. The injuries are such that in his collapsed head his eyes and mouth stay perpetually open, and when he lies still he looks stuffed. But Marjan lives on, led about by his mate, ignorant of his own ugliness.

*   *   *

The Mullahs have decreed that a government shall be formed, that ministries shall be opened. They've had me in their offices downtown filling out forms, explaining myself, establishing an identity.

They've taken away my passport and assigned a young man who speaks English to follow me when I go out walking. He isn't furtive about it. He's introduced himself and suggested we go walking together. But I've said no because I dislike him.

At the Inter-Continental I'm still the only paying customer. A few of the Taliban leaders seem to be staying here, but it isn't clear if they actually sleep here or just hold occasional meetings upstairs.

Sometimes a group of them stand below my balcony and look up, but shyly, with a desire not to disturb; after three minutes' study they leave.

DISTANCE, LIGHT, AND DREAMS

On the deserts of the American Southwest the nights are clear over the highways. It is a major temptation to drive with the lights off.

The first nuclear explosion happened in the American Southwest, in New Mexico. When they witnessed the rising of this sun they had created, many of the people working on the project began running toward it, overcome by something like the desire to offer worship. Oppenheimer later reported telling himself, "Now physicists have known sin." But Victor Weisskopf said he thought instantly, as he watched the orange fireball levitating amid its electric-blue halo, "of Grunewald's Christ ascending in *The Resurrection.*"

During the third quarter of the twentieth century the American Southwest absorbed atomic blasts equal to one-sixth the megatonnage projected for the thermonuclear holocaust of which we lived in dread.

The Southwest isn't all desert. Natural garden parks follow one another from the Idaho mountains down one river after another and into Mexico.

There is plenty of water in the Southwest—lakes and streams abound, and the citizens of Arizona own, per person, the largest number of boats of any state in the nation—but there isn't much water in the air.

Where only a little rain falls, the land keeps its level, shifted but not very much eroded or essentially changed by the winds, while the water of rivers cuts deeper and deeper into the world—thus the Southwestern canyons: Whirlpool Canyon on the Green River in northeastern Utah; and on the Colorado into which it feeds, Stillwater, Cataract, and Glen canyons; and then Marble Canyon, Echo Cliffs, and the Grand Canyon in Arizona. On the Virgin River in Nevada, Paranuweap Canyon is in places only twenty feet wide but a thousand feet deep.

These fissures, many full of violent streams, and many others as dry and silent as the bones that lie in them, and still others sleeping now under the waters of man-made reservoirs, are the secrets of the horizons. They aren't visible to a person standing on one of the highways to Las Vegas, perhaps stranded out of gas, or simply stretching his legs, along the road to the capitals of gambling and divorce and the tumbling rapids of money turning over and over.

The Colorado River was said by the Indians to have been laid out by God as a highway to Heaven for a man who refused to stop mourning for his wife until he'd seen her in that place. When the man came home, comforted to have seen his wife in the afterworld, God filled this road to Paradise with maelstroms and drowning in order to keep others from going there.

The canyons are the clear record of the past, the highways the clear record of the present. The future stands changeless and eternal in the deserts and the ranges. But like the future, the belittling stasis of mountains can be crossed.

Our only method for escaping the future is to move into it and claim it as the present. This is the great endeavor of the West.

The canyons of the Green and the Colorado rivers were first mapped by John Wesley Powell in 1869. From Powell's journal it would appear that his band of explorers spent a great deal of their time and made a good bit of their distance by carrying their cargo, and often even their boats, overland beside waters too rough to accommodate any passage.

Powell's party had reason to be cautious because, according to their best information, the Colorado poured into a hole in the earth somewhere in Arizona and rushed for an unknown distance through a void.

They began their journey at Green River City in what is now Wyoming. Within two weeks, within the first fifty miles, they had a boat dashed to pieces on the rocks of the Canyon of Lodore rapids. The three men in the boat made it safely to an island in the river's midst, from which the rest of the party rescued them. The three were lost and then recovered all in the space of a few minutes, but "We are as glad to shake hands with them," Powell wrote that night in his diary, "as though they had been on a voyage around the world, and wrecked on a distant coast."

The next day, a little way downriver, they came on the wreckage of the first party of white people ever to try this journey.

As Powell had it, hardly anything was known about those first explorers except that they were led by a man named Ashley. Some miles above the place of these disasters, the name ASHLEY can be read where he chiseled it into a rock, along with the date, which is illegible. Shortly afterward, according to Powell, almost everyone in the Ashley party was killed. Ashley and one other man climbed from the waters alive, and hauled themselves up the canyon's walls. Living on berries and cactus they made their way overland to Salt Lake City, took refuge with the Mormons, and earned their way by laboring on the foundation of the temple. Powell couldn't find anyone to tell him what became of Ashley and his nameless companion after they left that town.

But Powell was listening to local legend. In truth it's doubtful that the Ashley who carved his name onto a rock and then wrecked his party in the Green River ever saw the temple, or even its foundation, in Salt Lake City. A William Henry Ashley, who eventually became a congressman for Missouri, is credited with having navigated the

Green River in 1825 and with establishing fur trade routes in that country that made him a rich man; and in 1826 he led an expedition that reached the vicinity of the Great Salt Lake. He died in 1838. The Mormons, on the other hand, didn't establish their colony in Salt Lake until decades later: In the late 1840s, without a map, a stream of some twelve thousand apostles of Brigham Young—a New Englander with twenty-seven wives and scores of children—crossed the world from Nauvoo, Illinois. The first of them arrived in the summer, exhausted and starved, near the endless burning white flats of the Great Salt Lake, leaving in their wake four relay colonies and more than two thousand graves.

At that time Utah was a part of Mexico, forsaken by the American people and also, according to the mountain men who had first reached her, forsaken by God. Here, in the Salt Lake Valley, a full thousand miles beyond what had been, until then, the farthest American frontier, the Mormons settled down to build their temple and lay out a celestial city and await, as they continue to do, the destruction of the world by fire.

Parts of the desert, in themselves forbidding, are also forbidden: areas of the Nellis Bombing and Gunnery Range complex in Nevada are off-limits, especially Yucca and Frenchman Flats, the two dry lake beds where from 1951 to the early sixties America exploded its atomic weapons; in Utah, the Dugway Proving Grounds, the Hill Air Force Range, the Wendover Range, and the Desert Test Center are all restricted; and much of Edwards Air Force Base on the Mojave in California—where the sound barrier fell in 1947 and the first space shuttle *Columbia* touched down in 1981—is closed to us; and south of Death Valley, the roads to the China Lakes Naval Weapons Center and the Fort Irwin Military Reservation are barred. On the Sonoran Desert in Arizona, sixteen Titan II missiles bearing nuclear warheads stood through the Cold War in a circle of power around the city of Tucson. These are things the maps might tell you, or the newspapers. The people of the Mojave will tell you you're getting close to the Nevada line and that you can wander at seventy mph up Interstate

15 through Nipton and other towns without grass—towns made out of trailers and stunned by heat—to Las Vegas, a city that cherishes several green lawns and some trees and seems to take place in an enormous silence, like a phonograph playing in the wilderness. Even indoors the games clink and whir irrelevantly within the larger pursuit of time going after endlessness. Las Vegas is not forbidding. It's an inviting town; in fact it's a town that's hard to get out of. And yet it's a simple matter to walk after dark down the Strip to the border of neon and, whether you're a winner or a loser, to stare at a blackness that seems to reach down into the heart of all experience.

Other places seem forbidding or forsaken but are neither. Near the waterless Gila River in Arizona, a dozen miles from the trailer town (population twenty) of Sentinel, a mile past the ghost town of Agua Caliente (a main street, a collapsing two-storied hotel, and sand-drifted storefronts snagged with tumbleweed, once a small resort until the hot springs one day ceased) past these, a pie-shaped tin sign on a phone pole announces THE CHILDREN OF THE LIGHT/THREE MI. and points down a dirt path through a slag heap dreamscape of asteroidal desolation. The air along this one-lane path, and the atmosphere over Agua Caliente and over Sentinel, is a perpetually shimmering fog of dust out of which now appears a metal corral gate hung with another sign: WELCOME/KINDLY SHUT/GATE BEHIND YOU.

Beyond this gate the path is walled and roofed with date palms fifty feet tall. Crimson and yellow and pale blue rosebushes, oleanders, and morning glories pour up out of their roots. The mild, ceaseless desert dust-blow falls here, too, but now it comes down through the rainbow mist of sprinklers and descends on a number of low buildings and green lawns attended by venerable gnarled pine trees, and on a swimming pool. Truck gardens and small fruit orchards lie around the buildings. In the middle of each garden, a faucet planted in the dirt spills clear water all day long, bringing it up unreasonably out of the heart of one of the most arid regions in the world and bestowing it on the shoots and seedlings of the Children of the Light.

The Children of the Light are not children. Most of them appear to be in their seventies. They are the Elect, living as virgins and eunuchs in the Reign of Heaven, and they do not expect to die. They number nineteen—a dozen women and seven men. They grow their own food, raise their own buildings, and make most of their clothes out of white linen imported from Scotland. They offer nothing for sale and solicit no contributions. All but one has taken the name of a stone.

When I visited them in 1981 I found their leader, Opal, a tall woman in her late seventies, tearing turnips up out of the earth in one of the gardens. On her vest of white linen her identification was embroidered in gold thread: ELECT OPAL. She wore a denim skirt and tennis shoes and the sweat poured off her. "It'll be time for water soon," she told me. I wondered why she didn't just stoop down and drink from the faucet two yards away, but I didn't ask. I sensed that nothing I knew applied here.

Elect Opal took me around the buildings, glad to entertain a visitor, and showed me how the basements were shelved and rowed with two- and three-gallon jugs of canned fruit and vegetables, grains, nuts, and dry beans. Their main business was to grow and stockpile this food. They already had enough to feed the nineteen of them for several decades. The Children of the Light, she told me, were entirely self-sufficient and would continue to be so following the destruction of the world by fire. She didn't think highly of the descendants of Brigham Young and his followers. "The Mormons are storing up just for themselves," she said. "Our food supply is for anybody who finds us."

The Children of the Light had begun, under Opal's leadership, in Canada some thirty years before. They had lost their church and had wandered for twelve years through the central provinces and down through the United States, in a caravan of cars and trailers, seeking their place and praying for deliverance from this vagabondage. "One night," she told me proudly, "in a location in Florida, I was sitting out front of the trailer with Jewel, and there did appear before us in the air a flaming television screen ringed around with a halo of purple fire. In the middle of the screen we both read these words: *Agua Caliente*. We found it on a map and came here."

Near the largest building, a dinner bell rang.

"It's time for water now," she said.

We went into the central building, a place with a roomy, modern kitchen, a dining area like a small cafeteria, and at the end opposite the kitchen, a plate glass window looking out onto an arrangement of flower beds. Before the window was a kind of orchestra pit with a bass viola, a piano, some horns in their cases, and several music stands. "We have music on Sunday," Opal told me.

I greeted the others—speechless, smiling old women in white linen, and a few men who also had nothing to say to me—and we sat down to have water. We drank it measured out by the half cup, because, Opal told me, somewhere in the Bible it says, "And they shall drink water by the measure." Every two hours Elect Phil, the only one not named for a mineral of the earth, rang the bell; and they all drank water together in the kitchen, by the measure.

Water is the heart of the miracle of the Children of the Light. On their arrival in the town of Agua Caliente they found the empty hotel and the two dead streets and learned from the few residents of Sentinel, twelve miles away, that the hot springs had dried up, there had never been any fresh water, and nobody could hope to survive a summer here. The Children of the Light camped out in the old hotel, and with pooled funds, under the direction of God and the guidance of Opal, they bought eighty acres of black slag, using their last few hundred dollars to hire a driller to go down a hundred feet for water. The driller got nothing. They asked him if he'd please go down another hundred feet without payment. He agreed, and several feet lower tapped into a buried lake of fresh water more massive than the acreage above it. It hadn't been there before. The construction of the Roosevelt Dam, two hundred miles away, had somehow caused the formation of this underground reservoir sometime in the previous five years.

It was Holy Saturday, and I'd come here to the easternmost fingertip of the Yuma Desert, four days after the space shuttle *Columbia*'s landing on the Mojave, to see if I might help the

Children of the Light greet this Easter. But they told me that celebrations and holidays were never observed here. All the mornings, afternoons, and evenings are the same in the Reign of Heaven.

Elect Topaz, a tiny, round old lady with a sweet, befuddled expression, told me that each morning before breakfast they got together in the basement right below our feet to pray and receive their instructions. After breakfast they labored through the day, sewing, canning, carpentering, hoeing, planting—water every two hours; lunch; dinner. They passed the evenings talking or reading. Sometimes there was music.

"Who gives you the day's instructions?" I asked.

"The Voice."

"The Voice?" I said. "Where does the Voice come from?"

"From Opal," she told me, "out of Opal's mouth."

After water, Opal showed me around the main building. The sewing room, housing half a dozen electric-powered Singers, was off the dining area. Beyond the kitchen, in another wing, we looked into the men's dormitory—rustic and wood-paneled—and the women's, which was done in a kind of pink French Provincial. There were private bedrooms, lavatories, a study, a sitting room of meditative quiet.

Upstairs was a room they never entered. "The Voice," Opal said, "asked us to build this." It was a fair-size room with a fireplace, gleaming oak floors, and a tremendous table of cherry wood silently addressed by thirteen chairs. "We don't go in there," she said.

On the table a Bible—by far the largest book I'd ever seen, bigger than a whole case of most Bibles—lay spread open, but I never found out to what page.

"What is the purpose of this room?" I asked her.

She was amused by my question. "We don't know about any purposes," she said. "We were told to build it and we built it. Then the Voice said we'd better come up with a table and thirteen chairs. You have no idea the trouble we had getting that table built, getting it all the way out to this place, and then hauling it up here to the second floor." She pointed to our left, where they'd built a ramp from the ground up to this level. "It was the only way we could bring that table up here."

"This Voice," I said. "It just comes out of you all of a sudden?"

"Yes, it does," she said. "It's a great gift." Opal wasn't without a sense of humor. She seemed to be getting a kick out of my hesitation.

As I was leaving, Opal gave me a rose blossom almost the size of a cabbage in which four or five pastel colors swam together. "This is called Joseph's Coat," she said. "The coat of many colors." She gave me a cake of heavy bread mixed with dates, nuts, and honey, which she referred to as "manna"—"They were given manna in the wilderness," she quoted for me. Dust fell down all over everything.

I said good-bye to Sapphire, a woman in her teens, the youngest of the Elect, and to Topaz, who'd apparently adopted her. "How do you choose your names?" I wanted to know.

"Oh," Sapphire said, "The Voice gives them to us," and Topaz nodded and said, "The Voice."

The Southwest must be the only place on the earth with such a concentration of frightening names: Disaster Falls, Massacre Lake, Jornada del Muerto, Sangre de Cristo, Death Valley, Skull Valley, Bloody Basin, Tombstone, Deadman Wash . . .

Many of the landmarks along the Green and Colorado rivers were christened by John Wesley Powell. Some have kept their Indian names, and others have become what the Spanish priests or early settlers called them. A few have been officially redesignated: Toompin Tuweap (Land of Rock) is now Canyonlands National Park, Utah; Gunnison's Crossing has disappeared from the maps; and in Cataract Canyon, originally named by Powell, there are no more cataracts—at present it lies under the man-made body of water named for him, Lake Powell.

In his explorations, Powell learned that the Ute Indians weren't the first to live along the Green River. He located the foundations of ancient buildings and unearthed shards of pottery. The Utes knew of rocks, farther up the mountains, covered with pictures, but they had no idea who had made these things.

In Arizona, too, the dwellers first encountered by white explorers weren't themselves the first to dwell there. Some other civilization had preceded them, faded, and left no history. Its most extensive bequest to us is a great adobe structure surrounded by the remains of outbuildings, a sacred complex that stands within sight of the two water towers of the Arizona State Prison complex in Florence. The huge adobe ruins facing the prison are called Casa Grande, the Big House, named without irony by the Papago Indians who discovered it centuries ago, the phrase later translated by the Spanish fathers. The people who erected the Big House are called Hohokam, "Those Who Are Gone." The name they gave to themselves, the name they had every reason to believe was their name, is forgotten.

Something under the desert speaks to the yearning spirit, chiefly by refusing to speak at all. In the immenseness of sand that goes on communing with itself in a terrifying way, ignoring everything, answering itself with itself while the sky overhead wears out, the soul feels the same insignificance as the soul of the lost sailor.

Its look has been compared to the moon's, and the similarity is more than a visual one. Like the moon, the desert can't possibly be survived—but it has been. Like the moon, the desert is the place of distance, light, and dreams.

To a man or woman trying to get across it, it isn't a landscape but a hostile medium, a dusty and sometimes steamy glare of fortnights to the west, a hopeless waste very like the top of the sea, a place not so much to be looked at as lived through. Part of its beauty is this hard fact, that while we're seeing it, we're also surviving it; and the sight arouses in us the humble gratitude of refugees.

DISPATCH FROM WORLD WAR III

A guy rolls into the men's john at the Dhahran International Hotel complaining, "Hell, how do they expect to have a war without a bar?" This is a virtually intoxicant-free conflict, no weird concoctions circulating in these parts other than those brewed by a few enterprising GIs, or by Saddam's mad scientists. Maybe that's why in these first few days it's been a ticktock war, everything going off like clockwork, nobody driving backward over the latrine or dropping ordnance on a hallucination. The closest thing to a party punch was the wild adrenaline camaraderie that manifested itself during what has come to be referred to in Dhahran as K Day, which hit around three o'clock in the morning, Saudi time. In the basement of the Dhahran International, where the Joint Information Bureau tried to keep track of and somehow assist more than one hundred mostly terrified journalists in gas masks, the overwhelming impression was that of a demented Halloween party to which everyone had come dressed as the same monster, a sort of ant-eyed elephant with an amputated trunk. The pilot of a grounded commercial helicopter reveals he's just been processed out of the Marines, waving his military photo ID: "I'm going upstairs the minute this air raid's over," he shouts, "and I'm gonna sign right back up." An infantrywoman slaps her sidearm and says she's got a name scratched on every bullet. How does she know what the names will be? "Hell," she says, "they all start with Al."

At the Carlton Hotel nearby, we'd heard the planes taking off at midnight. At 3:00 A.M. the civilian support personnel suddenly spilled into the halls, shouting instructions to one another and hopping from door to door with their legs jammed halfway into MOPP suits, waking up their comrades. "Ron! Ron! Ron!" somebody shouted through my door. "Come on, man, it's happening!" I opened the door to confront a figure in a MOPP suit who said, "Steve! Steve! Get your gear on!" "But I'm not Steve," I told him, and a German reporter standing in his doorway in his undershorts said to me, "Yes. The war is started." My next-door neighbor, a computer operator named Dave, seized a brief silence to utter what will always be, for me, the first pronouncement by an American about this conflict: "The son of a bitch," he said, "was warned."

The war is started, yes. But which war? Isn't this a world war? And isn't it, as a matter of fact, the third? The question came up among writers watching CNN at the Dhahran International during the next exhausted day. Most say it's not a *world* war, it's just multinational. But how many countries have to join before you call it global? Aren't these several enough? Well, it's not a matter of quantity, it's the presence of major powers that makes a world war. How many major powers? France, England, and the United States aren't enough? Well, no, you need more: You need Russia. Russia, the country that for decades had been expected to start it, has neglected to show up for World War III.

During breakfast on K Day at the Carlton, one of the PX workers stands up in the dining room and screams, "How can I face the world when I'm not blow-dried?" We've been rifling through the kitchen for cereal and coffee because the hotel staff have all gone into hiding somewhere. CNN blasts over the hotel's public address, and we know by these reports what has happened before we manage to experience it. Isn't there any such thing as real life anymore? We end the night watching the news of ourselves and others in the region: tapes of the 82nd Airborne eating French toast made with white bread and swallowing nerve gas immunity pills.

At five o'clock the next morning, the chanters take up the morning prayer of Islam over the biggest loudspeakers in town, the first long syllable sounding precisely like the start of an air-raid siren: One by one by one, the voices raised to Allah drown everything out.

It's Sunday, January 20, 1991. We're heading toward the front. The coast of the oil-rich Gulf resembles Ocean Avenue in Santa Monica, and has the same atmosphere of irrigated desert meeting the blue sea. The highway north out of Dhahran burns straight through a historical emptiness, away from white beaches, toward the town of Khafji and the border with Kuwait. This part of the world looks like northern Nevada without the gas-stop casinos, without the beat-up trailer parks, though an occasional Bedouin encampment of tents and shanties serves as well, and then those are gone and the world resembles Nevada without even Nevada, a vast dirt Arctic on top of which nobody ever lived and nothing ever happened, while underneath, the minerals burbled. And now two armies of more than a million people have assembled in this region, which seems to have been created only to provide an arena for this battle.

Every four seconds another two-story military transport moves north over this road. Farther north is a shut-down restaurant with about eight hundred cars parked outside it—this is the place where Arab soldiers leave their private vehicles and head for their emplacements.

At the intersection of the Dhahran-Khafji highway and what is now called Dodge MSR (main supply route) by the military, three boys man a machine gun behind a stack of cinder blocks on which they've spray-painted PINK FLOYD/THE WALL. Their purpose is to give directions to lost transports. "I always forget what day it is," the sergeant from Colorado says. "Then I have to wait till Country Countdown comes on Armed Forces Radio. Then you know it's Sunday." "Hey, buddy, hold this for me," the Puerto Rican private from Manhattan says, and tosses me a grenade. Four kilometers to the northeast, a lake of fire burns on the desert floor—something to do with an oil refinery—burning so brightly it lights the entire sky as the night comes down, but the boys have no idea why it's burning. It just does; it burns and burns. I myself begin to tremble. It's the deep, primitive terror of History's devouring darkness. The boys see themselves as having finally found something more enormous than their own deaths. As I stand in the middle of this desert, I begin to suspect that this war's origins reach far back in time, to the recession of the first waters that left this land empty and waiting to be filled with conflagration.

It's been ten days since the bombing started north of the Iraqi border. The plume from the burning refineries in Kuwait has grown to a cloud and then to a general stink over the entire region. History's most massive oil slick is drifting down the Gulf. The troops on both sides, a million people with dust in their mouths, expect something terrible to begin any minute. The war is really on. The blood-carnival speechifying of Saddam Hussein has trailed off, and he now says he prays for the American parents, that their sons not be injured. The Veg-o-Matic apocalyptese of his rhetoric—the allies "swimming in their own blood," "the Mother of All Wars"—is reduced to a murmur as predictions give way to events, and reality seems ready to replace all our pitiful words.

And yet the Middle East's pipeline to rhythm—studios one, two, and three of the Armed Forces Radio and Television Service—keep on filling the desert nights with a certain military teenage bopalula that must be the only power on earth as wrenchingly American as these soldiers themselves. You get more for your music here. Everything has a double meaning, an import deeper than any intended by the composers—the chorus *I will survive,* from the Grateful Dead; a new version of Bob Dylan's "Knockin' on Heaven's Door"; "We've Gotta Get Out of this Place," the Animals' tune from the sixties; and "Wanted Dead or Alive," a song by Bon Jovi with the refrain *Goin' down in a blaze of glory.*

Meanwhile, in the Hotel Carlton's restaurant, officers of the armed forces of the Kingdom of Saudi Arabia, many of them guests of this hotel, linger over their meals of *mutabal,* lamb curry, calmly chatting, wearing uniforms of unwrinkled camouflage. There are no women—Western or otherwise—in the restaurant. It is a universe of men. The Saudi women, in fact, don't exist at all—they're small voids hidden completely under their vestments. A black-cloaked woman moving down a pale, sunstruck alley seems a shimmering, absent darkness headed out on some unfathomable, maybe fatal, errand. Outside, on the street, Saudi businessmen seem to move about with a calm assurance. Aren't they worried about this war? It's as if the war is taking place on another continent, some unholy environment far from Mecca.

Along the two main military supply routes, code-named Dodge and Audi, convoys crawl west and north—hundreds of miles of armaments and armored vehicles, and the ammunition and fuel they'll consume, also the men and women who will use them, hauled mostly by eighteen-wheelers. And coming back south and east on the same routes, the same eighteen-wheelers, empty, no longer hauling the vehicles needed to smash through defensive earthworks, the vehicles for plowing up mines, for hurling strings of dynamite across concertina wire—empty of the hinged steel spans needed to bridge defensive ditches, empty of the tanks and BFVs expected to cross them, of the men expecting to follow in bulky chemical-proof suits and gas masks, of the artillery that will light up the world ahead if they attack.

From in among the huge transport trucks, when a clear space opens for half a mile or so ahead on the straight, two-way desert road, suddenly a dozen or more small civilian vehicles pull out to pass—Honda Accords, Toyota Landcruisers, and little Nissan pickups carrying Saudi shepherds, piloted serenely by the citizens of Nariya or Hafr al Baten, the towns on the westward supply route—a kind of miniature convoy swinging out in unison from the obscurity of the larger one, racing ahead a few spaces and disappearing as it merges again with the monstrous vehicles of the military alliance. In the north of the kingdom it's like that now, the Arab lives moving in the shadows of these machines. They careen insouciantly in and out of this armada. Their fate is in the hands of Allah; the Westerners, by contrast, rely on heavy machinery.

They stream in and and out. All night and day, small personnel carriers pull up in front of the Carlton Hotel, and uniformed men and women toting M-16 rifles fan out into the lobby, as if ordered there to perform some unusual form of sentry duty, to stand at this bank of telephones, shouting "I love you, I love you, tell my boys, my little girl, tell her, tell him, tell them . . ." The ground offensive against Iraq is only days away, they believe, and they voice these feelings loudly and without embarrassment, some of them weeping, oblivious to the guests and other soldiers around them.

A young American woman in a jogging outfit leans against the same bank of telephones, shouting halfway across the world in a Southern accent: "No, she's not with me! I'm in Saudi Arabia, remember?"—very slowly—"Sow-dy Arabia! How are you doing? No, I'm in Saudi Arabia, remember? With the Army. How are things? Has it snowed? Has it *snowed. Snowed.* No, it doesn't snow in Saudi Arabia! It's hot! It's like a desert here!"

THE MILITIA IN ME

In July 1992, I went to Alaska to pan for gold, and to live out the
happy story, I don't mind admitting, of the American who finds
something fundamentally valuable and untouched in earth no person
has ever walked on. My first day in Anchorage I made the acquaintance of two men who fascinated me. John lived off the land and
well off the grid and on, as he put it, "the cutting edge of freedom"
in the hills outside Talkeetna; had built his own cabin, acted as mid-
wife at the births of his four children. His friend Richard prospected
in the Bonanza Hills southwest of Anchorage and hunted bears with
a compound bow. They'd set up a kind of headquarters in a booth
at the Arctic Burger, a coffee shop frequented by Alaska oldtimers—
they still call it "the Roadrunner" though copyright laws forced a
renaming years ago. Openhanded, cheerful men—winning to talk
to—these two had come into the city that summer to stump for presidential canditate and ex–Green-Beret-hero Col. Bo Gritz. Not that
they cared much for politicians or harbored any great hopes for government. Richard himself refused to pay taxes on his income. The
IRS was after him for over a hundred thousand dollars, but he
denied them any claim to legal authority, as the sixteenth
Amendment had never been properly ratified. "The whole thing's a

bluff," he said. He'd gone so far as to have himself deleted, somehow, from the Social Security system—his Alaska driver's license showed, where the familiar number should be, nine big zeroes all in a row.

"Bo Gritz is a true leader," Richard said. "He gave a speech in Colorado and eight thousand men in the audience pledged they'd follow him into battle if it came down to that. That's eight battalions," he pointed out.

And it was time to talk of battalions. Forty-three concentration camps had been built around the country. Under U.N. auspices, foreign troops conducted exercises on our soil; others, whole divisions, waited on the Baja peninsula. Both men believed that somebody had shanghaied the United States, that pirates had seized the helm of the ship of state and now steered it toward some completely foreign berth where it could be plundered at leisure. One of Bo Gritz's military contacts, they said, had verified all this. "The word's gone out, the order's come down: 1992 will see the last presidential election."

My wife and I honeymooned that month, just us two, at Richard's mining operation in the Bonanza Hills. A plane dropped us off, and a plane would pick us up nine days later. Meanwhile Cindy and I lived without any contact with what I had up to then believed to be the world, in a place without human community, authority, or law, seventy miles from the nearest person. We brought a shotgun with us—I'd never before owned a gun, somebody else always handled that stuff in what I'd thought of as the world—and I was surprised to discover that keeping it ready and handy instantly asserted itself as the bedrock requirement of our lives. And other things I'd never thought about became uppermost, matches and tools and, above all, clarity of thought and our ability to improvise—we had to stay focused in our senses, ever mindful of our tasks, because what we'd brought, and who we were, was all we had. At last whatever happened to us could only be *our* fault or bad fortune, and fixing it *our* responsibility. We realized our lives had never before been our own—*our* lives.

I had always lived under the protection of what I've since heard called "the Nanny State": Big Mom, ready to patch me up, bail me out, calm me down, and only a three-digit phone call away.

Just the same, it's a free country. I'd always taken for granted that the government looked after the basics and left me free to enjoy my liberty. Now I wasn't so sure. This little taste of real autonomy excited in me a craving for it. Maybe I wanted freedom from the government's care and protection. Maybe I wanted freedom from any government at all. I felt grateful for people like Richard, who'd run away from home and could get along for weeks at a time in places like the Bonanza Hills.

In the immense solitude of the Bonanza Hills somebody had been reading. In the prospector's cabin we found a few books: *None Dare Call It Conspiracy* by Gary Allen and Larry Abraham, describing the gigantic fraud perpetrated by the nation's Federal Reserve system. *Racial Hybridity* by Philip Jones, B.A. Also by the same author: *The Negro: Serpent, Beast, and Devil* —a stamp in the flap identified it as the property of the Aryan Nation Church in Hayden Lake, not sixty miles from our home in Idaho. We'd heard of them: eight guys in a rundown compound with a lot of wooden crosses and kerosene, taken seriously by nobody except those who were paid to do so, like the press and the FBI.

When we got back to Anchorage, Cindy and I attended the America First Party's rally for Bo Gritz, a small affair, surely fewer than a hundred people under an awning hastily erected in a light Alaskan rain, city folks and country folks, but mostly country folks, of all ages but mostly middle-aged, eating moose and venison barbecued right there in the small downtown park. There was one black kid present about eighteen, laughing at the world and enjoying the food. Nobody bothered him. Bo Gritz showed up, ate some moose, and made a speech. A man of medium height, barrel-chested and blunt-faced, he looked less like my idea of a warrior than like someone who'd hire himself out to collect delinquent loans. One loan in particular concerned him: He promised, if elected, to instruct Congress to mint a single coin "of the basest, most worthless metal we can find," to which he'd assign the value of one trillion dollars. "And I'll toss it down at the feet of the bankers and say—there, pick it up. That's the national debt. *Paid in full.*" The crowd, small as it was, managed to produce a roar. "It may seem our numbers are small. And they are," he said. "But I'm not worried. Do you know why? Because I've read the book, and I know how it turns out." And just as he said it, some in the audience nodded and said too: "*We win.*"

What book? The Bible's Revelation? *The Turner Diaries,* in which provocateurs touch off a racial Armageddon? I didn't ask. And what would we win?—an election, or a war? I didn't ask.

The people I talked with seemed to imply that the greatest threat to liberty came from a conspiracy, or several overlapping conspiracies, well known to everybody but me. As a framework for thought, this has its advantages. It's quicker to call a thing a crime and ask *Who did it?* than to call it a failure and set about answering the question *What happened?*

A year later, I'm traveling the Texas-Mexico border region in a rented car. The border patrol stops me well north of Big Bend National Park—sixty miles north of the border—and the officer asks me who I am and where I'm from and I tell him. "Can we have a look in your vehicle?" "What if I said no?" "Then we'd bring the dog over and he'd tell us we better search the vehicle." "You mean he'd give you probable cause for a search?" "Just your refusal to let us search," the officer says, "would be probable cause for a search."

In the elections last November a number of Democrats ran unopposed in our county. Republicans held on to their offices, but gained none locally. Nearly one-fifth of the people here receive some kind of public assistance—twice the rate of the New York boroughs—and our main industry is heavily subsidized by the federal government. But this isn't some hippie conclave next door to San Francisco. It's Boundary County, Idaho's northernmost district.

Perhaps above all our subsidized industry, logging—with access roads built free by the federal government and stands of timber in the national forest auctioned off to lumber corporations at a loss to the nation's taxpayers—makes this region a resentful hot zone. We live in these hills, we see them covered with tens of thousands of square miles of a marketable, renewable crop, but the government insists on letting too many of these trees grow up, fall over dead, burn to ash, come to nothing. Resentment makes a blind spot when it comes to extremists—you hate the government? So do we, even if between the two hatreds lies a vast, mainly unexamined, difference.

Three years ago the Weaver family, who lived south of us on Ruby Ridge, ended an eighteen-month siege in a firefight with U.S. marshals. In the first exchange of shots, one of the marshals and one of the Weaver children died. Two hundred federal marshals and FBI agents descended on the town of Bonners Ferry. None of us knew where all these people had come from. They instituted a curfew and banned gatherings, ran up debts in the stores, surrounded the Weaver place, killed Mrs. Weaver while she stood in the doorway of her cabin with her infant daughter in her arms. Bo Gritz showed up and talked her husband Randy and her surviving children into surrendering. The federal agents left town. None of us knew where they'd gone.

Then, too, here live a few folks like me—a city boy grown too neurotic to abide urban life, a lover of the wilderness chiefly for its solitude, but certainly no country boy—surrounded by a forest that would quickly extinguish him were he ever to lose his way in it, working half the day at a computer console and then stepping out to stumble mystified among the greasy barely functioning accoutrements of rural living, snowplows and well pumps and chain saws and pickups, things the local ten-year-olds can take down into piles and reassemble blindfolded. I fish poorly. I've never hunted, mainly for fear I'll shoot myself. And I like the trees, whether standing up or fallen over rotting. I don't like seeing clear-cuts like great big vacant lots in the wilderness. Yet I'm one who's lent sympathy to the militias, the throwback mountaineers, even the Christian Nazis. This is a free country. I just want to be left alone. I thought that's all they wanted, too.

During the eighteen months that Randy Weaver lived under a kind of self-arrest thirty miles away, it regularly occurred to me that if I were a real journalist, I'd be visiting him often and getting the story on him and his family before whatever was going to happen finally happened. But he clearly valued his privacy; and I must not be a real journalist, because I felt compelled to value it, too. What did they want? I didn't ask.

In the sixties I was a pot-deranged beatnik who remained in college mainly to avoid Vietnam. I didn't trust that particular government, but I thought that Washington could fix things if only *we* could take it over. Now I'm in the White House, or somebody a whole lot like me is.

At about three o'clock one morning in October 1994, while you and I were sleeping, Congress passed the Telephone Privacy Act requiring the phone companies to reengineer their equipment, and granting $300 million in federal funds to make the change, so that every phone in the United States of America can be tapped by federal agents from their offices.

At breakfast one morning, also that October, my family and I read the weekly paper together, captivated by its account of the recent sweep-search of the Sandpoint Middle School. Cops and dogs had locked the children down for three hours while they combed through lockers and belongings. They found a pistol and a bag of marijuana, not a big haul, but the principal was satisfied that he'd managed to "send a message." Indeed he had. My kids attended Mt. Hall Elementary about sixty miles north, and they heard it all the way up here. A couple of questions: What language is that, exactly? And one my son Daniel asked: "How come they didn't just use the intercom?" The response of North Idaho parents to this message was overwhelmingly favorable.

*   *   *

From Section 90107 of the Omnibus Crime Bill: "The President may declare a State or part of a State to be a violent crime or drug emergency area and may take appropriate actions authorized by this section." Such actions include sending in federalized National Guard, and "any Federal agency." Section 180102 authorizes Multi-Jurisdictional Task Forces to be funded with "assets seized as a result of investigations" to be used "to enhance the operations of the task force and its participating State and local law-enforcement agencies."

Ryan runs the surplus store down the road, the kind of surplus store that lives up to all the expectations about North Idaho, dealing in, along with the usual outdoor gear, gas masks, semiautomatic rifles, concealable weapons, literature like *The Anarchist's Cookbook*. I bought all four volumes of *The Poor Man's James Bond* there and that's all any writer would ever need in the way of reference material on murder, terror, or guerrilla war. I like Ryan. He's a student of the U.S. Constitution, and he keeps a stack of Informed Jury pamphlets on the counter right at the point-of-purchase. Often we talk politics, and we find a lot to agree about—he's become as suspicious of the State as I have. But when I suggested that maybe he'd like to check out the Libertarian Party, he was shocked at the libertarian notion that each person should be allowed to pursue happiness in his or her own way, even homosexuals. "But you could have a township that banned gays, as long as people weren't forced to live there, and as long as you didn't go over and bomb the gay township," I pointed out. "Listen: Do you know what they *do* to each other?" Ryan asked me. "We *would* go over and bomb them."

What about that college beatnik—was he in the government's sights? I wrote away to the FBI for my records a couple of years back. Three months later I got four pages headed *Student for a Democratic Society*. Here and there on these pages can be found bits and pieces, mainly about a demonstration I attended in 1967, at which I was arrested. But for the most part, the paragraphs have been blacked out with a felt-tip pen, and I have no idea what they say.

I'm standing by our mailbox on a two-mile straightaway on Meadow Creek Road between the Purcell Mountains and Deer Ridge, one of my favorites places on earth. In this alpine region the valley's bed is the largest open space I can stand in, four square miles occupied by our family and five others. In the mailbox today I find an envelope bearing no return address, and in the envelope two legal-size typesheets crammed with a six-thousand word tract entitled "BLUEPRINT FOR The FINAL TAKEOVER OF THE USA By 2 ALIEN Jews, Donald Goldberg and Indy Badh-WAR." It describes how the president starts a phony war and then uses demonstrations against this war as an excuse to suspend civil liberties. "Secret, elaborate plans for martial law and for directing military WITHIN OUR BORDERS IS already drawn up/distributed . . ."

About once a week I play cards at the Club Bar just across the state line in Troy, Montana. The Club is profoundly Montanan, a patchwork homemade-feeling saloon with a barrel stove and a fight every night and dogs and orphans wandering in and out, and a plywood coffin propped up in a corner. The bar itself is no great shakes. They used to have an impressive one, but in the sixties a powder-monkey for the Highway Department came in during his lunch hour wired with dynamite and ordered everybody out, then blew himself up, and the bar too. The establishment's owner, Tony Brown, explains that the coffin is for "the next guy who dies in here."

In the eighties, Tony served as the mayor of Troy, and perhaps by reason of this former prominence the Militia of Montana approached him almost two years ago. In a series of private meetings "right here at this table," he says, slapping the poker table, a group of three men assured him that they intended to protect the rights of citizens and discriminate against none. Tony Brown agreed to book the local high school's auditorium for a meeting of the Militia of Montana.

In the meantime, he read the militia's literature, and he had some questions. "Do you mean to tell me," he asked them, "that if a little faggot boy wanted to lead the charge, like blowing on the trumpet, you wouldn't let him in your militia?" John Trochman, head of the militia, told him no— "Not unless he converted to our religion."

Tony Brown makes his way across the small west end of Troy, Montana, a town with no section on the other side of the tracks— all of Troy is on the other side of the tracks. Tony Brown makes his way to the high school, to the militia meeting, where he's agreed to serve as MC. He cuts through a neighbor's backyard, gets hold of one of the neighbor's hens, and plucks from its back one feather.

Interested citizens, mostly men, have filled the auditorium. At this time resentment against the national government runs high in Troy—the U.S. Forest Service has just floated a list of proposed regulations that make it hard to imagine any human could set foot in the federal forests without transgressing them, and it's rumored also that 30,000 rounds of ammunition have been issued to the officers in anticipation of having to enforce the new rules. Better than two hundred angry Trojans have come to hear what the Militia of Montana has to say about all this.

Tony Brown, holding a chicken feather in his left hand, places his right one over his heart and leads the gathering in the Pledge of Allegiance. He reads Articles I and II of the U.S. Constitution, and the Declaration of Independence, and the Constitution of the State of Montana, and then, by way of introducing Mr. Trochman, he reads a nine-page speech lamenting that "the current state of America is truly alarming to any man who is capable of reflection," a speech all about Thomas Paine and the Founding Fathers and the Kennedy assassination and the Warren Commission and the forest service and taxation without representation, and about the night in 1773 when American colonists stuck feathers in their hats and dumped out tea in Boston Harbor.

Brown finishes his speech by refusing to endorse the Militia of Montana, and then sticks his feather in his hair and walks out of the meeting, out of the building, back to the Club. Back to the poker game.

"I was the first one to tell those assholes they were assholes," Brown likes to say these days. "But I want it understood—all these extra laws, extra police, extra oppression: I just don't think that's the way to go."

As I watched the TV coverage of the Waco tragedy in 1993, I kept in mind that the trouble there began over the nature of the firearms the Branch Davidians had stockpiled for themselves, over the question whether their weapons were military but legal, or *too* military and forbidden. It occurred to me that the attempt to abridge or deny what people see as a basic human right can result in more misery and carnage even than the people's abuse of that right. I began to feel personally involved in the question. I don't want to see whole families killed in order to protect me from the threat of random violence.

The government's vigilance led it to pass in 1992—by no means an unusual legislative year—1,397 new federal laws and to generate 62,928 pages of regulations protecting me from, among other things, the possibility that I might make a bad deal on a nectarine. Have I checked my nectarines lately? The bureaus employed 125,666 people to write these regulations, return them to Congress, and wait for a response. After sixty days a regulation becomes law.

It is illegal to sell a peach smaller than two and three-eighth inches in diameter. Nectarines are covered, too. But nectarines have no fuzz, and are therefore legal down to a diameter of two and five-sixteenth inches.

But if freedom means self-responsibility—what about the people who can't take care of themselves? My friend, I'm one of those people. Every day I don't bring down something fatal on my head is another miracle. And every day I experience such a miracle, I want another one. Leave me alone. I'm in love with these miracles.

Last summer our family took a cabin in the Canadian Yukon, forty miles from the nearest neighbor. I wanted to live again for a while out from under authority. But the local conservation officer came around regularly just to visit—there wasn't anybody but us to talk to—and also one day an immigration officer showed up and interviewed me and wrote things down about me on a pad. I started to wish we'd gone back to Alaska instead.

The life was basic—wood, food, water, weather. I read books about the U.S. Constitution and the Founding Fathers. At night we listened to the shortwave—the VOA, the BBC, Monitor Radio, and also a couple of Christian Right stations whose constituents had obviously become embroiled in the whole question of what the U.S. government thinks it's doing. Looking in my books, reading of the great people and tremendous ideas that had once found a home on this continent and produced the U.S.A., I wondered, too, about the revisions we've since allowed. This isn't the United States I was taught about in school, and it's not the one the Founding Fathers founded. Meanwhile I listened to Linda Thompson, a fiery critic of everything governmental, babbling on WHRI's *For the People* about bringing down U.S. choppers with .308s, and the more modulated voice of the show's host in response, both voices mourning the death of something even more precious than human life, and above all crying out, of Ruby Ridge, of Waco: *What happened?*

The lamentation stirred my heart. The incomprehensible actions of federal agents at Ruby Ridge and Waco had taught me that people willing to make a stand for their rights, run the risk of martyrdom. Always and everywhere that's been the story. But my life long I'd believed the promise that here in America we tell a different story, of a nation created by and for those very people, and no home for bullies and tyrants. A government made, in the words of its first Declaration, "to secure those rights." Not to *grant* them, not to ration, license, or prioritize among them. To *secure* them.

My own unexamined assumption had been that the world's gotten so much more dangerous since the late eighteenth century that only a fool would expect George Washington or James Madison to stand by the original Bill of Rights today.

But I'd forgotten that when they gathered to frame the Constitution they did so in a country full of Tory infidels, just after a revolution, on a continent where several powers vied for rich territory, in a world full of terrorists and saboteurs, in a nation very, very wobbly on its legs. Yet they counted the security of this infant nation less important than the freedom of its citizens—and so they honored the rights of those citizens to speak and think and worship and freely trade, and the right to keep weapons as sophisticated as anything the military could acquire for itself, even to the point of buying a cannon and positioning it on one's front lawn right downtown.

What happened? If I ask the government, if I ask my leaders, they'll say nothing happened. This is still a free country. If I ask the stations broadcasting in the upper bands, the voices from Nashville and New Orleans and Noblesville, Indiana, fading in and out in the ether, they have an answer, but it's an answer to a different question, and it goes like this:

God made the world in eight, not seven, days. Two branches of humanity were fashioned, from one of which descended the Twelve Tribes of Israel; the others, the darker races, God created on a different day. Early in history Sephardic people came down from the north into the Middle East and supplanted the original Jews, drove out the Chosen People, and for centuries these quislings have conspired to rule the earth through the institutions of finance. The true Chosen of God, the descendents from the original Twelve Tribes, are the white race.

Just before the Great Depression the U.S. federal government and the nation's economy itself were hijacked by the Jewish families who run the banks of the Federal Reserve. They seek to own everything and enslave everyone by extending their power over the earth through a one-world government to be developed out of the current United Nations. They foster high-level groups committed to this goal. Anyone who's anyone in U.S. statesmanship, for instance, belongs to the Council on Foreign Relations, and some of them openly espouse the idea of a single world government, though that isn't necessarily the council's stated goal.

These people use the federal income tax, never legally instituted (the amendment fell one vote short of ratification, a fact afterward covered up) to rob us of our wealth. The Federal Reserve prints worthless money and lends it to the nation and gets it back as true value, backed by the good name of the United States, and gets it back with interest.

These ideas have been floating around since before the invention of the printing press. They found a new perch when the Federal Reserve and the League of Nations were formed. People saw them taking a solid shape in the policies of FDR's New Deal, looming large when the U.N. came to be. Who did it? Behind it all, behind all of modern Western history, lurks the Master Conspirator Jew.

The young French nobleman Alexis de Tocqueville traveled the U.S. for nine months in 1831, and in his writings on young America he makes no mention of conspiracy. He found no Jewish plotters. No Secret Service, FBI, BATF. No FDR, no LBJ. Karl Marx, Father of the Communist Conspiracy, had written nothing yet. The Federal Reserve did not exist.

How did America's future look to the Frenchman? "An innumerable multitude of men, all equal and alike, incessantly endeavoring to procure the petty and paltry pleasures with which they glut their lives. . . . Above stands an immense power which takes upon itself alone to secure their gratification. . . . to keep them in perpetual childhood. . . . It covers the surface of society with a network of small complicated rules . . . men are seldom forced by it to act, but are constantly restrained from acting . . . a flock of timid and industrious animals, of which the government is the shepherd . . ."

Alexis de Tocqueville didn't smell a conspiracy, just the natural course of politicking, what we now call "politics as usual," candidates trying any way they can to attach themselves to emotional issues. What do you covet? What do you fear? We'll fix it. Come election day even the national, federal leaders want to be part of my family, putting food on my table, money in my pocket, a zone of safety around my children. That's why so many federal laws duplicate state laws already on the books—the feds want to help run my hometown. The New Republicans call it "micromanaging" a hi-tech phrase that itself just duplicates a couple of old sayings: "All politics is local." Or "Everyone runs for sheriff."

The U.S.A. was meant to be a collection of small governments kept from oppressing minorities and each other by one limited but overarching federal system of laws and courts. But people *prefer* to oppress each other, each one *wants* all the others regulated, and the Feds took a lesson from local politicians who used this basic desire to their advantage by promising to honor it in exchange for votes.

I want to float above the fray, want to be like Walt Whitman, "both in and out of the game, and watching and wondering at it." But when the violence starts, I'm not aloof. I'm in the middle, pulled both ways. When the violence starts, the one in the middle, if he's honest with himself, must feel the guilt for the excesses of both sides.

When I heard about the bombing in Oklahoma City, I felt sick to my soul . . . My God, what have I done?

I believe the State should be resisted wherever it encroaches. But the bombers of that building will demonstrate for us something we don't want demonstrated: There's no trick to starting a revolution. Simply open fire on the State; the State will oblige by firing back. What's harder is to *win* a revolution, and the only victory worthy of the name will be a peaceable one.

Why should I be talking about resisting government? Take it all around, we Americans are the freest people on the planet. Our riches afford us mobility, variety, and opportunity enough to drive us crazy, as well as the time to go crazy in—more and more of all of these as time goes on. Like other systems descended from English law, ours offers certain protections from government intrusion—fewer and fewer of these as history marches forward.

If I'm not on either side when the shooting starts, and I don't like being in the middle, then where do I belong?

I'm one among many, part of a disparate—sometimes better spelled "desperate"—people, self-centered, shortsighted, stubborn, sentimental, richer than anybody's ever been, trying to get along in the most cataclysmic century in human history. Many of us are troubled that somewhere, somehow, the system meant to keep us free has experienced a failure. A few believe that someone has committed the crime of sabotaging everything.

Failures need correction. Crimes cry out for punishment. Some ask: *How do we fix it?* Others: *Who do we kill?*

My family flew back from the Yukon in a plane. I drove home in the pickup across a thousand miles of North American wilderness, sleeping beside streams and moving at my own pace and answering to no one.

Some miles north of Smithers, British Columbia, one of the tires went flat. I kept two spares aboard, but the jack, it turned out, wasn't working, and so I stuck out my thumb in hope of a lift into Smithers. A pickup with Alaska plates stopped a quarter mile up the road, and I ran up there and explained the problem to my rescuers, two young men hauling a big stock-trailer overflowing with antlers and a self-possessed, unperturbable dog of the sledding type who sat between them in the front seat. "We've got a jack," the driver said, and began backing his rig up along the shoulder toward mine, slowly and expertly—he didn't stick his head out the window, but only eyed the jutting side mirrors.

These two, I saw when they got out to put a jack to my bumper, were country boys from quite another era, guys in overalls and big shoes and blackened jeans and red suspenders, with boyish, wispy beards, like ghosts from the War between the States. The driver was thick and blond and as becalmed as his dog, only more of a golden Labrador, the other man much like a retriever too, the thinnish intelligent kind, and both of them with the true clear gaze of dogs.

"Lot of antlers," I said. They had hundreds piled in the trailer, to the roof. They told me they made furniture out of antlers and drove around anywhere and everywhere, selling it. For the past month I'd been reading about the old days, missing them as if I'd lived in them, and I said, "You sound like free Americans."

"No," the smaller man said, and thereafter did all the talking while the other, the blond driver, changed my tire. "No American is free today."

"Okay, I guess you're right. But what do we do about that?"

"We fight till we are," he said. "Till we're free or we're dead, one or the other."

"Who's going to do this fighting?"

"A whole lot of men. More than you'd imagine. We'll fight till we're dead or we're free."

Ghosts indeed. Rebel ghosts wending through the Appalachians to enlist in time for Gettysburg.

"Listen: I'm asking: Just tell me: What do you want?"

"Freedom. We just want freedom."

"But I mean—what happens if you bring down the government? What do you want to replace it with?"

"We'll need strong men, strong leaders. I believe the time will provide them," he said.

"And is that the only way to get it? In a war?"

The young man was chewing tobacco. He had big, kind eyes and his lips worked around his chew. I feel it worth mentioning that he didn't spit in my presence. He said, "Freedom has to be bought with blood."

In that landscape of mountains and empty distances, the statement resonated with profound authority. Blood sacrifice—it's as old as human spirituality itself, it's the thread that binds the Old Testament to the New, that binds in faith the Christian people to the God who bought their freedom from sin with the blood of his only son. But hasn't the price been paid, according to the Bible? Or does it seem we've been abandoned here unredeemed, confused, trying to decipher a strange new text?—a Third Testament cobbled together out of bits and pieces of the other two and interpretations that don't bear much examination. Prophesies of blood sacrifice and a war between good and evil, prophecies not yet fulfilled.

RUN, RUDOLPH, RUN

Caves in the earth get lost and found over and over. A cave in Pennsylvania was apparently occupied by an unbroken chain of prehistoric human occupants for thousands of years, but then inexplicably it was abandoned and forgotten until white Americans stumbled onto it. The cave in western North Carolina's Nantahala National Forest where Eric Rudolph lives now with (according to the Federal Bureau of Investigation) half a year's supply of BI-LO California raisins, BI-LO Harvest Choice Cut Green Beans, BI-LO Old-Fashioned Oatmeal, Planters Peanuts, and StarKist Tuna: if anybody but Rudolph knows its location, nobody's telling, not even for one million dollars.

Eric Robert Rudolph is wanted for every bombing that somebody else wasn't already wanted for. He's charged with creating explosions that killed one person and injured a hundred others during the summer Olympics in Atlanta in '96; damaged the Northside Family Planning Services and the Otherside Lounge (described in the papers as a gay nightclub) in January and February of '97; killed an off-duty policeman and maimed a nurse at the New Women, All Women Health Care Clinic in Birmingham in January of '98. Witnesses around the Birmingham crime scene remembered seeing a Nissan pickup. Agents traced it to Rudolph. Rudolph took to the mountainous Nantahala Forest outside the town of Andrews in Cherokee County, North Carolina, where he'd lived off and on since boyhood.

The Nantahala and neighboring forests cover the corner where Georgia, North Carolina, and Tennessee come together, a region of green nappy mountains where, as of this hot Labor Day Weekend, weekend of the full moon, only a few leaves have begun to turn, and only perhaps because of thirty days of drought. Where east-west Routes 64 and 74 encounter small towns, they're lined with the appliance dealerships, Wal-Marts, and Taco Bells, the generic hair salons and the factory shoe outlets that mark out our shared national culture. But off these major arteries all of that drops away quickly into the rural South, the olive lakes and the Rebel Lanes and Johnny Reb Motels, garden patches of tobacco and sweet corn, roadside stores proclaiming BOILED PEANUTS AND PORK RINDS; and it seems every local road comes to a fork between the stairway to Heaven and the slippery slide to Hell. ETERNITY, as one bumper sticker has it,—SMOKING OR NON-SMOKING? A hand-lettered board by a house jammed close to a narrow back road says WHAT ON EARTH ARE YOU DOING FOR HEAVEN'S SAKE. Traditionally this time of year the numberless little churches hang out signs calling the faithful to renewed salvation—REVIVAL SEP 7-11—REVIVAL WITH PASTOR MIKE—REVIVAL—REVIVAL—REVIVAL . . .

Andrews is small. It looks to have no promise, with several vacant storefronts along Main Street and two digital bank signs disagreeing slightly about what time it is. The one barbershop in Andrews has only one chair—Arden the barber's done his work there on three generations of the males of Cherokee County. Where a second chair might go, a man in a hunting cap stands with his hands clasped behind his back, casually addressing the others there: a bent old man and a teenage boy on a bench, and a prosperous-looking gentleman in the chair, returned to town for his thiry-five-year high-school reunion. "They ain't going to find Rudolph up there," the standing man says. "There's seven hundred and sixty-two and one-half caves don't nobody know about them, and let me be the one to tell you, son: That country is complicated. All up and down and twisty. And full of echoes: I went hunting down in a draw there and seen a quail pop up. I pulled that trigger at six minutes to eleven. And son, it's still a-thunderin."

The teenage boy says he makes money gathering wild ginseng in the hills, claims he's stumbled onto caves up there plenty of times. "You have to kind of get lucky," he says. Afterward he forgot where he'd seen these caves. "They seem like they move around a little bit sometimes," he says. "I know those folks are all up there hunting Rudolph, but they ain't going to find him."

Elizabeth, the young woman who keeps the desk at the Valley Town Motel in Andrews, collects such Rudolph memorabilia as the hand-drawn poster brought around a couple weeks ago by a woman Elizabeth had never seen before, a pencil sketch of Eric Rudolph with flowing hair and the mild beautiful eyes of Jesus Christ—PRAY FOR RUDOLPH the caption reads.

"He was good-looking," an old friend of Rudolph told some of the countless reporters who came to Andrews and filled up the Valley Town Motel after the fugitive was spotted in July: "He could have been a movie star if he dressed up."

But Elizabeth says, "Don't even *think* I'd pray for him. He's crazy. I don't care if he's handsome or not. He's a *bombist*."

At Arden's barbershop the men say, "He's dead by now of natural causes. Anybody'd starved to death by now."

"He's dead. They killed him. He's part of some outfit like that Army of God or the militia, and they killed him to keep him quiet."

"He's got away. He's in Money Carlo or Tahiti or something. Money Carlo or the Caribbean or I don't know."

"He's still in the Nantahala. In a cave. They'll never get him."

This is the area harboring Eric Robert Rudolph, white male, thirty-one years, 5'11", 165–180 pounds, eyes blue, hair brown, part-time carpenter, accused murderer of the living and defender of the unborn, months-running Top-Ten fugitive despite the efforts of up to two hundred (but currently down to eighty) FBI agents, their choppers and vans equipped with sonar and infrared sensing technology, several dog teams from the Georgia Department of Corrections, forty uninvited civilian volunteers under the leadership of Idaho's Col. Bo Gritz (all wearing red, white, and blue) and an undetermined number of bounty hunters, both amateur and, to the extent they can be, certified (for instance by the "Fugitive Recovery and Bounty Hunters Association" of Fort Worth or the "National Association of Bail Enforcement Agents" of Rancho Cucamonga, California). From the weekly *Andrews Journal*:

> *James Robin Bach, 49, of Chattanooga, Tennessee, was arrested after a disturbance at the Andrews Post Office Friday afternoon. Officers removed a very large hunting knife strapped to his hip, found drug paraphernalia while patting him down, and found a loaded .357 Magnum hidden in his vehicle. Bach told officers he was a bounty hunter.*

It wasn't Eric Rudolph himself who brought these hordes to Cherokee County, but rather George Nordmann. Mr. Nordmann, who owns the Better Way Health Food Store on Main Street in Andrews, reported in July that he had spoken with Rudolph and that the fugitive had later taken one of his trucks and what the authorities have ever since referred to as "a six-month supply of food." George Nordmann waited a couple of days before reporting this encounter. He's an earnest, very decent-seeming man in his sixties, passionate to communicate his feelings on diet and health, willing to spend an hour with a customer who buys nothing, recommending a book called *Tissue Cleansing Through Bowel Management*, showing off ten pages of color prints of people's feces and close-ups of skin sores, and citing in particular a chapter titled "Intestinal Flora and Bowel Gardening."

His kids have posted a note to the public on his storefront: PLEASE SEND OUR DAD HOME AT 5:30. He's been dogged by journalists as his former neighbor Rudolph has been dogged by the Prison Bureau's actual dogs, and the FBI is still scrutinizing his story as to how all this food got into the hands of their quarry. Woody Enderson, inspector in charge of the Southeast Bomb Task Force, said Rudolph was "given the items in an encounter with a local witness." Mr. Nordmann hasn't been charged with anything.

*   *   *

"This is for the FBI and the media," Daniel Rudolph, brother of Eric, said into a video camera he'd rigged in his garage near Summerville, South Carolina, last February, and then turned to a whirring radial-arm saw and cut off his left hand at the wrist. Dressed in a white shirt and tie and wearing a tourniquet on his upper arm, he wrapped his stump with a towel and drove himself to the hospital. Paramedics retrieved the hand. Doctors reattached it. The local police chief said of investigators who viewed Daniel's videotape, "They never want to see it again." Apparently feeling implicated, the FBI issued a statement: "Daniel Rudolph's decision to maim himself is regrettable and totally unexpected." Neighbors questioned by the media claimed Daniel had never struck them as anything but completely stable. Reporters hunted down a former landlady in Florida who highly recommended Daniel and his wife as tenants and said they'd once baked her elderly mother a cake. The videotape was sent to the FBI Behavioral Sciences Unit.

Soon, in October, Col. Bo Gritz, having disbanded his volunteer force, having commemorated their failure in a brief ceremony by shaking each man's hand and pinning a small decoration to his T-shirt, and having returned to Idaho to discover that Claudia, his wife of twenty-four years, has served him with divorce papers, will drive out on a back road and shoot himself in the chest, but not fatally. Claudia is fed up with the colonel's quests to rescue hostages, fugitives, people under siege. "What kind of life do I have without my bride?" the colonel will ask of an interviewer.

As a kid Eric Rudolph spent summers with a man named Thomas Branham, a close family friend, in the Nantahala area. After the death of his father, an airline pilot, mother Patricia moved from Florida with her three boys and their sister and bought a small country home near Branham's place. In 1986, when Branham was arrested on a federal firearms violation, Patricia Rudolph went his bail. Branham on this occasion refused to recognize the court's authority and described

himself as a "freeman." The case was dismissed on appeal, as the
agents who found Branham's machine guns were actually authorized
to search his premises only, according to the warrant, for counterfeit
Heinz discount coupons.

The previous year, Patricia Rudolph had taken Eric and another
brother, Jamie, to a commune in Schell City, Missouri, run by the
Church of Israel, which was at that time, but no longer, associated with
the Christian Identity movement. Christian Identity doctrine claims
that Jews descended from the union of Eve and Satan, and that Anglo-
Saxons are the true Chosen People. Patricia, Eric, and Jamie stayed in
the commune about six months, according to pastor Don Gayman.

In high school Eric wrote a paper arguing that the Holocaust never
happened. Patricia Rudolph wouldn't disclose her children's Social
Security numbers to school officials. Eric Rudolph later rented homes
under aliases and registered vehicles under phony addresses. He has
never applied for a credit card or opened a bank account.

While Eric may have been influenced by his early associations, his
brother Jamie shrugged them off and currently lives in Greenwich
Village as a techno-pop composer. He recently issued a CD entitled
Evolve Now.

The mass media and modern mobility have homogenized the speech
of the urban South, but many folks in Cherokee County still speak
with an accent so thick a person not from around here is tempted to
conclude they're just playing with him. Andrews, the "Little Town
with a Big Heart," belongs to an area with a sense of itself, a region
with a self-image, whether or not it's entirely accurate or current—a
place of honest and self-reliant mountainfolk, God-fearing, Bible-
believing, stubborn, exclusive, and proud. Andrews hosts the headquarters of the Southeast Bomb Task Force, a borrowed office in the
local police station whose spokespeople take no questions from journalists but periodically issue upbeat statements that fail to reflect
what must be a growing frustration with a populace less than coop-
erative in the local manhunt. At the Cherokee Restaurant in
Andrews ("Home of Country Cookin") a sign out front advertises

RUDOLPH BURGER, RUDOLPH BROTHER BURGER, FBI CURLY FRIES, SKY-CAM COKE WITH AN OPTION: EAT THEM HERE OR GET THEM ON THE RUN.

It's not that people are still fighting the Civil War, or even that they're mildly, vaguely antigovernment. Locals object to that kind of labeling. "Sure, I don't agree with everything the government does. But I don't agree with everything my wife does either."— "Just because people like guns and fishing doesn't mean they're antigovernment." But apparently the kind of intelligence, the tips, that a million-dollar bounty ought to be generating, haven't been coming in. "We started out appealing to citizens' sense of civic duty," will be the Justice Department's statement in October, when Eric Rudolph is formally charged with the Olympics bombing; "then we offered a reward and appealed to their greed; now we appeal to their sense of conscience." But— "I don't see where he did anything so all that wrong," citizens of Andrews will tell the TV cameras. "I wouldn't turn him him in for even *ten* million dollars."

An ad on the local-access cable station in Andrews: REVIVAL SEP 9-14/WITH J.D. HOLMES/1 DOOR WEST OF NAPA AUTO PARTS/TENNESSEE ST., MURPHY, NC. Then another immediately following: YOU COULD GET UP TO $1,000,000/FOR INFORMATION LEADING TO THE ARREST/OF TOP-10 FUGITIVE/ERIC ROBERT RUDOLPH/5-11 WHITE MALE/165-180 LBS/1-800-575-9873.

In the vestibule of the Garden Restaurant in Andrews a quart-size Tupperware container painted red and blue rests on top of one of the twenty-five-cent toy machines. A six-by-eight computer-printed sign above it:

DEAR RUDOLPH,

YOU HAVE GOT TO COME HOME SOON.

AS YOU KNOW, ALL THOSE LITTLE BOYS & GIRLS WILL BE HAVING THEIR PICTURES TAKEN W/ME AGAIN THIS YEAR AT WAL-MART

I DON'T KNOW WHAT I AM GOING TO TELL THEM WHEN THEY ASK ME: "WHERE IS RUDOLPH?"

SO PLEASE, DROP YOUR ADDRESS IN THIS BOX SO I CAN BRING THE SLEIGH OUT AND GIVE YOU A RIDE HOME.

LOVE,
SANTA

P.S. MRS CLAUS WANTS ME TO TELL YOU THAT SHE MISSES YOU!

Beneath is a sheaf of paper for replies, each sheet headed in caps:
MEMO FROM ONE OF SANTA'S FRIENDS/YOU WILL FIND RUDOLPH AT:

You bet!
I am with my Elfs in the South Pole—you can reach me at the
FBI office in Andrews, SC

—offers one correspondent who didn't bother to shove his answer in
the slot, but left it out on display.

The staff at the Garden Restaurant have no idea where this box
came from. It wouldn't seem to have been placed there by law
enforcement, who have their own tip hot lines, and another logical
candidate, bounty hunter Ray Santa, claims to have no knowledge.
Ray Santa has spent time in the mountains looking for Eric Rudolph
on two separate visits from his home in Baltimore. He says he'll be
back again soon. As he rode the fire roads through grass as high as
the handlebars on his mountain bike, Santa says "I had the feeling
Rudolph knew where I was."

Mr. Santa owns the Gator's Pub in Baltimore, so named because
he spent time in the seventies hunting alligators in Belize. And in
Costa Rica he collected poison-dart frogs, among the most toxic
varieties of animal on the planet. He ended up hospitalized and semi-
famous in San Jose after handling the amphibians.

"This type of adventure—I live for it." Small and well built, in his
early forties, Mr. Santa nevertheless admits he was a little shaken
when a man banged on his station wagon at the Bob Allison
Campground in the Nantahala Forest, where Santa was sleeping
alone. "It was three in the morning. It flipped me. The guy was completely drunk, that's all, it turned out. He just liked to come up there
away from it all and drink, is what he said. But it definitely got the
wheels motioned in me that— 'what am I doing here?' But hey, if you

walk out looking for poisonous snakes, and you do it the way I did—no socks, boots, or equipment, or nothin' —well, a guy, he's got to be a little crazy."

According to Mr. Santa, the night Bo Gritz's volunteers spotted someone with a lantern and flashlight off in the depths of the woods— "That was me." He refers to Colonel Gritz's force as "these clowns," and says, "At times they were right beside me and never saw me."

Ray Santa hasn't yet spotted the fugitive, but he did find two shirts spread on bushes as if to dry, deep in the thickets, as if hidden intentionally from view, one white and one blue. He believes Rudolph might have left them there. Santa didn't disturb them. He left packets of dried food out along game paths for Rudolph, but they weren't touched.

This bounty hunter travels unarmed. And what if he should find the fugitive? What then? "Well, basically I hope to see him first. That's my ace in the hole." And what about Rudolph's gun? Supposed to be an M-16 or something similar? Santa insists, "I don't think he could kill a person face-to-face."

Ray Santa claims to have seen Patricia Rudolph, sixty-nine-year-old mother of Eric, drive through the Bob Allison Campground twice in a big black Cadillac, accompanied by one man. He says that more than once the FBI sensors were turned on him from roving vans, but they never stopped him. "That Bob Allison Campground," he says, "that's the key." The FBI searchers were camped there for some weeks. Colonel Bo Gritz's volunteers also stayed there. Of Colonel Gritz and crew he says, "These clowns, they wanted to give the reward money to Eric Rudolph's mother. To me that's like—*What?* After what he did? What about the victims? What Rudolph did was absolutely wrong.

"I'm not saying abortion's right or it's wrong. Just that the government shouldn't make those rules. You look in any penal system— ninety percent are probably unwanted—I mean when they were babies—and some of them probably killed people who were pro-life!" He repeats, "This type of adventure—I live for it." And adds, "Sometimes I wonder about myself."

At the Lake's End Grille in the hills a dozen miles east of Andrews, a sign above the counter says, ERIC RUDOLPH—1998 HIDE

& SEEK CHAMPION. The seekers have quartered themselves nearby at the Appletree group campground on Chunky Gal Mountain. In the September heat the FBI sentries blocking the campground's entrance spend their time chatting with each other, dressed in black T-shirts and black pants and black hiking boots—the same outfits they can be seen wearing in news footage of the disaster at the Branch Davidians's Mt. Carmel retreat in Waco, Texas—and lounging under a giant green nylon safari-style gazebo.

"They're nice fellas," says the waitress at the Lake's End. "They come down here sometimes and they've got their dogs in the back of the trucks,"—drawn perhaps by the large sign standing out front of the Lake's End: RUDOLPH IS HERE.

Meanwhile, across the road from the Piggly Wiggly supermarket in Murphy, the seat of Cherokee County, a black-lettered message on a red-bordered billboard advises IF YOU CAN READ THIS/YOU WERE NOT ABORTED./CALL YOUR MOTHER AND/ [in red italics:] THANK HER

One door west of Napa Auto Parts on Tennessee Street in Murphy twenty-six adults and four children have gathered for the purpose of spiritual revival with the Reverend J.D. Holmes. Men of the Barnett Construction Company are tearing up the sidewalk out front with a giant jackhammer, working on into darkness with floodlights, obscuring the sounds of the hymns and the preaching of J.D. Holmes, who has come from out of town. Mr. Holmes is a blond man in his early thirties wearing a brown suit and pale yellow shirt. Amiable and sincere, he introduces himself quietly to individual arrivals, then steps onto the small stage before an eight-foot-tall plywood cross and a brilliant metal-flake-red set of Pearl drums, as these are the premises of a local youth center, and talks for a while about his own aimless but basically harmless youth, which, nevertheless, would have led him eventually to Hell. "Do you think anybody warned me about it? Not really. What they mostly said was, 'Watch out!—or you'll get religion!' But, thank God, I didn't get religion. I got Jesus Christ.

"God cannot know of a sin that he doesn't hate," Mr. Holmes declares in the course of his sermon. He lists some sins that God hates:

pride and lying and wicked imaginations expressed in pornography and bloody slasher movies; feet that run to mischief—that is, busy-bodies ("If you are on God's business, you got *no time* to be in any-body else's business!")—and above all, he says, *above all:* the shedding of innocent blood. Which means, in our nation at this time, abortion.

"Eighty-five percent of abortions is repeat business. And more than eighty-five percent is for convenience's sake—not to save life!" He could easily be talking about the Northside Family Planning Services in Atlanta about a hundred miles away. Since January of 1997, when a bomb went off outside the clinic, the staff will disclose its whereabouts only to women actually making appointments over the twenty-four-hour telephone line. Despite the bombing, medical staff at Northside Family Planning still perform first-trimester abor-tions seven days a week for a fee of $305 on weekdays, $339 Friday through Sunday.

"Their innocent blood cries from the ground, like Abel's did!" On this subject J.D. Holmes gets really *waxed*—and here is the point of describ-ing such a gathering in such a place: It's easy to see that tonight, at this meeting, nobody's arguing points of medical ethics or examining the right of privacy. This is about eternal salvation and irremediable damnation. The two sides to this debate have nothing to say to each other.

Eric Robert Rudolph will be formally charged in October for the Northside clinic bombing. Some Bible-based Christians believe that any business offering to stop the human organism's growth in the womb deals in murder, and that whoever kills a man or woman working there saves lives. This was the argument offered by Paul Hill, who gunned down a doctor and his bodyguard at a clinic in Pensacola, Florida, in 1994. In an article titled "Why I Shot an Abortionist," Hill wrote: "The Lord is at work to deliver the unborn."

But did Paul Hill actually save any of the unborn? Has Eric Rudolph? Appointments interrupted by bloodshed can be rescheduled. On the other hand, Deborah Gaines sued Preterm Health Services Clinic in Brookline, Massachusetts, four years after John Salvi III attacked the clinic in a brutal shoot-out that left two people dead. She was there for an abortion that day but didn't reschedule and instead

gave birth to daughter Vivian seven months later. She claims she's entitled to compensation for the cost of raising her daughter, says the clinic should have had better security. Two guards on duty at the time and
presumably responsible for providing that security have sued the clinic, too, alleging emotional trauma.

Eric Rudolph may have something to say about all this should he
someday be dragged to the surface. Until now he's sent no letters to
the newspapers or to the law, posted no messages in the dead of
night. He may be long gone.

David White, of Reliable Investigations in Murphy, won't make a
definite guess as to Rudolph's whereabouts. "I learned a long time
ago not to try and predict the activity of a criminal. But if I were him
I'd still be back in those mountains." Mr. White, retired from, as he
vaguely states it, "a life-long career in law enforcement," is the only
private eye in, or anywhere near, Cherokee County. He's quick to dis-
associate himself from bounty hunters, bail agents, and the like.
"We're moral, ethical, and professional."

Stephen Cochran, Nantahala area resident, knew Eric Rudolph in
recent years, calls him a skilled woodsman, says Rudolph frequently
camped alone in the winter with nothing but a poncho, a sleeping
bag, and a rifle. "He considered himself a survivalist. He always
went places in the mountains where nobody else went." Can the the
searchers find him? "They might be in spitting distance of him and
not know it."

FBI and Georgia state investigators met with about seventy-five
bear hunters recently and showed them "raisin and oatmeal canisters, vitamin bottles, and tuna fish tins" like those Rudolph has,
according to hunters who attended the lecture. Bear season will open
in mid-October. "He may have a nine millimeter, an M-16, or a
Colt-91 automatic rifle," said Bill Lewis of the Georgia Bureau of
Investigation. "This is not your typical hunting weapon. He also is
likely to be antisocial." As to the FBI agents who might stop and
question hunters out in the woods, Lewis made this request: "Please
bear with them."

Hunters indicated they were more concerned about a lot of armed agents sneaking all around the forest. "There's going to be confusion and panic with all these hunters and all these FBI agents out in the woods," said one.

The Saturday after Labor Day, "Doc Holiday," a mesmerist from Atlanta, performs for the annual mass meeting of the area's Electric Membership Co-op at the fairgrounds outside Hiawassee, Georgia, just over the line from Cherokee County. The Doc hypnotizes a group of twenty people onstage and climaxes his act by inducing a state of "rigid body catalepsy" in a teenage girl, stretching her taut body between two stools, and standing on her belly with his arms upraised while co-op members snap photographs.

The next day the fairgrounds hosts a much smaller gathering of area musicians at a potluck lunch and dinner that lasts all afternoon and into the night. Not many more than forty people play for one another and feed themselves at long tables heaped with plates of fried okra and every other manner of vegetable, chicken— "gospel bird," because all preachers love chicken—ham, potatoes fried and mashed, iced tea, and soft drinks. Groups play such old-time standards as "Golden Slippers" and "Will the Circle Be Unbroken." There are clog dancers. Dorothy Smith, a plump grandmother with abundant black hair, sings her own composition:

> *He never meant to hurt no one,*
> *He wouldn't harm a fly,*
> *The Lord knows Eric Rudolph*
> *Didn't want that man to die,*
> *But he could not justify*
> *Knowin all the things they done*
> *So to stop that baby-killin factory*
> *He made a home-made bomb*

She and her band, Scott Ferguson on bass, Don Fox and Wade Powell on guitar and dobro, have taped the song and placed it on sale at gas stations and general stores around the tri-state region. A copy costs

$6.50. "They won't have it on the Murphy radio station," Dorothy says. "But it gets played around Asheville."

You gotta run, Rudolph, run, Rudolph, run
Or the FBI's gonna shoot you with his gun
A modern-day Billy the Kid
Boy you better do just like he did—
You better run, Rudolph, run, Rudolph, run . . .

"Abortion is the same thing as murder," Dorothy Smith says. "This is the same feeling of anybody around here—if you ask anybody, they'll say, 'Well, I'd take him in and feed him.' I maybe wouldn't take him in, because that's against the law. But I'd feed him." As for the deaths attributed to Rudolph's work: "He should've got up a little earlier and made sure nobody was around to get hurt when his bomb went off."

It may be a long while before we learn what's become of Eric Robert Rudolph. But we've got almost forever, because the evidence isn't going anywhere: According to speleologists, a footprint in a cave can last for 200,000 years.

The Mammoth-Flint Ridge cave system in Kentucky has 340 miles of explored and mapped passageways. Geologists think it extends much farther into the darkness under the earth. There's no telling where Eric Rudolph might have got himself to by now, and without ever having had to show himself above ground.

In 1914 Count Bégouën and his three sons discovered the Trois Frères Cave in the Pyrenees. A tunnel that can only be wriggled through ends in a massive chamber covered with Paleolithic 12,000-year-old images of the hunt, including creatures half-man, half-beast: a chamber used for initiating adolescent boys in a ritual of death and rebirth. Students of humankind have long seen the link between the cave and the womb. In 1956 the anthropologist Jean Gebser suggested in a piece called "Cave and Labyrinth": "The cave is a maternal, matriarchal aspect of the world. . . . To return to the cave, even in thought, is to regress from life into the state of being unborn."

THE LOWEST BAR IN MONTANA

With mixed feelings I have to say that the Club Bar of Troy, Montana, though still owned and run by "Downtown" Tony Brown, isn't quite the region of danger and chaos it once was. I used to describe the Club as a patchwork homemade-feeling saloon with a barrel stove and a fight every night and dogs and orphans wandering in and out. The stove and the feeling remain, but Tony has repainted and refurbished—even the bathrooms are downright hospitable—and he insists there were never any orphans around in the first place, but I claim some of the dogs probably were. It's nice for Tony and for the saner patrons that the establishment hasn't seen a fistfight or a drawn firearm in quite some time. But it's kind of depressing for those (admittedly few) of us who enjoyed dropping in at the Club in pretty much the same spirit in which Elizabethan Londoners used to visit the bear pits.

Troy is a little town in Montana's northwest corner, up near the Yaak River. For a while, Tony Brown was the mayor of Troy—I think during that brief period in the seventies when American politics went way off the tracks. He bought the Club in '73, lost it ten years later, got it back in '89.

The Club sits across from the railroad tracks on Yaak Avenue,

also known as Bar Street. I visited recently during the regular
Thursday Open Mike Night, when local talent assemble and entertain a few folks, mainly each other. The joint was crowded, and
while several really gifted and a few astonishingly awful musicians
had at it, Tony Brown showed me photos taken in the bar and pointed
out memorabilia on the wall, much of whose origins he can't seem to
remember. He's hung the environs with bric-a-brac and posters of
James Dean, Marilyn Monroe, John Wayne. There's a six-foot-long
blue marlin caught by a friend whose living room was too small for
it. "Actually," Tony said, "his wife caught it. If *he'd* caught it, they'd
have found room." Above it hangs a rod and reel, but it's got nothing to do with the fish. It was hocked by one of the gamblers to stay
in the poker game.

I think you could describe Tony most briefly as a small man with
a big face. Somewhat elfin. This night he was all slicked up in dress
pants, dress shirt, and fancy suspenders decorated with musical
notation, as if he intended to MC, but he didn't get on stage except
occasionally, and then just to blow his trumpet until physically
restrained by some of the other musicians.

Tony's very proud of his postcard collection, messages from loyal
patrons who have wandered into the unlikeliest places—I was surprised to find that one from me had reached here all the way from
Afghanistan, a land without a postal service. I'd only sent it so I
could say I'd tried. Tony said, "Hey, the mail service is great around
here. My mom told me she got one this morning just addressed to
'Betty'—no last name, no zip code, no nuthin. Came right directly to
her. Didn't even say 'Troy, Montana' on it."

He showed me several pictures, kind of a photographic study,
actually, of this one bald guy who passed out at the bar and then
someone drew a face on his shiny head with a blue magic marker and
red lipstick. Apparently this man never woke up, never noticed. Joy, the
barmaid, told me he stumbled later to the john, where he tilted forward
while doing his business and left the imprint of his cartoon eyes on the
wall.

Tony is also inordinately impressed with the Elvis-theme thank-you card he got from the junior high basketball team he coached last spring. He insisted strongly that I put something down about it in my notebook.

I asked if my coffin was still around, and Tony took me back to the storeroom to see it, a cheap one made of half-inch plywood that looks as if a big man would fall though the bottom when his pall-bearers gave it a heave. I have always believed the coffin will be mine when I die, so I can be buried in it in my backyard next to my wife Cindy and my dog Harold (Cindy's not there yet; Harold is), with Tony Brown saying a few words in farewell (Tony performed the service at our wedding, too), but I believe he's sold my coffin to, or promised it to, or used it for collateral on small loans from, a great many people. I haven't actually paid for it yet myself. Generally he says it's "for the next guy who dies in here." He's got a lot of other stuff piled around it—old beer signs and unidentifiable junk. His storeroom's half the size of the barroom itself.

The Club is the only place where I ever witnessed an actual barroom brawl. This was on a Friday night five or six years ago. Everyone in the place was up and fighting except for me and one old veteran of WWII, both of us hanging on to the poker table for dear life and hoping we'd have enough uninjured players to get the game going again when this was over. It wasn't the choreographed, stool-slinging slugfest you see in movies. There was just this squabble that the customers kept attaching themselves to until a kind of mass or glob of Montanan animosity heaved itself this way and that, shoving into the pool table and knocking over stools and repositioning the booths. Every time they got near the plate-glass window I thought they'd go through it, but they didn't; not that time; some time later it got busted and was boarded over for several months, if I remember right.

I was in there one slow night when the assembled clientele—about a dozen winter-weary Trojans (half a dozen gamblers and not many more drinkers)—were entertained by a couple who went into the ladies' room to consummate some unholy wine-illumined dalliance. For five minutes there wasn't a sound in the place but their cries of abandon, until they came out smiling shyly and smoothing their garb and everybody applauded.

Plenty of the old spirit remains. It's just that you don't need twenty-four-hour life insurance and a big dog to go inside and feel comfortable—though dogs are still allowed. "Not all dogs," Tony advises me—"some dogs."

This Open Mike Night the atmosphere is loud and happy and the patrons are certainly enjoying themselves. Tony introduces me around, going in particular for the respectable citizens: high school teachers, a hospital administrator. Tony says he managed to bring peace to his domain by instituting a lengthy "86" list. Though the new policy means a cut in the establishment's income, he says his clientele is down to "friends only." Anybody's a friend until proven otherwise. But any trouble and you go right on the List.

Tony still runs his poker game three nights a week. Often the Club hosts professional bands, and occasionally a comedian. Last February Tony put on a Poetry Slam that brought more than two dozen versifiers in from the woods around Troy to read to an enthusiastic audience. For all such events Tony makes dinner—sandwiches, stews, things like that. Tonight it's enchiladas and beans and chips and salsa. You get it on a paper plate and if you don't like it, well, then don't pay—the jar labeled DINNER DONATIONS sits next to the register.

I stayed in town overnight, two blocks from the Club at Tony's residence, which used to be a boarding house and still boasts a sink in every room and numbers over the doors. I got Number Seven, and Tony, his wife Valerie and their three kids were lost somewhere else inside the place. Part of the film *The River Wild* was shot in this house, but was ultimately cut out of the movie. Tony didn't mind—they remodeled the downstairs for free.

The next morning I got up early to observe Charlie, a retired ironworker from the Southwest, who starts the fire in the barrel stove and gets things opened up in the mornings at the Club. There's a morning coffee crowd who show up about 7:30 every weekday.

Charlie counts last night's Dinner Donations while Uncle Jack comes in with Uncle Jim, both men well into their eighties. They admire last night's dinner take—about ten bucks—and start in guzzling java and swapping jokes, really old jokes, jokes that were ancient when these guys were young.

They introduce me to a younger couple, Cindy and Darryl—"Cindy keeps the language halfway clean around here," Uncle Jack assures me. Darryl's a big guy, and Cindy's a tiny blond. Behind the bar Tony Brown keeps a photo of Cindy out front of the Club with a seven-foot-long mountain lion she'd just shot dead in the hills outside town. This morning they're heading back home to set sixty muskrat traps before lunch. Cindy's been skinning muskrats all the previous day.

Uncle Jack likes that idea—"I'd love to see that. And stirring gravy. Stirring gravy. I could sit on the couch all day and watch a woman stirring gravy." Uncle Jim agrees it's one of the most erotic sights on earth.

They've all been here for decades, for close to a century in the case of the uncles, but nobody present can remember when the Club was founded or can guess how old it is. They all agree on one series of statistics, however, that distinguish this tavern from all others:

The point in Montana closest to sea level lies twenty-some-odd miles away, where the Kootnai River flows across the state boundary into Idaho—elevation 1,826 feet. The morning patrons guess Bar Street to sit at 1,877 feet above sea level. And since the Club has a basement, it goes down to 1,860 or so, making it "the lowest bar in the state."

In celebration of this distinction, Charlie puts a shot of something in each of the uncles' coffee. I'm not sure that's a good idea at all. But I guess he knows what he's doing.

Just as I'm leaving, a guy out front in a big gold Buick with Washington plates wakes up with a dead battery. I recognize him as one of last night's patrons as he rolls out and looks at his car. "I been sleeping in it all night," he says—maybe with the door cracked open or his head on the horn, and that would explain his lack of power. He studies the whole situation and delivers his conclusion:

"You can have one hell of a good time in that place."

AN ANARCHIST'S GUIDE TO SOMALIA

THE TERRORIST FROM THE HABAR-GIDIR

On a February morning, early enough that the heat's not yet terrible, a twin-prop Ethiopian Airliner sets down outside the town of Dire Dawa, in the dry, high elevations of northeastern Ethiopia, to allow the dozen passengers to stretch their legs while the ground crew lugs aboard six one-bale-size burlap sacks of "greenleaf," or "khat" or "chaht"—a stimulant herb, the African Horn's drug of choice. Next stop, Shilabo, about fifty miles from Somalia; then across the border by land. Two decades of war have strangled Somalian commerce, but chaht moves everywhere across the Horn as easily as water might, if water ever moved in this desert country, trickling steadily into every hamlet and hooch.

Among the passengers heading for Shilabo with the chaht is forty-two-year-old Mohamed Farah Artran, an officer for the Somali National Alliance, which has emerged under Gen. Mohamed Farah Aidid as the country's most powerful faction. Around the hangars of the airstrip he moves not with tropical languor, but actually with considerable nervousness: The truth is he's red-eyed, palpitating, chomping on a mouthful of chaht and no longer enunciating intelligibly. He's been up all night eating this stuff. He's heading to Somalia's seaside capital, Mogadishu, to wave good-bye to the U.N. troops as the international body pulls up stakes and sails away from his homeland, and in his company there travels an American of extremely doubtful competence, a confused and desperately friendly and, Artran hopes, well-bankrolled American who continually smiles and nods and repeats, "Salaam," to anyone who'll listen: somewhat the idiot nephew.

Artran's friends call him by his nickname, "Billeh," which means "long-awaited child"—the long-awaited son born to a family of the Habar-gidir clan and grown now to slightly less than medium size, carrying fake Ethiopian ID and a pair of extra jeans in a plastic shopping bag and making small, strange, surreptitious hand signals, as they wait to get back on the plane, to his American, whom he insists on calling "Mike," which isn't his name. In fact for this journey Billeh has invented a number of aliases and cover stories, stratagems that seem to spring forth boldly but swiftly pass along, like entities on a carousel; and Billeh has also decided they should sit separately and not talk to each other—but he can't help it, he's ripped on "greenleaf" and feels eminent and sociable, ignores his own instructions, tells the American he's glad they're making this trip because in Marka, south of Mogadishu, his brother has placed their uncle under a form of house arrest, threatening to kill the uncle if he steps foot outside his door, and Billeh would like to travel down there and get the trouble between them smoothed over, possibly by threatening to kill his brother. The American, a writer of some kind, is masquerading, for the moment anyway, as a German welling engineer— the water kind, not the oil. Somalis like water, and they like Germans. Better than they like Americans certainly.

However dizzying their strategies, Billeh knows he can keep the American alive in Somalia. Trained in terrorist tactics thirteen years ago in Israel by the Mosad, the Israeli secret service, he's been involved in the Somali struggle since the fighting started against the dictator Siad Barre in the late seventies, a struggle that only intensified after Barre was brought down in '91. Lately Billeh's been living in Addis Ababa, Ethiopia's capital, but he's a distant relative of Gen. Mohamed Farah Aidid, head of the SNA—they both belong to the Habar-gidir clan—and his contacts back home are the best. Although he delights in behaving like a secret agent with dementia, there's probably not much danger.

Billeh only worries about the state of Mike's money supply. If there's enough of that, he can help this white guy, whatever his aim. The American's aim: to see the U.N. off and remain behind as the Last Journalist Out of Mogadishu. Billeh's aim: Cash Extraction and Total Assets Transplant. He brings the American's wandering attention continually, gently, through timeworn Somali proverbs and patient explanations of Reality, back to this overarching purpose. "Where are we?" Mike keeps asking, "is it on the map? Do we have plan?" Billeh quotes venerable wisdom: "With money, you can make a road"—he points aloft now—"up in the sky. This saying," he assures the American, "was in existence long before the Wright brothers."

Shilabo is only a village, but it gets a place on the map because it has water. Also a dirt runway. The plane puts down in the brown darkness blown up by its props and taxis to a patch of pavement about the size of a basketball court in the midst of the East African desert. Billeh and Mike and the sacks of chaht disembark, and the plane is gone. Not a building, not a road in sight, just dried-up scrub and runty trees like big toadstools floating randomly on a sea of red dirt. A couple of trucks in the nowhere. This is still Ethiopia, though the inhabitants, when they find them, will be Somali.

"You must get your story straight," Billeh suddenly declares. "We are *visiting* the *area*."

"And I'm German?"

"Visiting on the Ethiopian side—only Ethiopia. Never the border. We visit Lobopar. Parmaguc. Fer-fer. Kaprigar."

"How do you spell that? Is it on the map? Am I still an engineer?"

Some boys wearing tattered cammies and armed with pretty funky-looking Kalashnikovs turn up to load the chaht onto an Isuzu pickup. For fifty Eithiopian birrh they take the new arrivals into Shilabo, which materializes suddenly out of the general dead vegetation not a half-mile away, a town of sticks and dried mud and a couple hundred camels creaking upright off their knees to sidle out of the way as the travelers come across the square. A couple of nice-looking women pass by doing the slide, draped from crown to instep in wild rags. Children stand stock-still in the shadows, staring. Most of the buildings seem to be teat-shape huts, each with a fifty-gallon drum nippling out the top for ventilation, but others, low structures of adobe, front the lanes as well.

"Our overland trip begins here," Billeh says. "We hire a car for Lobopar. There's a Landcruiser. You have a lot of money? It will cost."

"Is this a story, now, or the actual plan?"

"To get," Billeh says, "you must spend."

PHONY GERMAN WITH A NOTEBOOK

The hundred dollar bill's no good—"It's not correct"—they want one made in 1990—don't ask me to fathom the meaning of such considerations. But I've got one—I have three hundreds left, and thankfully one is a 1990. Otherwise we'd be making our home here forever in Shilabo. Billeh's banging away with his jawbones at that chaht. He's one masticating mother. And then a caravan—nine camels with big wicker water baskets either side of their humps. The Landcruiser's going to melt. But that's no problem—we'll camel out of here. There's a dust-devil about half a klik tall whirling outside of town.

They make the currency exchange, and then there's the petrol thing, there is always, in Africa, the petrol thing—somebody knows about a gallon somewhere in a jug hid like moonshine. And we intend to burn it up across this desert. They say Shilabo burned down in the '64 Ethiopian-Somali war, then again in the war of '77, and then once more in the nineties during the Ethiopian internal troubles when Ethiopia's most recent dictator was getting ejected. You'd think the fire was yesterday, looking out across this desert like rusty ash dotted with bushes burned black in the seasonal drought. Sitting in a three-legged chair propped against a tree, waiting for the petrol to happen,

I try some of Billeh's chaht—he's a poor man, yet like all but the most devoutly Muslim Somali males, he spends a couple of dollars to supply himself with an ounce each day. No ritual has attached to this greenleaf; you just pick up a handful and shove it into your mouth. A cilantro-looking herb, but tasteless. It doesn't kick much, not compared, say, to a pinch of Skoal, but after a few mouthfuls we're skating out over the desert in the hot-wired Landcruiser in the company of two guys toting AK-47s with the wind licking our heads, hauling a hurricane of dust. The Somali gunmen blast us along an old tank track (not on the map) toward the unattended border, stampeding livestock into the waste, the inexplicable burros, the idiot goats and the buoyant, trotting camels, and I'm thinking, Hey, of course I can do this, I just point the way I'm going and trust these people. They've got half a pound of chaht among them. A chalky radium-green residue froths their lips, as if they've been devouring fireflies.

Over the fifty miles between Shilabo and the Habar-gidir village of Lobopar the vehicle breaks down five times. Billeh and I remain seated while the other two stand in the shade of the raised hood, apparently praying, and when they get back aboard and the driver touches together the two dangling wires beneath the steering column, the monster starts again, all five times. One more stop at sunset—we're close to Lobopar by now—while the two get out and fall to their knees at the roadside beside their Kalashnikovs, bowing northwest toward Mecca. Billeh puts his feet on the dash and smirks. He was raised Islamic but he's seen enough of this world to convince him it's all a lot of crap.

SECRETS OF THE OGADEN

They arrive at today's destination. Just the way Shilabo did, Lobopar turns up around them as if conjured, a wavering flimsy habitation of straws and sticks and patchwork canvas domes, goats on frayed pickets or fenced around by corrals of uprooted mesquite, fifty camels kneeling in the dirt. Huge birds that might be ostriches bred with storks pace the outskirts, tearing at trash—Billeh calls them "guzuru." The sunstruck quiet gives over to a general melee as the clan turns out to study the visitors, in particular this first Caucasian to make an appearance here in years.

Billeh settles Mike, whom he's also taken to calling "Idaho White Boy," on a straw mat under a thatched port before the entire population of the village—women in long wraps, and children almost naked and the several elders with their hair and Vandykes bleached out orange—to hear the villagers' tales. Only the elders speak. They explain to the writer that this is the Ogaden, the border region inhabited by nomad Somalis in makeshift hamlets linked by the tank tracks from then-dictator Siad Barre's war against Ethiopia in 1977—an attempt to annex these Somali-populated areas of Ethiopia. Barre lost, leaving his kinsman under the doubtful protection of the Ethiopian Army, who quarter in scattered encampments throughout the Ogaden, subsisting through a casual and meager shakedown operation among these villages. Lobopar itself is without facilities, not even a well—water's brought by camel from twenty miles off. They have no money, no medicine, nothing to trade with but what they can raise up out of the red-powder desert around them. Mostly goats and camels that forage in the surrounding earth, the goats for slaughter and the camels for milk and for transport. In the Ogaden, life comes hard, but these have won through yet another day, unlike all the others they've lost to sickness, famine, massacres, battles. The villagers sit close together, everyone touching someone else, steeped in a contentment that seems, at this moment, perpetual. It occurs to the writer that the secret way to happiness is in knowing a lot of dead people.

The session ends at nightfall, when the muezzin calls like one astonished by, skewered, even, by a great grief; and the villagers, a hundred or so, kneel down in a line on the track through town for the day's last prayer . . . and rise up transformed by the evening's prospects—because now is the holy month of Ramadan, during which they deny themselves food, drink, or sex during the daylight hours, those hours ended now, entirely forgotten.

The women bring out metal plates piled with chunks of goat and spaghetti—which they call "macaroni"—and Del Monte tomato sauce. Mike is, as always, bewildered by these things offered to him, and with mingled amusement and pity Billeh shows him how to eat pasta the Somali way, without utensils, taking a shock of it in his right hand, turning it this way and that and gathering the long strands up into his palm, and then shoving it into his face. Mike prefers the *anjera*—a floppy pancake the size of a hubcap which they tear apart and dip into a thick, tangy sauce.

And then the chaht, and then it starts. Nobody jumps up dancing, but in several tents groups of men engage in a kind of headlong socializing, chomping greenleaf and conversing all night in the ancient way of nomads run across one another: One man holds forth in a near-monotone for many minutes, maybe an hour, encouraged by one-syllable interjections from one of the others, coming at five or six second intervals—"Oh—oh—oh. Aw—aw—aw. Ha—ha—ha," et cetera—and then the next one starts—chewing, chewing, verbalizing all night long, pausing only to hock and spit or gulp some tea.

Just before dawn, as the men go down, the women get up, and the roosters. Not half an hour later the men roll out again for the morning prayer. When do they sleep? The writer suspects that in a certain sense, they just never wake up all the way, but rest continually, simultaneously moving and surviving.

Even Lobopar has its Toyota, a dinky sedan with three of its windows shot out, and Billeh and Mike, escorted now by two more guys named Mohamed—one's nicknamed "the Lion" and the other they just call "that one"—climb aboard and head out of Lobopar straight toward the sunrise, straight into its fiery throat it seems, alongside termite berms like primitive monuments, eight, nine, ten feet tall and five feet through, skirting obstacles—old tires, busted axles, piled stones—laid in the way by camel herders who don't like vehicles using their roads. When a camel looms up on this close path, the beast ends up harried ahead for as much as a mile before it hits on the notion of stumbling off, exhausted and far from its pasture, into the scrub to let the car get past.

Close to the Somali border, the party stops to check out the weapons. Billeh's been lent a Kalashnikov, sand-blasted smooth and dull like those of the other two, each with a thirty-shot clip that may or may not be full, they refuse to say, and also Lion carries a sort of rocket, or grenade, that screws down onto the muzzle of his Kalashnikov and appears not to bear experimenting with. Lion produces from his waistband, for the writer's use, a 1917 model U.S. Army .45 caliber sixshooter, probably a Colt. It's got three forty-five automatic rounds in its cylinders, which are chambered for the long .45s, not the shorter automatic rounds. But Lion and Billeh both promise it'll shoot, all three bullets, anyway. "One for each of you, if we're attacked, and one for me," the writer jokes—they laugh like hell for twenty seconds, then shut down tight and inform him seriously that Muslims don't do suicide, it's banned by the Koran. He assures them the Bible's against it too, and everybody's comforted.

They travel on. The writer's sleepy, the Somalis jazzed as ever. Billeh nudges him at one point, asking, "Do you remember when we came to the fork, five kilometers ago? That was the border. Now it's Somalia."

AMONG THE SUBMITTERS

Mataban, Somalia, looks like an actual town, with a sector of European-built stucco houses, and a tarmac highway passing through— Billeh says it's known as "the Long Road," and soon enough Mike will find out why—and a larger sector of hooches cobbled together out of sticks and straw with a stray piece of cardboard maybe and the more prepossessing ones roofed with "galvanize." On either side of the road, several shops trade from a modest store of sundries and canned goods, and two nameless dirt-floor cafes under tin roofs even have generators and electric lights, and one old refrigerator each. The town fades quickly into desert pasture where the livestock, Mataban's most numerous inhabitants, forage surrounded by scavenging birds. A few rickety pickups cruise the streets, and a burro hauls a fifty-gallon water drum up and down the block on a two-wheeled cart, unattended by any driver.

Lion stays, but That One heads back home to Lobopar with a

fifty-dollar bill. Billeh parks the writer before a plate of steaming goat parts at a long table in the larger cafe. Nobody else is eating. Somali men bunched around a shortwave radio listen with screwed-up, painful faces to the Somali BBC's description of the misfortunes of the U.S. super middleweight boxer Gerald McLellan, beaten into a coma by Nigel Bend of the U.K. Quiet men, most of them bearing rifles. "They like Germans very much," Billeh reminds the writer.

The drought of '89 has passed, and the resulting famine of '90, and folks look fed—there aren't any fat people sitting around, but there's food when you want: goat's meat, onions, camel's milk, pasta or rice, and bread slightly scorched in the adobe ovens. Dates. Watermelon. Mirinda brand orange drink. When Mike orders coffee, the old man running the place spoons Taster's Choice Freeze-Dried directly into a cup of hot tea. No alcohol on sale, but in addition to chaht many seem addicted to Sportsman cigarettes made in Kenya of Kenya-grown tobacco. By their possession of cigarettes it's easy to tell the lapsed Muslims from the pious ones. Even the smokers and green-lipped chaht-fiends turn out five times a day for prayers, however—all but the very few non-Muslims, like the writer, and such jaded warriors as Billeh, who spends the noon prayer time getting his party quartered in a hooch behind one of the cafes and learning that the town's only two-way radio, by which he'd hoped to call his SNA contacts down the highway, doesn't work. He shrugs and cops a bag of greenleaf from an elderly hunchback in rags and sits down to elevate his spirits.

In fact chaht, or "plant," or "vegetable" appears to be the chief focusing point for these guys—at about $1.75 an ounce, each goes through a couple of ounces in a twenty-four-hour period if he can, taking a pinch now and then through the day and at the cocktail hour going at it seriously, and then, after the day's last prayer, absolutely single-mindedly, heading through until almost dawn. Nothing stops the flow of commerce in chaht, not even civil war. It's mild but they treat it like a big bad drug, tripping out on it for days as if it were crystal meth. The warlords use it to pay off their militia. Thus its mystique: chaht, the warrior's drug of bloodshed and ecstasy. *It certainly works for Billeh,* the writer writes in his notebook. *He stays . . .*

> *He stays for the most part comprehensible although he hasn't slept for two days and claims it won't be necessary for two more weeks and enjoys making jokes I don't get or take as serious statements, and feels compelled sometimes to inform me suddenly that, for instance, Bill Clinton is a Democrat, or that he himself has seen many UFOs, and he's constantly changing the cover story, frequently reversing our plans or abruptly contradicting his previous explanations, and generally adding to the state of desert-dusted windblown confusion around these parts and particularly in my head. Or he speaks in strange metaphors— "The river is very wide and we can't swim to Belet Weyne because our hands are broken" means, I eventually discover, that there are bandits camped between here and there who want to shoot our asses off, and we'll need more than two Kalashnikovs and twelve bullets and one Mystery Surprise Rocket Grenade to dissuade them—and his diction sometimes caroms off figures of speech: by "self-taught difference" he means, I guess, to say "self-defense." Like every person I've met here, he hates the U.N., from the lowest minion to the secretary general, whom he refers to as "Boutros Boutros Boutros Boutros-Ghali." He likes my Visa credit card and has determined our highest aim should be to convert it into its cash equivalent, which is what he thinks the credit limit actually is. He informs everyone that I'm German, then asks me to tell them about Idaho. As for me, I have chewed enough chaht this session that my scalp is crawling around pleasantly on my head. In fact what it reminds me of is ephedrine, an asthma remedy sold over the counter at California truck stops to keep you driving all night . . .*

But nobody's driving anywhere, not out of Mataban.

In three days the strip of shacks along the straight band of tarmac has been transformed into a little city of nearly twenty cross-country vehicles and their occupants. Trucks hauling goats, trucks hauling camels on their knees, hauling sacks of salt, or empty fifty-gallon drums, and trucks going back unloaded to the capital for more of whatever they've been selling up this way. Passengers collect, folks just looking for a better place, dozens, and then scores of them, straggling in out of the desert. The two cafes can't feed them all—the trucks have turned into shelters for all the people sleeping on straw mats underneath them as they wait—but what, Mike wants to know, are we waiting for? For militia to escort us. For word it's safe to travel. For a bridge to be repaired. The story keeps shifting across the screen of these patient faces, the explanations glimmer in the endless monologues out of iridescent lips. But *something's* wrong, something threatens, in the next forty miles. In every truck at least two men carry Kalashnikovs, and a couple of rigs are even topped by belt-fed machine guns on tripods—just the same, this desert armada doesn't rate the military challenge ahead from the bandits, or the rival clan, or whoever they are. Mike suspects it's the bandits themselves who'll be escorting them in the end, or that the bandits aren't really there but provide the basis for some militia garrison's existence, and so their protection is completely unnecessary but nevertheless required—one of those African things, the result of deliberations made without reference to logic or utility. When logic and utility fall from grace, the mystical authority of subtler concerns rises up like an intoxicating incense, and everything is done for reasons no one understands.

Mike lives in the interim in an eight-by-ten hut with a revolving gang of young Habar-gidir guerrillas, as many as nine at a time trying to sleep in here, rather a close situation, skinny though they are. Suave men in ragged counterfeit brand-name apparel—"LIVE'S 501s", for instance, made in China. They've discovered Mike's taste for goat's liver and rice and make sure he gets it for breakfast, lunch, and dinner. He doses the cloudy well water with iodine, but he's overlooked the disease potential in the casually handled chaht, and now he's feverish and sinusy and given to fits of trembling. They've issued him his own AK to sleep with, but he doesn't think it's one that shoots. He's weary of their stinking feet, their incredible patience, their monotone bull sessions and fake clothes. Lion looks after him like a child after a puppy.

Muslim means *submitter*. Lion is devout in his submission. He doesn't smoke or drink or chew, observes the daylight fast of Ramadan. He and a few of the other guerrillas rise before each dawn to worship standing upright in the hooch with their heads bowed, not only out of piety but because the roof is low. At day's end he joins the hundred others kneeling outside on the tarmac, where the desert wind mingles in the softness of dusk with the chanted prayers, which sound like forlorn questions in this emptiness, and with the goats' terrified bleating. Afterward Lion takes a small meal and hunches over Mike's tiny fifty-dollar shortwave, getting the Voice of America in Real Slow English. Lion has been shot twice, once in the right leg and once through the left shoulder and out his back, and recovered without medical treatment from the first wound, was treated in Mogadishu for the second, still carries a bullet fragment in his neck. Tonight the radio talks about the tragic super middleweight title fight. Lion reacts with intense interest, then with alarm, finally with deep sadness, with genuine pain. McLellan remains in a coma, floats in a darkness six thousand miles away.

DOROTHY'S DESPERATE NOTEBOOK

Evening, Sunday: Well, we still haven't gone anywhere. And here I am once again in Africa, waiting. Waiting for tomorrow. At which time something may or may not happen. I remember now how hateful is this place for an impatient man.

Looks like better than two dozen trucks bunched up in this town now. Last night we lay out on a mat talking and watching meteors in the cool night while the warmth came up out of the ground beneath us. "We": are me, called the White Boy, or sometimes Mike (for no discernible reason), and two Mohameds—Billeh from Mogadishu and the Lion from Lobopar. We're going to Mogadishu

with extremely vague notions as to what happens then . . . "The Lion"—
I suppose Billeh's the Tin Man, and we're looking out for the Scarecrow—
and naturally I'm Dorothy, and I guarantee you, Africa is as close as you
can come to the Land of Oz, or as close as anybody would want to
come.

In the dark it seems as distant to the horizon as to the sky overhead. No moon tonight, only every star there ever was, and satellites
coursing by, and occasionally but rarely some blinking thing that
might be an airliner seven miles up. Another night under a strange
sky in a different realm. I listen to the reports on the shortwave of
bombings, attacks, plagues, even witch-burnings (seventy elderly
women burned in South Africa in the last ten months) and I feel I'm
living in a world where such things are all there is . . . I've got a pocket New Testament, but I can't read much of it—because I'm living in
the Bible's world right now, the world of cripples and monsters and
desperate hope in a mad God, world of exile and impotence and the
waiting, the waiting, the waiting. A world of miracles and deliverance, too. Add the invention of the Kalashnikov in 1947 into the
mix, and life gets exciting. So it's hard to read the Acts of the
Apostles as I have been and consider that it's been going on since the
Creation. It shakes your faith—my faith, anyway.

Mohamed from Lobopar—we called him That One—shows up
suddenly. He's driven all night to tell us that after we left there, the
Ethiopian army locked down the village for eight hours and
searched every hooch, looking for the White Guy. The Somalis
stonewalled them, told them nothing. "Why are you helping the
White Guy," the soldiers asked, "when you're black like us?" And
the villagers replied, "Our goats are white—they give us meat and
milk. But we've never gotten anything but shit from the Ethiopian
Army."

Morning, Monday: And now, the latest from the Horn of Africa:
We're going nowhere, we're doing nothing, and I'm not getting any
better at either one.

*   *   *

Afternoon: I'm out of the sun in the hooch we've been staying in, and little coins of sunlight get in through the gaps to make it kind of pretty in here.

In his vague half-joking semicoherent ambiguous way, Billeh seems to be indicating that the Ethiopian Army's interest in me has elevated me to the status of international fugitive, and that I should definitely plan a route home that bypasses that beautiful country. I'm guessing I can somehow get to Nairobi and from there to Frankfurt . . . But I'm getting way ahead of myself, which, in Africa, is step number one on the road to mental chaos . . .

Morning, Tuesday: The passengers are boarding the convoy now—Toyota pickups, Mercedes and Fiat diesels. Maybe a hundred people, fifty goats, eighteen camels on their knees heading into the big city, bedded down in a double hauler and gazing out of their tremendous serene eyes at the Horn of Africa. I'm sitting up front in a big throbbing blue Nissan diesel. We're preparing to go. There were never any bandits—a bridge was out . . . we never waited . . . we were never here. . . Now we've come to the edge of town, nothing before us but the absolutely straight strip of tarmac across the absolutely flat desert. And we stop. The bridge *is* out. We were always here . . . We've never been anywhere else. The driver speaks only a few words of English. I ask him what we're doing and he tells me, "We're waiting."

Ten minutes later: We're moving—somebody had to radio ahead—evidently there *are* bandits, or *were* bandits . . . Five miles later: We've stopped. The truck just ahead of us has a flat tire—actually it doesn't look flat, but they're changing it. Two miles later we stop again at a little roadside settlement. Apparently it's "time for a break" . . .—it's teatime! There are no—repeat, no—bandits. All the trucks pull aside, everybody gets out. We've been on the road ninety minutes and we've come about twelve miles. A dozen people, six or seven hooches, but this place has a name—Per Gerit. There are hundreds of folks on this convoy—or say one hundred, at least, almost all adults, men and women—and of all these I'm the only one who thinks there's anything wrong with setting out to go somewhere and then stopping immediately and repeatedly.

Suddenly (thirty minutes later) everybody's leaping up, scattering, peering down the road, cocking the actions on their guns. Then we all jump in the trucks, drive to a deserted village a kilometer up the road, and stop again . . . Now we're going again . . . The road's lined with gunmen—then a detour fording a dry river, and we maneuver around two trucks blown up last week, as the driver tells me now—the bridge is out, and there are bandits . . .

The tarmac ends—400 kilometers between Mataban and Mogadishu, into which distance they've managed to cram seven billion miles of bad road, and all kinds of hot weather. We've entered a wasteland of two-rut tracks in confusing proliferation, because where the ruts get too deep a detour develops, and then a detour off the detour when that one gets rutted out, and so on. The folks on top of the trucks holler advice as to which detour looks most promising. We're averaging well under ten mph, when we're moving at all. We stop in the middle of nowhere for the Muslim prayer time just before sunset. Distant plateaus . . . lonely mile-tall dust dervishes dangling over the land . . . bushes like claws, and flattop trees, none of them taller than three meters. Everything's in silhouette at dusk, the earth suddenly vermilion . . . as if a page had turned and its shadow fallen over all the world.

Two days later and two dozen miles from the coast the checkpoints begin, only three or four before the city proper, boys tensing a rope across the road, others leveling rifles from behind oil drums. Burros bent over the patchy fodder, urchins asleep in the shadows of adobe kiosks. Machine gunners in the shade: They call themselves "Technicals"—all-terrain trucks with their roofs cut off and antiaircraft guns or recoilless rifles set up in the back. Lion suddenly says good-bye to us here—he's been drafted. He lives at this checkpoint now, and that's that. In this land without a government, the Technicals generally call the tune. They want money from the convoy. The drivers pour from their rigs in a crowd, jostling and sweating and making their points. The price goes down, they strike a deal, the rope descends, and the line of trucks heads east again, passing more swiftly along beat-up tarmac between two large ponds surrounded by rice paddies and populated by storks, guzuru, cattle, buzzards, flocks of smaller fowl. The air gets damp, almost tropical. Cresting a rise the caravan looks down on a maze of stucco walls fronting torn-up streets, a low skyline of European-style buildings, Mogadishu spilling toward the Indian Ocean.

It's plain that few people inhabit these stone structures—even in the cities they raise up hooches of sticks and straw, no more interested in preserving, restoring, or stealing the big windy dwellings of the Europeans than the Europeans would be in moving into scrawny shacks beneath the shadow, say, of the Eiffel Tower. No building stands complete anymore anyway. The town is a labyrinthine ruin, looks almost archeological. Trash moves along like tumbleweed and gathers into drifts and it's starting to bury small structures. Children swing on lines dangling like jungle vines from the concrete power poles. Surprising to see, in the hands of kids on the streets—toy guns: toy machine guns, pistols, cap guns, electric ray guns. A boy of kindergarten age holds a gun to his friend's ear. They both wince— it's all quite realistic. Maybe they've seen it done.

The convoy slows down in a market run amok over the avenues. This must still be the thoroughfare, or must have been once. Whatever it used to be, it's everything now, the center and origin and destination of all things—anything but a place for vehicles—carts and stalls under canvas jammed together almost to the point of piling up; they've taken over the highway and have to be beaten back, nudged by the huge wheels of the first truck before the vendors wrench their stores just slightly out of the way of being crushed and stand atop their wares screaming through the windows at the drivers. The Nissan labors forward like a raft through a swamp—a swamp of people black as obsidian. They look like silhouettes draped with clothing. "Bakara Market! You can get anything here," Billeh shouts down to me— "Clothes, medicine, many kinds of food. Guns! Bombs! Slaves! Gold! Silver! Petrol!"

Farther downtown, Billeh and I leave the convoy. The truck lets us off onto a street of shops where commerce continues, on a survival scale, in canned goods, soft drinks, powdered milk. Here and there small browsing herds of goats, even camels, as the nomad lifestyle, like the eternal sand, drifts back into the city out of the desert, out of the seaside dunes, out of the middle ages, as if the urban twentieth century had been a ripple across the screen of heat, a curious ghastly mirage . . .

There's little traffic—but much more, on reflection, than there ought to be: Miraculous to see cars and trucks, these things running off drops of petrol sold out of five-gallon jugs at the curbside by just a few lucky vendors, still moving way after they've turned to junk: vehicular Frankensteins that look as if they'd been rolled down the sides of mountains, corroded and battered and lurching along on tires of varied unmatched sizes, and laden with people, anybody who'll pay a coin or two. Here, whatever moves is commercial.

Climbing aboard a van full of passengers, Billeh and his charge excite some flurry of debate: the others think the White Boy ought to get the hell out, or pay a hundred dollars, because his presence is hazardous. Suppose he attracts a grenade or something? Billeh concedes the point, and reintroduces himself to a couple of cousins, and suddenly everyone makes them welcome. Some begin complaining about the Marines, and others point with pride to the water trucks and big guns stolen from the U.N., to the blown-up troop trucks upended and wheelless in the streets, and the corner, a monument now, where eighteen U.S. Rangers died fighting Somali militia. The U.N.—what did it accomplish? The tons of food and medicine, it's all forgotten. Only the police effort and the bossing stay fresh in the minds of Mogadishu. The outfit that saved, by its own count, 150,000 lives here seems almost universally derided and resented.

When the ill-timed efforts of nation-states to impose their idea of stability unbalances the tribal powers, the return to balance is violent. A case in point: U.N.-imposed peace talks in Djibouti in July of

'91 led to Ali Mahdi's swearing himself in as president the following month. But Mahdi had no real following. The mistake resulted in fighting that killed as many as 30,000 people in Mogadishu and virtually destroyed the city with mortar fire.

MOHAMED OF THE AL SAHAFI

Mohamed Jirdeh Hussein, owner and manager of the Al Sahafi Hotel in Mogadishu, a standout figure of a man, a full head taller than the average Somali, bald, smiling, quietly alert and eminently helpful, drives north through the capital accompanied by three gunmen in his Nissan Patrol. They negotiate the checkpoints out of Aidid's territory and across the Green Line into Ali Mahdi's domain, and continue clear out of town along a lonely seaside track, past centuries-old brick ovens set in the sides of bluffs, past the prison turned into a hospital, the kind of place where a foreign legionnaire would recuperate with grinning forebearance from his wounds, past shantytowns that look deserted in the noon heat.

Mohamed and his men stop at a desert airstrip in sight of the ocean. For quite a while he waits chatting with the handful of militiamen who run this operation—Ali Mahdi's men, of the Abgal clan—in what he likes to call "Terminal A," a stifling metal cargo crate furnished with seven theater seats. West of the road the red desert goes forever. On the east beautiful barrens and white dunes roll down to the Indian Ocean. But the water's said to be hazardous. A bit farther north there was situated, for years, an abbatoir for camels, that dumped its bloody waste into the sea. And the shores of Mogadishu became a haven for sharks.

And journalists come down out of the sky. Meaning, in this case, the South African video crew Mohamed came here to collect, three whites and one Zulu taxiing toward him in a charter from Nairobi.

The hotelier welcomes them in the blowing dust. He remarks that almost all the Western journalists have left town. They float offshore now with the last few thousand U.N. troops, waiting to get out of this place. "For that part of the world, the story's over," one of the South Africans acknowledges. "But for our part it's just beginning."

Mohamed takes them into the city, along avenues shellshocked and drifted with sand and half-gone back to dune, among houses blown apart and shot up and then, it would appear, burned by fire and finally crumbling under the simple weight of time and ruin. "It's a *nice* little town," he says. "It's *devastated* now, but . . ." He points out the sights—hulks with the blue of the sky and the sea showing through, former mansions looking purified by the sweet hot seaside African light, but absolute ruins— "Ah! The French embassy . . . Here are the residences of American diplomats . . . This," he says of a pile of rubble, "is a *wonderful* night club—and here is the town's most beautiful hotel," he tells them, adding, "It's a shell now."

The Nissan makes good time, driving right or left of the medians, taking the roundabouts clockwise or not— "You can have any lane here," Mohamed explains, his face lit by a jovial mood as they hurtle through the apocalyptic streets jammed between sweating gangsta gunsels, the horn buzzing nonstop— "Not like the U.S.!"

On a thoroughfare of buildings eaten away by small-arms fire, the Al Sahafi Hotel stands scarcely marked by bullet holes, its three stories completely intact, the last shred of civilization in the capital, like a museum depicting life in the twentieth century. The generator works, there's hot water in the showers and electric light all night; air conditioners and iceboxes function turgidly in the rooms. Yes, the phones have quit, but only recently.

Downstairs Mohamed manages to serve three full meals a day. Eggs, meat, pasta. Tropical fruit and green salads. On a pillar in the hotel's dining room: an enlarged black-and-white photo of Mogadishu as it once was—a city like Honolulu in the fifties, a restful place of sea and sunlight.

A half-dozen Western reporters, British and American, remain upstairs waiting for a chaht flight out in the morning. In the meantime they've barricaded themselves in a room among stacks of beer and soft drinks, flak jackets and Kevlar helmets lying about, the six of them half-drunk and celebrating moreover with chaht and a bag of Somalian reefer— "all of it fucking legal, mate!" a blond Englishman cries when they greet the new arrivals. They've made it through another story, the work's over, the competitive game-playing, too— temporarily. Everybody's buddies, temporarily.

But the South Africans' work is only starting. They've got to venture out into the city. Idaho Mike tags along, most grateful to share Mohamed's Nissan and his squad of guns. The truth is Mike can't afford his own bodyguard. He's down to one gold Krugerrand, a medium of tender the Al Sahafi promises to view with the greatest respect as soon as it can be authenticated (meanwhile he please mustn't charge drinks), and credit cards are considered pretty funny in this town. Billeh's off making the rounds among an infinitude of cousins, bearing hundreds of U.S. dollars.

The South Africans want footage of Mogadishu's chief players: General Aidid, and Aidid's bankroller Osman Ato, and their chief rival Ali Mahdi. Their host ferries them to the gates of power. But they're only admitted a few feet inside the high walls, into the yards of the big houses, and stopped by men with rifles and factotums with apologies—nobody's talking, nobody's seeing journalists while the U.N.'s still in town. The video cameras record only these tense faces, the crowds of the self-important outside the doors of the truly important, those men inside who broker the momentary peace and cut up the spoils and hold the crumbling future in their hands. Men living in great mansions, but on streets buried beneath chaos. Leaving Osman Ato's home, the Nissan skirts blown-apart vehicles drifted over with sand and the sand-piles topped with fresh rubble from buildings. In all the streets they take note of a kind of sedimentary devastastion—the latest devastation covering yesterday's devastation, and the devastation before that.

Perhaps the visitors would like to see the hospital?—the Isbetaalke-Guria, five stories high, a building as filthy as a New York subway station and smelling like one, full of echoing screams? Meet a kid blown up by a mortar, hooked to a drip and a catheter, waiting for his third operation in a room like a tenement basement, with his plastic toy gun beside him on the bed? Get a view of his abdomen, which looks like a shark went at it? Talk to guys without legs, without arms, without faces? The power's off. It's hot. Women sit by some of the wounded waving little fans of woven straw. Not a doctor in sight. No medicine here. Somebody has to find it outside, downtown, in the Bakara Market, and bring it in. The elevators don't work. The journalists climb from floor to floor as if sentenced to do it, interviewing people without voices, getting footage of people without feet.

Something's different about Mogadishu when they get to the streets. People are scarce. The traffic's disappeared. The hush anticipates two transitions in the city's life: the departure of the U.N., which comes tonight, and the breaking of the month-long fast of Ramadan, which comes tomorrow. The fixtures of certain factional realities remain, the cruising Technicals, the checkpoints, and clumps of gunmen ready to assume a new authority. Others loiters in limbo: here and there the Mogadishu Police, in crisp obviously quite new olive outfits, policing not at all. They're U.N.-funded. Out of work now, and hourly less and less evident. One guesses that by nightfall those uniforms will have found their ways deep into storage.

At midafternoon the journalists stand at the city's dead center, along the Green Line, the boundary between Ali Mahdi's sector and Aidid's South Mogadishu. It looks as if somebody rolled an asteroid through town and out to sea. The Somali Parliament building's rubble stands smack on the Green Line. The monument to the Unknown Soldier—from which war? Mohamed can't remember. That's the rubble of the gas station. Rubble of the car wash, the Bank of Commerce. "Now," Mohamed says—why? Why does he think it has to be said?— "now it's a ghost town."

"The Marines will be leaving," the journalists remind him. "We'd better get down to the port,"

"Yes, it's time. I don't think I'm going with you."

Mike says, "We'll get Billeh."

4:11 P.M. Thurs.

A Huey helicopter flies east overhead as the last of the U.S. Marines make ready to leave the beach; a buzzard dangles in the thermals closer over the town. Troops have vacated all but the port, leaving behind in the city itself a vacuum, as under a hand just raised to flatten something. Or it's as if the gates were swinging open on a bastille, and soon comes the moment when the prisoners within either rage out into the streets, or step forth blinking into peace and freedom. Over loudspeakers the calls to prayer start up, the muezzin moaning from the minarets in the hush. A big gun starts up somewhere in the distance but then stops—the silence everywhere—then the sobbing music of the Muslim prayers.

4:25 P.M.

Billeh and I stand with a few last journalists overlooking the port, directly next to a sandbag emplacement of U.S. Marines under a palm-thatch shelter, one of three Marine positions left now on the port's inland side. These American boys muttering into their radios and sighting along their gun barrels at suspicious figures below them among the cargo crates are the last U.N. troops in the country, along with some platoons, a half dozen at most, dug into the beach below and camouflaged by stacks of lumber that would look more incidental if the boards weren't brand-new. As we watch, three platoons suddenly vacate their positions down there and put hurriedly to sea in a black rubber raft. They rock a minute in the low surf, then accelerate out toward a larger landing craft full of more Marines. Beyond them floats the *Vergina*, a Greek charter loaded with 1,500 U.N. troops, most of them Pakistani.

4:32 P.M.

Now the eight Marines next to us leave their emplacement and file quickly past, the last saying, "Go! Go! Go!" They break into a run.

We follow behind, running, too, and catch up around the corner of a wall as they board an amphibious transport as tall as a semi. The vehicle makes a tight corner with its outer tread clawing at the sand and swings past kicking up dust in our faces, and I feel—I hadn't expected this, but I feel personally ashamed. The transports, three of them now, crawl onto the open ramp of landing craft. We watch them go, but I don't think we want to turn around and see what they've left. Billeh pinches me on the ass: "You're not the last journalist left in Somalia," he says, "but I'm happy to tell you that you're the last American."

A Somali immediately begins grabbing up the electric communication wires strung along through the dirt underfoot, but another stops him. "Wait until the journalists are gone—" Billeh translates. Down on the pier the looting starts—the journalists call it "Affirmative Shopping"— as locals gang together to tip over the cargo crates and set dozens of empty fifty-gallon drums rolling along everywhere like big cookies in some burning black fairy tale of war in the sunset of our idea of civilization. It doesn't look as if there's a whole lot left to steal. A man shouts, "Journalists! Time is up! Now is danger come!" How does he know? People are clumping up together out of nowhere, and they look panicked. Angry faces bloom all around us. "They're saying the journalists are making it dangerous," Billeh says. The shooting begins— here, there—where? Who? You never know, you never see, it's one of the strange laws of urban warfare, you can never *see* who's *shooting*. "We must get off the streets," Billeh says. But the gunfire's sparse, scattered—celebratory fireworks. It's a party, not a battle.

That night Mike and Billeh and the South Africans stand on the Al Sahafi's roof in the cooling dusk. Just after dark the Marines, putting out to sea beyond the harbor, send up flares that boom at first like mortars and then pop open into silence, frail orange suns dangling in the sky and making an eerie dimness below, in which nothing is familiar. One last firefight down at the beach—they hear the AKs popping in their characteristic way, and then, from the boats, the triple-snap of U.S. M-16s in three-burst mode, every third round an arcing crimson tracer. It's over in minutes. For a couple of hours the flares rise and set over Mogadishu, and then it's dark—without electric lights, the city disappears as completely as the international presence has.

ONE MORE WIZARD WITH A MICROPHONE

The next morning the city of Mogadishu breaks its fast. It's over—little parties all around town, including one at the residence of Gen. Mohamed Farah Aidid, a hundred people laughing and eating bits of jelly and pastries handed around on paper plates. The journalists are glad to see the bottled water. But they didn't come for water. Where's Aidid? He'll make a statement soon. Deeply, deeply, Mike feels the need for a cover story—but Billeh introduces him all around the gathering as the Last American in Somalia. "We have him now!" he jokes, gripping Mike's wrist in both his hands. Ho-ho! Mike doesn't touch a bite. In celebration of the end of Ramadan, the cap guns are going off all over—harmless, but disconcerting—eerie that kids should hold toy weapons in their hands as they stand in the bullet-riddled alleys . . .

Later the journalists are led upstairs and out onto a veranda with a floor of white and black shiny tiles and seated in an arrangement of green and orange wicker chairs. For some time the journalists wait facing a long table on which rest a shock of plastic flowers in a straw pot painted gold and a little blue Somalian flag with its one yellow star. A half hour passes. Occasionally someone steps up and lays a tape machine or a microphone gently on the wrinkled white tablecloth. The wind comes over the veranda's railing, laying down the red dust that owns everything, and its wife the sand. The little flag blows over. Africa: the sudden passionate fixing of attention to some ridiculous trivial detail—the position, now, for instance, the *line* of the *angle,* of an electric cord for a microphone. Perhaps the tall assistant's fumbling ministrations parallel the neurotic superstitions of gamblers—the charms of one who's survived over and over the lottery of random destruction. "Ladies and gentlemen," he says: "General Aidid to speak with you."

The warlord who has driven the world from his domain, who snookered the West Point generals and transformed himself from a man with a U.N. price on his head into the chief negotiator of the U.N. departure, the one person they could deal with in getting out of the country without bloodshed, this one strides forth and looks out at the assembled press and smiles.

How appropriate that this should feel above all like the moment when Oz, the great and terrible, steps out from behind his curtain, uncovered now as a plump man with coffee-colored skin, short, bald, in a pinstriped shirt and conservative necktie, an avuncular man, a weary man, only somewhat freshened by triumph. He lays his gold-knobbed cane against the table and stands beside it, touches the tablecloth, takes up his statement in trembling fingers. "I am extremely very happy," he reads in English, "to meet with you today here at my residence."

He reads that the Somali people were "conducting the most desperate struggle ever to happen in the history on the Earth." He reads the future: Security, rehabilitation, resettlement of displaced people, development and elections . . . It's clear he hasn't the slightest idea what happens next.

As for the transitional government, he says it will be "a government to unite, to rebuild, to solve all the Somali problems." He assures those assembled that he is going "to save my country."

The journalist from America has decided to cling to the notion that out there, in the countryside he passed through to reach this crazy city, the people know what they're doing. Their leaders don't, and we don't. But they know. All this destruction is shaping tomorrow—a tomorrow without a lot of Idaho White Boy ideas in it.

They got along for centuries on their own. No reason to think that in two decades they've mislaid the skills entirely, but the skills aren't honed. The main rehabilitation won't be structural, but human, spiritual.

Meanwhile General Aidid states that he intends to repeat the age-old errors, as he prepares to institute some sort of modern democratic government that will turn, if successful, to the other nation-states for endorsement, support, military muscle.

But the nation-state, the twentieth-century geopolitical entity held together by the government's monopoly on the use of force—it's finished. The Kalashnikov rifle and the Stinger missile, and the worldwide dissemination of these weapons during the proxy conflicts of the Cold War, have changed things as much as the invention of gun-

powder did in the thirteenth century. A determined Third-World
people can now hold out against the greatest powers—witness
Vietnam—and even a loose coalition of determined clans or factions
can drive away the strongest armies—witness Afghanistan—and
now in Somalia and the former Yugoslavia it's been made plain that
even factions at war with one another can, with their left hand, as it
were, stalemate the U.N. in its efforts to stop the fighting among
them.

It begins to waver and dissolve, but still it stands, humanity's
mass hallucination: the vision of a planet of united nations, the great
delusion that the nation-state doesn't work *yet,* but someday *will*—
that the governments who killed each year of the twentieth century,
on average, a million of the civilians they claimed to protect and
serve, can be trusted to cease their wars.

Another general makes ready to join them, all those people
who've proven they can't run the world. Still they go on seeking
order by making war, because anything's preferable to anarchy—so
say the survivors.

The general is open for questions. A reporter just arrived from
Madrid lifts up his hand. "Can you say the war is over?"

Pause. The general nods, he smiles, happy to demonstrate his ability in this regard. He pronounces the words perfectly: "The war is
over."

JUNGLE BELLS, JUNGLE BELLS

Friends who know me to be of weak character might be interested to learn I was once nearly saved from it: In the winter of 1962 I underwent initiation into the Boy Scouts. But it seems to be true, character is fate, and the flawed one will follow its flaws. After my first Scout camping trip, which took place in the Philippine jungle during our Christmas vacation period, I soon quit going to the weekly meetings, and never even bought a uniform.

This failure had a lot to do with the physical experience itself. December in the Philippine Islands is appreciably cooler than some other months, but it's still the tropics—not just a welter of heat and steam, but a real cauldron of organic strife. The soil is dark and red and wet, every square inch a complicated battleground of insects, reptiles, and funguses, and any living thing that lies still—or, let's say, "camps out"—on the ground there can expect to be devoured.

What was I doing in the Philippines? My dad was with the embassy, and we moved several times during my childhood. Every move meant a chance to reinvent myself. My style of adjustment was to arrive in a new universe, lie low while striking up a few acquaintances, and then start distinguishing myself with bad behavior. Advancing age alone would soon elevate me from Cutup to Hoodlum, and it was only my eventual discovery of the Beatnik category that saved me from the penitentiary. In the interim I made a try at Beachboy, but was frustrated by my lack of a surfboard and my failure to locate any surf. As to what attracted me, this Christmas vacation, to the Boy Scouts of America, I'm still baffled.

I underwent this transition late: Boy Scouts start at age eleven, and I was already well past twelve. In the Cub Scouts, I'd failed to progress. I'd earned the Wolf badge, and the Bear badge, but I'd wandered into a swampy obsession with the gold and silver arrows that could be earned by tiny achievements and sewn beneath these badges in long glittering strings, and my career had foundered in these near-irrelevencies until I'd become the ten-year-old equivalent of a fifty-year-old first lieutenant. And I'd failed inspection routinely, because of my Elvis Presley haircut. So why would I want to try the Scouts again? Let's just agree that one symptom of a weak character is a sick passion for making the same mistakes over and over.

We arrived at the campsite on a sweaty Friday afternoon, about two dozen American youths, most of us in crisp green uniforms, in a convoy of family sedans driven by volunteer parents or Filipino chauffeurs, all of whom immediately drove away while we set up our tents. Tents today are like four-ounce, inflatable apartments, but in the sixties the Scouts used the same kind our fathers had used in World War II. Olive canvas, no floors, taut ropes jiggling in the wind that swept over this hillside, a wet wind, a flabby wind, while in the valley below the local people had gathered from outflung jungle villages to, of all things, slaughter pork one hog at a time, with blows of sledge hammers—this probably in preparation for Christmas celebrations.

As we gathered miscellaneous half-rotten sticks for firewood, our scoutmaster instructed us in the ancient incendiary arts. Our scoutmaster frightened me. I think his name was Jerry, a bald, spectacled figure who looked as if he'd been only recently let out of a Japanese prison camp; but this impression was wrong; he'd been let out some seventeen years before. Like many Euros who've lived for decades in the tropics, he'd lost a lot of his body hair and all of his fat and seemed fabricated out of cords and paper. He regarded those days of captivity and torture at the hands of his enemies as the primary character-building experience of his life, and he was bent on duplicating it, in every way possible, for his Scouts. He was enthusiastic about this opportunity. The other boys took Jerry's attitude in stride, as far as I could tell.

The Scouts aim to build character and impart a wilderness savoir-faire with Native American overtones that would meld the Lone Ranger and Tonto into one small young self-sufficient good guy. The atmosphere on this campout was one of military discipline constantly marred by sobs and outbursts, because the Scouts were children, after all.

Unlike a lot of Americans who find themselves overseas, we youngsters had no connection with the military. The U.S. bases were far from the capital, Manila, where we all, the sons of corporate executives and career diplomats, attended the private American School. For the most part we presented the usual picture of well-to-do suburban American boys, healthy, happy, innocently evil, anxious to start fires and chop things up with hatchets.

The most spectacular character-building was being undertaken by one of my classmates, a paralyzed kid in a wheelchair. His houseboy pitched his tent for him on a metropolis of jungle fire ants and drove away, and this boy spent the weekend trading his supply of ice-water—a big jug of it he had—for insecticide and bug repellant. Although we weren't friends, just vaguely acquainted, under these unusual circumstances I suddenly recognized that we were a lot alike. He allowed himself to be enrolled in everything, clubs, Little League, choir, and so on, but he refused to stick to his script—we were supposed to admire and pity him and he was supposed to be cool, but actually he acted like a big brat, uncontrollably dissatisfied and constantly sneering or complaining or acting defeated. I still see him slumped over in his wheelchair, flushed with baby anger, squirting poison fumes into the dirt around him.

The first day we dug rain ditches around our tents and policed the area of litter and then circled the campfire and listened to our scoutmaster reminisce about his days of dysentery, starvation, and terror, and we roasted weenies and devoured flaming marshmallows while the screams of dying hogs lofted up from the valley. According to Jerry, the best way to manage with dysentery is to wear nothing but a jockstrap, so you can get down to business quick, without having to negotiate, and it terrified me that everybody but me seemed to feel this was information worth filing away.

Staring into the flames brought on a kind of hypnosis that added to my sense of dislocation. Hacking away with a hatchet at some kindling for our fire, I managed to opened a hole in my tennis shoe and sheer off the tip of my right big toe. This turned out to be a smaller wound than I feared at first, but it had to be bandaged, and, before that, disinfected. Our leader dumped a pint of Merthiolate into a canvas bucket and took me away from the circle of fire, as it was night by now, very dark by now, and into the jungle where he sat me on a rotten log and plunged my foot into the Merthiolate. I was proud to be told by the others, "We could hear you screaming all the way back here at camp," and I was glad, also, that I'd managed to do some serious agonizing for the scoutmaster's benefit. I hoped it meant I had a future in the Scouts—not that I intended ever to have anything to do with them again; but I wanted the scoutmaster to be pleased with me while he had us in the dark jungle, and above all I didn't want him to understand that he had on his hands here a little Scout who intended to desert the ranks first chance he got. In fact if this had been a real army, one with an enemy, I would have joined them and pinpointed this location on a map for their artillery. All of this was unknown to me in any specific way. Inside, I was blank and blameless.

When midnight came, that first night, three or four of us underwent the initiation rites, which took several hours and which I don't remember much of—tired and disoriented, also blindfolded, and wearing only one shoe—except that at one point the veteran Scouts in charge of my transformation poured cooking oil all over me and claimed I was being peed on by a water buffalo. I seem to remember also that I had a length of rope, symbolizing something mythological and Native American, tied around my neck, and that I wasn't supposed to talk until it was removed. I'm not sure whether or not I kept the silence, but I'll certainly believe it if somebody who reads this small memoir calls me up and tells me I babbled the whole time.

The actual camping was cut short the next night by a downpour that flattened our gathering of tents like so many small cocktail napkins. It came from the source of all such tropical storms, from absolutely nowhere, and it filled our pitiful rain ditches in a couple of seconds and started rapidly eroding the hilltop itself, so that the muck went sliding out from under us. The sopping canvas tents collapsed and we youngsters succumbed, in their monstrous, drowning embrace, to panic completely unbecoming the ranks. We didn't know whether to hang on to the tents and go down with them or abandon ship and be swept away on the heaving seas of mud. Jerry stalked among the weeping scouts like Captain Ahab, reminding us that he'd not only gone through this many times in the war, but gone through it wearing only a jockstrap. But his voice was tiny in the wind and rain, and eventually he gave up exhorting us to be men and led us off the mountain. We slept on the floor of the church in the nearest village, the building all the villagers slept in when it rained like this, listening to the water roar down the hillside in cataracts. Early in the morning we left that place forever, some of us strengthened after adversity, and some of us with our weaknesses unspoiled.

THE SMALL BOYS' UNIT

In the winter of 1992 *The New Yorker* magazine invited me to travel to Liberia and write an article about what I found there.

I lived with my family in Iowa City at the time. I taught writing courses at the university. My two children walked a couple of blocks every day to what we'd been assured was one of the nation's best public schools, and my wife worked as a volunteer there several days a week. The people around us in this small city seemed prosperous and happy. I made a great salary. And yet I agreed to go.

Two years earlier I'd published a piece about a very brief visit I'd made to Monrovia, the Liberian capital. On the strength of this experience alone, I was offered the second assignment.

Some of my creative writing students had become interested in a book called *The Writer's Journey* by Christopher Vogler. In one place the book said, "Unless something is brought back from the ordeal in the Inmost Cave, the hero is doomed to repeat the adventure. Many comedies use this ending, as a foolish character refuses to learn his lesson and embarks on the same folly that got him in trouble in the first place."

I was going to write a profile of Charles Taylor, commander in chief of the National Patriotic Reconstruction Assembly Government

(NPRAG) and self-described president of Liberia. After two years of civil war, President Taylor's forces claimed to control the Liberian countryside, all but the capital city of Monrovia. A force of peace-keepers, mostly Nigerian military, had kept him from getting this last bit of territory, where half the country's population lived. Recently a tense peace had given way to battles between, mainly, the Nigerian peacekeepers and the NPRAG, but other factions harassed Taylor on the west and the south, and this amounted to the Liberian civil war's having started up again.

Commercial flights to Liberia had been suspended since the start of the violence. Visitors to Taylor's territory had to go overland from neighboring Côte d'Ivoire—the Ivory Coast.

At four o'clock on a December morning I got off an Air Afrique jet in Abidjan, the capital of the Ivory Coast, having arranged to be met by representatives of the National Patriotic Reconstruction Assembly Government. I'd spoken with the NPRAG's Foreign Minister in Washington, a gentleman named Momulu Sirleaf, and Mr. Sirleaf had assured me that everything was arranged. I had forty U.S. one hundred dollar bills stuck in the seams of my pants and a quart of clean water in a plastic canteen and the number of somebody to call if the arrangements went wrong.

With the other arrivals I moved under gray fluorescent light and down the bald concrete halls and past the jaundice-eyed men of Customs in their starched and serviced khaki uniforms. I wandered around a while smelling the tropical rot and general cologne until I was sure nobody had turned out to meet me. Then I hired a car to the Intercontinental Hotel.

The room was small and very clean and wetly air-conditioned, faintly mildewed and dimly lit by a circular neon tube. The fake marble floor had been mopped and would never dry.

I called the number I'd been given, the only local telephone number I had, the number of a Liberian national named Robertson, who was supposed to meet me at the airport. Mr. Robertson was in, but he didn't know who I was.

I mentioned the Foreign Minister, also Mr. Taylor's American attorney. They'd assured me, I told him, that everything had been arranged. That I'd be met at the airport, and then escorted first to Danané, an Ivoirian border town, and from there to Charles Taylor's headquarters in the small city of Gbarnga, about a hundred kilometers inside Liberia.

Mr. Robertson seemed unacquainted with any of this, but after a while he recalled that yes, he'd heard somebody was supposed to interview the president.

I told him it wasn't an interview, but an extensive profile. People close to the president had arranged for me to spend up to a couple of weeks at his side. I tried to imply it wasn't anything to be casual about.

My contact promised to check with his people and meet me in the lobby in twenty minutes.

I guessed this could mean as much as two hours, and I waited that long before I went downstairs to wait some more. But when he hadn't come after four hours, and he didn't answer his telephone anymore, I guessed he wasn't coming at all.

From my room I tried to call the States but was informed the long distance telephone operators were on strike. You could receive overseas calls, but you couldn't call out. They'd been on strike a long time, and they were expected to go on and on.

I took out my correspondence with the important magazine that had promised to arrange everything, with the Foreign Minister who'd assured me that everything had in fact been arranged, with the prominent Maryland lawyer who represented Charles Taylor's interests abroad and who had reiterated the arrangements.

Now incomprehensible incantations covered the pages. The words of the messages, the names, the places, even the letterheads pulsed with mystery and a joyous insanity.

I had visited West Africa only once before, but I had a good idea what was happening. And I knew it was useless and idiotic to try to resist it.

On a circular couch in the center of the lobby a dozen coal-black whores waited almost motionlessly, and I thought I should go get one and come back to the room and just stay here until I'd spent all my hundreds and then go home. But after another hour Mr. Robertson turned up. He phoned me from the lobby and I went down to meet him, a friendly middle-aged Liberian in loose sports apparel and sandals.

"Everything is arranged," he told me happily.

I would travel to the border by commercial bus, accompanied by Mr. Robertson's son John. I'd be escorted across the border into Liberia, met by a presidential staff car, and taken to Gbarnga and to Charles Taylor.

But first, tomorrow, I'd have to meet with a press officer, a young woman named Miss Raefley, who would give me the background. I wasn't interested in meeting her, but I knew it would be impossible to skip any steps or find a shorter way.

The next morning I had breakfast in the hotel's dining room with Miss Raefley, a woman in a pink pantsuit, late twenties, more articulate and clearly smarter and more seriously educated than the folks I knew back home. She told me that right now the biggest problem for Greater Liberia—so Taylor's sector of the country was called— were the Nigerians and their heavy-handed efforts to impose a peace. Because they couldn't seem to extricate themselves without losing face, Liberia had become known as "Nigeria's Vietnam." Their peace- keeping efforts didn't exclude random bombing raids on the Liberian countryside. I already knew all of this. My question was, was Charles Taylor expecting me, had it really all been arranged? Everything had seemed so simple: Hop over to Abidjan, to the border, to the head- quarters. Now I couldn't even get out of this hotel.

Miss Raefley spoke of Charles Taylor with obvious respect. She and all the Liberians I met on this trip referred to their president as "Charles Taylor" or "the President" and never "President Taylor." I make noth- ing of it but only observe the fact. She listed his accomplishments: con- solidation of the countryside, elections and a democratic government, general peace and order interrupted only by outside factions.

I didn't know much about him really, and neither did anybody else, it seemed. I'd made the acquaintance, on my previous visit to the region, of a French journalist who'd been ordered executed by Charles Taylor. But the gun they put to his head wasn't loaded. It had been a kind of joke. Early in the war Taylor's faction had captured Monrovia's AM radio station. He delivered a report at six each evening, saying things like, "We now have one thousand prisoners of the peacekeeping forces and already I have personally killed seven hundred and fifty-three of them and they die easily, it takes only one bullet to finish two of these cowards and murderers who think they can stomp all over Liberia." He gave these speeches in a loud, high-pitched voice. Maybe this was just a style of oratory, but it got him a doubtful reputation.

Miss Raefley the press officer admitted it: "We've definitely lost the propaganda war." But she insisted the Reconstruction Assembly Government was actually that—a true government—bicameral, consisting of representatives democratically chosen in a recent election. By the will of the majority, Charles Taylor was the president.

I agreed that to the little extent he'd been noticed, Charles Taylor had been demonized by U.S. journalists, myself among them, but here came a chance to fix that, if somebody would only get me back on track to write this profile. I would write up to ten thousand words. The magazine had a huge U.S. circulation. President Clinton would probably read it.

"And," said Miss Raefley, "I understand they've worked out your itinerary."

"Yes," I agreed. "There were just a few hitches."

Mr. Robertson's son John Robertson was a sincere young man in a tight striped long-sleeved jersey, although, to me, the weather seemed very hot. His father had told me we'd be leaving the hotel at 8:00 A.M. to make the first bus for Danané, the air-conditioned luxury bus. The two men arrived at my hotel about one in the afternoon and took me in a cab to a terminal in a muddy market downtown where long-distance buses stopped. The air-conditioned bus had left at eight, unaccountably right on time, so on an open-air transport we bought three seats for the two of us, which gave us room to lay our packs aside and keep a breeze between us.

The driver refused to estimate our arrival time in Danané. He said, "It's bad luck."

We headed north and west on the four-lane highway, the driver gunning his motor and, like everyone else, honking his horn—celebrating the miracle of automotive transport. People staggered wearily along the margin while down on them looked a billboard that said, GUINNESS IS GOOD FOR YOU. Côte d'Ivoire has many good roads, and in 1992 this was the best of them, passing as it did alongside Yamoussoukro, once the tribal village of the aged President Houphouët-Boigny and now the site of his vast palace and also of the monument to his spirituality, the Basillica, which was built for half a billion dollars, to some people's great disgust. The Pope visited it reluctantly, viewing it as a symbol of top-heaviness and African big-man excess. But the people loved their president, had loved him ever since he took power in 1960. He kept crocodiles in the man-made lake alongside the palace. Attendants fed them live chickens in a small ceremony each day at dusk. Our bus sped alongside the high concrete walls of Yamoussoukro and into the surrounding arboreal chaos, the people in the towns and along the country roads so thrilled by its passage—even though there were six a day, and plenty of other traffic—that they howled and shouted greetings and the kids leapt in the air as it flew past. When they actually wanted the bus to stop, they stretched out an arm and silently waved it up and down as if petting an invisible pony, looking completely bored.

After dark we came to Danané, the border town, which really did feel perched on the edge of an immensely different zone. We stopped at a kiosk cafe—a bare bulb dangling, a tape blaring, and one child dancing in the dust. Herdsmen and their lanky Brahman cattle were settling down for the night on the highway's tarmac, which still held the heat of the sun. The pavement ended here and a dirt track headed off toward Liberia, a region three hundred miles long and half as wide without electricity or running water or commerce to speak of, a land fallen into the hands of wild young men with automatic rifles.

We were supposed to go the Hotel Lianes, an adobe place in a dirt yard, very inexpensive, and there rendezvous with a man named

Winston Holder. In the night, with only a few lamps burning here and there in the town, it was impossible to tell who among the shadows wandering around might be Winston Holder. John asked but nobody could tell him. Information came his way that maybe we should actually be looking for a guy named Lincoln Smythe. About midnight we turned in having found nobody at all.

"Everything is arranged," John Robertson told me.

"Thank God."

"I forgot to mention that we appear to have one small problem," he said.

"Okay . . ."

"Evidently it seems Winston Holder has already left this morning to the border and Gbarnga. He took a journalist in."

"A journalist? Who?"

"I don't know who. They thought it must be you."

"But it wasn't me. I'm me," I said, though from the first hour in this country I'd begun to doubt it.

"I have Lincoln Smythe's address. He'll put us right. Everything will be arranged promptly, and we'll work out your itinerary."

"I thought everything *was* arranged," I said.

By the bare bulb hung above our straw beds I saw, far back in John Robertson's eyes, the eternal West African question: *What is this guy going on about?*

"Naturally," he said, "but we just have to work out your itinerary."

Everything is arranged doesn't mean you should expect to get anywhere or accomplish anything. In fact, for sanity's sake, those two ideas have to be banished: the idea of getting somewhere and the idea of accomplishing something. Everything is arranged means that all is complete, the great plan of the universe is unfolding before our eyes. So eat, drink, sleep. Everything is arranged.

As we drove around the next morning in a hired car, looking for Lincoln Smythe or Winston Holder or somebody who could help us find either one, it came clear that Danané, a town of about a thousand serving to administrate a larger surrounding population whose number I couldn't guess at, hosted a sizable bunch of Liberians who did not enjoy much status here. Some served as agents for Taylor's faction, others just preferred a place where a few things worked and people lived in peace.

The second time we visited his address, we found Lincoln Smythe at home. He answered the door in his underwear. He didn't know who we were, or who Winston Holder was. He asked us for cigarettes. He got dressed and took us to a kiosk cafe where I ate fried eggs, and he and John turned me over to a new man.

The new man was in his thirties, well spoken, neatly dressed, ready to take me to Liberia to see what he called "the situation on the ground." He shook my hand and introduced himself as Augustus Shaacks. He spelled his name. I didn't ask him who the hell he thought he was because John was gone, and Lincoln was gone, and Winston Holder had never materialized. Augustus Shaacks was all I had.

"I understand one of Charles Taylor's staff cars is waiting for us at the border," Augustus said. "We'll pick it up, go to Gbarnga, and meet with the press officers and get you immediately to the President."

"Can we hire a car to take us to the border?"

"Most definitely."

"Well—" I said, "let's go!"

Augustus's face was small and round and beat-up, with big, droopy eyes that made him look burdened with grief and wisdom. "I forgot to mention," he said, "but it's unfortunate that at this time we cannot particularly cross the border, because first we have to see the Commissaire de Police. We need to permission to cross."

We hired a car to the police station, an imposing edifice, comparitively, housing five offices, also one jail cell behind a heavy wooden door. People slept on the red concrete floors of the lobby and the hallway using their shoes or sandals as pillows.

The desk officer sat behind a high counter telling anybody who entered to sit down and wait. Augustus and I waited an hour or so on a stone bench in the lobby, then we waited a couple more hours on a wooden bench in a hallway. Repeatedly I asked him to show me somebody around here I could bribe. Each time, he shook his head. "Not yet. The moment will be right."

That afternoon we sat before a khaki-uniformed man in an office decorated with health posters and an ad for tires, across a desk covered with little rubber-banded bundles of identity cards. This official explained in French that we needed to go to Abidjan and apply for and wait for and eventually be issued an official press identity card. Then he'd be happy to let me cross the western border.

Today was Friday. So I'd have to wait until Monday to start the application process—to drop down into a bureaucratic web and let them devour the shreds of my reason.

Augustus and I put our heads together. "Let me just bribe this guy," I whispered.

Augustus, who could do all sorts of magnificently expressive tricks with his face, made his eyes swim in a sort of fatherly contempt and said softly, "Now is not yet the time."

"But look—now he's getting on the telephone," I said. "If he calls a superior or ropes in anybody else at all, it'll be too late to pay him off."

When the man got off the phone, he said he'd just talked to his superior, the mayor, and the mayor had said we must go to Abidjan. I now grasped that this man was the Commissaire de Police. I slipped a twenty-dollar bill inside my passport. I handed the document to him and asked him in English to look again at my visa. He opened it, studied the twenty dollars, smacked it shut, and handed it back across the desk. He shook his head.

"All morning I've been saying, 'Who do I bribe, who do I bribe?' Now we're screwed," I told Augustus, "because this was the guy, and we missed our chance. The staff car won't wait up there at the border another three days, will it?"

"Ah! these people," he said.

"Can we call up to the Liberian side and tell them what's going on? Get the car to wait?"

"That's an excellent idea, Denis," he told me. "Unfortunately, the telephones on the Liberian side are temporarily out of order."

We went across the hall to get some sort of permission to leave the town for Abidjan or—I didn't know what. They wanted to dec-

orate my passport with another clearance, that's all I knew. I handed my documents to a young boy who asked my destination.
"Liberia," I said. He stamped a page and we were out of that place,
prepared to go back to the capital and start all over again.

"Look at what the boy stamped here." I showed Augustus my
passport. "It says 'Liberia.'"

Augustus looked amused. "You fooled him by mistake."

"I can cross the border with this?"

"If we hurry," he said. "At any second these people might realize
the mistake."

"If they do—can they radio ahead of us?"

"They have a telephone to the border station on the Ivory side.
They might give a call to stop us."

He found a car for hire and we leapt inside. The cabbie switched
on his ignition using a bent nail.

At the edge of town we reached a police outpost and a barricade,
showed my documents, and were waved along onto a red dirt road
that headed over grassy hills to the border. The scene was pastoral but
desolate. Dusty yellow flowers on tall stalks. Sea gulls. Goats. An
occasional thatched hut made of sticks and khaki mud. Ten miles
along we reached a collection of shacks and large sheds, the village of
Gbé-Nda. We dismissed the car and walked to a crude roadblock—a
long branch jammed onto two posts beside a red sign saying ARRETEZ.

"Is this Liberia?" I asked.

"It's still Ivoire," Augustus said, "the last border station,"—a
shed with a man in it holding a gun in his lap. The telephone, housed
in a box on a pole about ten yards away, looked unfortunately like
a good one, but apparently it hadn't rung yet. The guard searched
my knapsack and stole my maps. He asked for money, and Augustus
told him, "I coming back. I see you soon. I coming back." The guard
accepted the erroneous stamp in my passport. I gave him a disposable
butane lighter. He went through my pack again and stole my flashlight. The telephone kept quiet.

We crossed a plank bridge over a narrow gorge and entered
Liberia. A hundred yards along we came around a curve in the track

to find Loguatuo, a village wandering over a green plain under gigantic acacia trees. There were signs of commerce—a shack called "Uncle Pee's Tee Shop," and the like. We saw a few women and kids, but the population seemed mostly to be barefoot teenage men wearing the rags and tags of camouflage outfits and carrying rifles.

Augustus knew his way around. We approached a large wooden kiosk, passing the stares of scores of these young men, many of whom seemed red-eyed and slack-jawed and decidedly messed up on something. They knew Augustus—"Gus, can I see you?" they said, "Gus, you got something for me?" "I coming back," he told them all, "but right now I'm with a personal friend of the President." One made a gesture quite new to me—discreetly pulling down his lower eyelid with his forefinger. "Man, I'll see you when I get back!" Augustus shouted at him, while another one bird-dogged us with his gun barrel nodding down discomfitingly toward our spines until Shaacks asked him if he was going to shoot us and he replied he didn't know. About these guys nothing could have been clearer than that they didn't know what they were going to do—what on earth *thing* they would *do*—the very next second.

"There's the car!" I said. "Isn't that the car?" The car that would get us out of here.

Two monstrous gleaming Daihatsu SUVs waited beside the kiosk while a few Euros in clean khakis spoke with the boys guarding the roadway into their country. In the forward Daihatsu sat a beautiful white woman with red hair.

Augustus went and talked for a long time to the guards and to the black driver of the Europeans' car.

"Well, unfortunately, according to some people here, the staff car came yesterday and picked up a journalist and took him to Gbarnga."

"Great! The mystery journalist! He stole my ride!"

"I couldn't say. I think we're all right. We could be dealing with a miscommunication," he said.

"Well—how about these people?"

"They're from MSF."—*Médecins Sans Frontières*, or Doctors without Borders. "They won't give you a ride."

"Did you ask them?"

"But the staff car is coming."

"How can it be coming if it already came and went?"

"We'll radio to them."

"I gotta talk to these folks," I said.

"Please, listen to me," Augustus said. "The staff car is coming." I gathered he thought it rude not to wait for this staff car even into our final years as old men. The staff car was a gesture from the President, after all.

I approached the doctors and smiled and tried to talk French and asked for a ride. I was grimy and tired and probably wild in the eyes. They declined to take on this passenger, as anybody would, not out of fear that he's a criminal, but you don't want to be killed by anyone else's ridiculousness, or catch the disease of bad luck.

The Doctors without Borders went away in their small beautiful caravan.

Augustus left me with a Coca-Cola while he set off to find our staff car and change some money for me. He came back with an absurd multitude of worn-out five-dollar bills. "What's this?"

"Liberian JJs. The man on the money is Joseph J. Roberts." A Liberian Founding Father who looked like George Washington in a powdered wig, only he was black.

"What are they worth?"

"They're not worth anything," he said. "But we can use them to pay off the boys along the route."

"What about the car?"

"They're already returning to pick us up."

"Where did you get this information?"

"I'm sure they realized the mistake."

"I don't think anybody around here realizes anything at all. Not one goddamn thing."

"Everything is arranged. We'll radio tomorrow."

"Can't we radio now?"

"There's a very minor problem that prevents the radio from functioning."

"WOW," was all I could think of to say.

"They've gone to work on it."

My parents raised me to love all the earth's peoples. Three days in this zone and I could only just manage to hold myself back from screaming Niggers! Niggers! Niggers! until one of these young men emptied a whole clip into me.

A Toyota van pulled up to the kiosk now, and a man leapt from it as if sprung from my own demonized heart, a vivid man, the most vivid on earth, shouting mysterious things.

"Gettemi!" he shouted, "Gettemi, Gettemi!" He strutted around waving his arms and crowing passionately. I'd say he was in his sixties, a European, and you could see he'd been in Africa quite some time, because as a physical soul he had almost disappeared and been left with not much more than the tendons and skin and astonishment of a baby bird. What astonished him beyond his capacity to contain himself, at the moment, was the guards' request for some money. "MONEY! You think I give you MONEY? You think I *Mister* Pay! *Mister* Pay! You sonabitch I never give you money you kill me come on I DON'T care, I DON'T care you kill me seven thousand time!"

The young men laughed. They'd get no JJs, only this entertainment. When the man noticed me he pierced me with a look of complete understanding and sympathy and fellow-feeling.

I told him who I was and asked him if he could take me somewhere. He said he was Antonio Rainieri from Gbarnga, going back home, and of course I was welcome to a ride. I asked about his origins. He'd come from Italy, where exactly in Italy he seemed to have forgotten or to consider irrelevant.

He screamed, "Ay! Ay! Ay! Rainieri he a fountain he squirt to you MONEY MONEY MONEY!" He yanked at the zipper of his khaki pants and chased the boys around, pretending to urinate.

"It seems this man is crazy," Augustus warned me.

"Which one?"

"Allow me to suggest that we wait until—"

"I'm going."

"—until we get your itinerary sorted out. Tomorrow—"

"I'm going," I said, and Augustus had to join me because he owed it to his president to stay by my side.

We climbed in amongst Antonio Rainieri's immense African wife, their gorgeous mulatto daughter, and their Lebanese son-in-law. They'd stocked up on supplies in the first town of any size inside Côte d'Ivoire, and now they traveled home hauling boxes and sacks in this unlucky-looking vehicle with its fractured headlights and mismatched tires.

We set off into the West African dusk. I'd never been in the bush before. In Sierra Leone some local journalists had once offered to take me to distant villages to meet men who could turn into snakes, stretch their arms to tremendous lengths like rubber, who could be shot repeatedly from close range without effect. But at that time I'd been stuck in the urban capital, and this was my first look at these thatched shacks of sticks and adobe plaster in brief clearings of tawny muck. For dozens of miles the road was just a mud-filled trough, then it turned to battered tarmac. Mr. Rainieri cursed each pothole like a personal outrage.

The checkpoints hindered us more than the condition of the road. Not a hundred yards outside Loguatuo we came to the first one—sleepy youngsters draped in ragged shawls or blankets in the humid night poking their gun barrels into the car. "I wan' see you, you got something for me?" they asked, and Rainieri jumped out of the car each time, as outraged as an infant at birth: "MR. PAY! GETTEMMI GETTEMI GETTEMI," which eventually I deciphered as "goddamnit." "This man," Augustus added every time, referring to me, "is a personal friend of the President." The checkpoints followed one another relentlessly, the bullet-riddled shacks keeping close enough to signal one another by gunfire in the event of attack, and the men were expected not to fire their weapons just for fun. Mr. Rainieri had limitless time to deal with these delays, to lambaste the guards, and Augustus wanted everybody to shake my hand in lieu of money. They met the friend of the president, we squirted money, our antenna banged under the raised gate and we proceeded to the next barricade through a land lit by a half-moon and fireflies—"Wan, see you, you got somet'ing for me?—" "Mr. Pay! Mr. Pay!" Rainieri screamed. He talked like Chico, walked like Chaplin, smoked a long not very aromatic cigarette called "Fine" —in his own language close to "the end."

Driving one-handed and waving his cigarette, Rainieri told me, "I love Ahfreeka, I love everybaddy, we all one family, we all one family!"

"Where did you learn your English?"

"Where I learn? Here! Here!" he said in a way that left some doubt as to whether he knew of anyplace else.

It was quite clear that with Mr. Rainieri around, nobody needed to expend any energy. His wife and daughter seemed to hold no opinions. They'd landed in this situation only as observers. I couldn't get them to talk to me, though I could get Mrs. Rainieri to laugh like mad just by addressing her. The son-in-law was soft and plump, sweetly imperturbable, quite silent inside and out. He confirmed everything Rainieri said, but I don't know how he did it.

Whenever I glanced at Augustus beside me, he delivered a whole speech with his talented face—I was a rude child who would lead us both nowhere and I'd be sorry (but as my caretaker he would stick by me to the end and fish me out when I sank myself), and he looked forward to my tormented apology.

In the town of Barla we stopped to give some supplies to Mrs. Rainieri's family. A half dozen of them were sleeping on the walk and may have been there for days. They all jumped up celebrating as soon as Mr. Rainieri's one headlamp lit the buildings. Everybody hugged and kissed. Gifts were handed out. We pulled away. Everyone started to weep. "It's no good in that town," Rainieri assured me tearfully. "I tell them to live my house—come on Gbarnga! But they no. No! No! No!"

We went at a lurching crawl. Each time the van banged into a hole he went berserk with disappointment, which, it turned out, wasn't so strange, since his business was construction and he'd paved much of the road himself. In his unique Italian Creole he talked of his experience here in Liberia, almost entirely unintelligibly, but it amounted to a diatribe against nobody in particular—he blamed nobody for the surrounding chaos—and a lament that with the coming of war, business had stopped, death had ruled the land, and although now the worst was past, Charles Taylor's recovery seemed stalled. "Charles Taylor is good man. I meet him! I like Charles Taylor! He took my D4 Caterpillar. He can have it, he good man. I love everybaddy!"

"Mr. Rainieri, why don't you leave? Go back?"

"To where I go back?"

"To Italy."

"Italy! Italy! I have friends all over—all over Italy! Greece! South America too I got friends!—and they just like me, the same—can't get work! All over same! Nobody no work! I gonna stay here!"

The road got better as we neared Gbarnga. On the outskirts we dropped Augustus at a friend's home. He would find me tomorrow after contacting the press office.

"A good, good, good man!" Mr. Rainieri said of Augustus.

We pulled into the yard of the Rainieri home, a large one-story ranch-style dwelling. Fully a dozen people—servants, family, friends, I couldn't tell—surrounded the van. Our bunch got out and the clan came together in the bare yard laughing and crying. As the unloading began, he introduced me to each of them, and then he showed me around this house in which they camped rather than lived. The walls were solid concrete painted turquoise. Blankets covered the living room floor. Everybody slept below the level of the windows because bullets sometimes went flying through the neighborhood. Nothing in the house actually worked, nothing worked anywhere in Liberia as far as I knew, and we lit our way with penlights and a hurricane lamp. Mr. Rainieri said he had a generator, but he didn't turn it on. During my short visit I didn't speak directly with anyone but him.

He took me into the kitchen and warmed up some pasta on a Primus burner, and we ate while he continued the garbled story of his life. It's not necessary to describe him at length, but I find I want to describe him and even to repeat myself. He hardly had a physical existence, was rather just a cloud-chamber of emotions in which all his hopes and expectations stayed as bright as they'd been on the day he'd arrived—he accepted nothing, expected better, harangued each wrong that blocked him; at the same time his heart rained love. Love for humanity, particularly for Liberians, the people who'd adopted him, the only people who could return his love with matching intensity. He didn't seem aware that he himself existed; meanwhile this large family celebrated him continually. Passions ran over him like an army, one minute his color darkened, ropy veins stood out around his eye sockets, his throat constricted until he crowed his words. Suddenly a joyful thought, and his face popped like a flashbulb and he was smiles and light laughter until, seconds later, the cloud parked over him again and he spoke in the deep tones of prophecy. On top of everything, he was sick. His eyes ran and his voice was soupy. Standing in his dirt yard in the dawn he complained about it, but then a rooster hurried by, chasing a young hen, and he suddenly laughed, all his troubles obliterated by the humor in this small spectacle. "I take you to my restaurant in Gbarnga!" he said. "I have a restaurant!"

As the sun started to bake over the morning, we drove the couple miles into Gbarnga.

The highway was in good shape, but the short main street of this very small town had crumbled back to dirt. Hand-lettered signs announced the stores, the WHAT DO YOU THINK CAFE and the WELCOME TO THE SOLUTION INN and the DON'T GIVE UP BUSINESS CENTER. Mr. Rainieri opened the doors of his Ciao Restaurant and showed it proudly—no mention of the fact that it was closed and probably had never been opened. A rough wooden table, a couple of chairs. I was spared having to comment by some children who came to the door and spoke to Mr. Rainieri.

"Somebody looking you!" he said. "Come!"

Outside, the people on the street stood still, observing a late-model burgundy Mercedes as it raced going maybe sixty to the end of the block and whirled around and raced back to halt quivering before us in a choking fog of dust.

Two big black men leapt from the front doors and came out and shook both my hands simultaneously, one on the left and one on the right. Dress slacks, sport shirts, sunglasses, and purple berets. Perhaps you've seen the movie *The Blues Brothers* . . . They introduced themselves as press officers. I won't even try to pretend to remember their names.

"We're here to take you to the President."

"The President!" Mr. Rainieri shouted, and clapped me on the back. "Go to the President! Good-bye!"

I got into the backseat of their Mercedes and we headed onto the highway at a speed exceeding 100 mph and then screeched to a crawl at a checkpoint. But we didn't stop. The Mercedes nudged against the rope stretched taut across the pavement. A guard spoke shyly: "Please excuse me, sir—"

They sang of their contempt, their weary outrage, in three descending notes—"*Drop* the gate. *Drop* the gate."

The guards dropped the rope as if it packed a jolt, and in twenty seconds we were breaking a hundred again. Finally! People on the move! Serious people! And powerful too: Checkpoints melted away as they approached singing, "*Drop* the gate, man. *Drop* the gate."

We spent the morning driving crazily from place to place without explanation, possibly because I asked for none. Like my press officers, I felt life was complete, the car was enough, everything was arranged. High speeds and bullying the punks at the checkpoints—this was revolution! *Drop* the gate, child, *drop* the gate! After noon we entered a realm of tall rubber trees. Cool suffused light and perfect little golf-course gravel roads, the Firestone rubber plantation, one million acres of tall slender trees. The Firestone people themselves had all left. Now the Revolution owned it. Twenty miles into this astonishing forest devoted to a single life-form we came out from under the trees and into a square mile or more of groomed lawns with a few buildings scattered across them like toys. In the largest building we were met by a servant woman in a white uniform who handed me a dripping ice-cold bottle of Coca-Cola and asked me if I'd like a chicken sandwich. The place appeared to be a huge lodge encircled by rows of rooms—scores of guests might be accommodated here. A chicken sandwich? Electric lights burned in the ceiling high overhead like Christmas constellations. Clean water from a spring that flowed out back. Hot showers, air-conditioned bedrooms. A chicken goddamn sandwich? Why on earth not! In this place I remained for several days before I understood I'd been taken prisoner.

I didn't lack companions. A handful of NPRAG legislators had gathered here, or liked to hang around here, or were also being held here. Just weeks earlier they'd been elected by a process they admitted was hasty but insisted was sincere, and they certainly didn't need to convince me of anything, but they tried. I have all their names written down some place.

One of them, Dr. Sebo, who resided principally in London, had preceded me here by just a day or two. He'd come through Danané.

"How did you get past the police?" I asked him.

"The only way possible: I bribed the Commissaire," he told me, "with a fifty-dollar bill. And when I crossed to Loguatuo—a staff car was waiting though I wasn't expected! What a blessing!"

There was a journalist here named Joseph Baba, a Ghanaian who lived in London and wrote for *Talking Drum*. He laughed when I pointed out we weren't getting anywhere. He'd been here seven or eight days, he said, or nine. He'd lost track. He liked it fine.

And I don't think anybody thought it rude to keep me here, because it couldn't possibly be done against my *will*—what could I lack in this place? There was even an elaborate satellite telephone I was permitted to use to call my wife in Iowa City, Iowa, a place whose very name now sounded like unbelievable nonsense . . . The problem was that the folks from the NPRAG, while extremely polite and genuinely friendly, didn't take me anywhere, although they promised to do so every time I could buttonhole one of them, and I couldn't walk away on my own, because I'd wandered twenty miles deep into a forest tattooed by a maze of small dirt roadways.

All day I drank freezing Coca-Cola and clean spring water brought to me by black maids in white livery. I resided in the great house of a plantation so vast it constituted a region known on the

maps simply as "Firestone." This clearing, and the small habitation
nearby where workers lived, were called Harbel. I chatted often with
the legislators as we partook together of the colonial spirit in this
country which, rarest among all those of Africa, had never actually
been colonized. Dr. Sebo was a fit-looking man of medium size,
physically warm and intellectually vibrant, very winning. He laid out
the situation in Liberia: Elections were done, the land was governed,
order had returned, the youngsters with guns had learned some
restraint—Dr. Sebo himself had witnessed, right in the street, in
Gbarnga, the instantaneous summary executions of three checkpoint
guards for the crime of firing their weapons without cause. Things
were settling down, but the Nigerians had turned their peacekeeping
role in Monrovia into a sporadic nationwide bombing campaign
from the air. Meanwhile the Nigerians ignored the factions troubling
the borders to the southwest, from Sierra Leone, and the Nigerians
themselves contributed to the ongoing smoldering battle at the front,
just this side of Monrovia. Taylor's people held Roberts Field, the
airport, where nothing flew in or out. "The country is irrevocably in
the hands of its people," Dr. Sebo said. "Nigeria has floundered into
its own little Vietnam." The others agreed.

My second night at Harbel, nine or ten of us gathered in my room,
where Dr. Sebo scattered out across my bed a batch of ID cards taken
from dead Nigerian soldiers. The men combed through the cards
with their long black fingers. Max Willie, manager of the plantation's FM radio station, held up one card with a bullet hole through
it. "1969," Max said—the year of that soldier's birth. They started
telling me of Nigerian atrocities against innocent Liberians, but these
tales had come to them secondhand and unsubstantiated and had the
ring of legend. Their enemy was bad, they believed anything of him.

They had closer enemies also. The other government, the one in
Monrovia, supported by the world press and given the slightest nod
by the U.S., had split off from this bunch after the last president's
ouster and violent death. In Monrovia they had a completely different President of Liberia, a man named Sawyer. All these bold
upstarts from both governments knew each other—they'd gone to

good schools together here and there, in London, mostly. But if they had to, they'd kill their former friends. They'd chosen their sides.

Some of this bunch visiting my room hadn't seen each other in a long time, and this was a regular party. To be here tonight made life complete, they were overjoyed, their voices traveled the scale, they began to scream, contraltos and altos singing together as much as talking, lapsing into Creole. They spoke to me of "the wind of change," and I could feel it sweeping upward through this room in a small tornado of good-fellowship, of beery respiration and pomade and cologne and sweat. Yes, people had to be killed. The process of change must be fed with blood. Dr. Sebo illustrated for me, his voice thick with delight— "If I happen to have a boil on my thigh for instance, a boil full of pus, I must squeeze out the poison," working his two thumbs together, performing this operation, getting his shoulders into it, "you squeeze and squeeze, don't you, and you expel the rotten pus—but you're not satisfied you've got the whole of it until you see some blood flowing." I remembered what a local journalist had told me in Sierra Leone as I left on my first visit into Liberia, a university-educated black man in a white dress shirt, shaking my hand like a British schoolboy: "When you come to that land, you must go to its God. And you must make a sacrifice."

Crowded into this room with these men made richly alive by the irrevocability of their choices and the prospect of sudden death, I felt ease and relief. Relief among black people I hadn't done anything to, deeply black Africans whose history omits to implicate me. Of course the sins of the U.S. government touch this region as all regions; but I can repudiate those sins effortlessly. They're merely the sins of people with too much power. I'm not one of those. I didn't wreck this place.

Suddenly Augustus Shaacks stood in the room, bowed and slumped, as if cut down from a hanging-tree but refusing to crumple, his face looking up from the depths of some great wrong, my wrong, my betrayal of him. He'd been staying in town, on somebody's floor. He'd taken me all the way here and then been dropped like a boy and cheated out of this luxury.

"Augustus," I said, ashamed of myself and also hating him for making so much of it, "you stay with me from now on."

Thereafter Augustus ranged around the plantation on my behalf,
trying to get a sense of whether or not I'd ever get going on the magazine's profile of Charles Taylor, an assignment I cared nothing
about now—I just wanted to get free of this place, get back across
the border. Augustus seemed completely sincere in trying to help me
with everything but that. Morning, noon, and night he turned up
and told me, "There is nothing to report."

Max Willie provided me daily with the same report: "There is
nothing to report."

"What am I doing here?" I asked repeatedly.

"Everything is arranged," they said. "We'll report to you again
tomorrow."

At night I fell asleep with the refrains of West Africa playing past
in a kind of mental rondelle: *I forgot to mention. Nothing to report.
Everything is arranged. We have just one small problem. We'll work
out your itinerary and then. . . And then we'll work out your itinerary . . .*

Tall streetlamps surrounded the lodge, and the compound stayed
lit up through the night like a sports event. When the town of Kakata
twenty miles off was rocketed one night by Nigerian Alpha-jets, or
so the reports went, I pointed out to Max Willie and some of the
staff what an inviting target the compound made. Max had just
returned from Kakata, where he'd transferred a load of corpses in
his pickup truck from the demolished areas to the local hospital,
which, understaffed and absolutely without medicines or equipment,
served only the dead. "We'll be dead, too," I pleaded, "if you don't
do something about all these lights." "We can't turn them off," one
of the maids said, "the switch is in the utilities room, and we don't
have the key." I demanded they break the door down and get the
lights switched off before the next batch of Alpha-jets cruised overhead.
The staff, mostly shy young women, couldn't imagine authorizing this
kind of destruction. "Well, how about shooting out the lights?" I asked
Max, who never went anywhere without his Kalashnikov looped to his
shoulder. Max didn't think he had the authority.

My kind of activism made Augustus uncomfortable, too. He wouldn't support my suggestion. The wait-and-see approach won the day. I concluded they probably knew more about their own war than I did.

Somewhere in the second week of my . . . visit, my internment, my quarantine, . . . Max came to me and said, "I have something to report."

Let me say I was astonished. "You do?"

"You're going to go to the President this evening. Please be ready at eight o'clock.

"The President?"

"Exactly, my friend—Charles Taylor!"

"Where is he?"

"He's in Firestone now quite possibly. He's definitely in the region."

About eight-thirty or nine that evening, only a few minutes after Max had pulled up in front of the lodge to take me to the President, as we stood by Max's Nissan Patrol waiting for Dr. Sebo and the Ghanaian Joseph Baba, something like a low wind began off in the distant night and grew closer and closer and became a terrible loud wailing that erased all other sounds—an air-raid siren, I thought. The noise passed right overhead. People shouted, "The plane! The plane!" We heard the *whump whump* of exploding rockets to the east, quite nearby.

There was no drill for this other than that people ran around screaming, "The plane! The plane!" until the explosions stopped. The aircraft's commotion diminished in the distance. The country-side was silent. The ladies of the staff had clumped themselves together under the building's portcullis.

Max said, "Nigeria plane!"

"Where did it hit?"

Augustus said, "They're launching on the village!"

Max and Augustus and I climbed aboard the Nissan Patrol with three young gunmen. We headed toward Harbel Village, two kilo-meters away.

In order not to draw attention to ourselves we drove without head-lights, yet without any trouble, because the sky was clear and the region washed in light from a colossal yellow moon past three-quarters full.

I wasn't happy about the seating in the Patrol—I ended up in the rear, in the middle, the last one out should the Nigerians return for more destruction and spy our vehicle, the only thing moving on the landscape. However, when in just a few minutes we heard the terri-ble noise of the plane coming over us, escape turned out not to be a problem, as I was translated instantly to a point two hundred feet from the car and found myself on my knees, clinging to the trunk of a rubber tree, before I consciously understood that we were under attack. We watched the plane's silhouette against the night sky and watched the pipes lighting up crimson beneath its wings as the rock-ets came. I went deaf. Bits of civilization spilled out of my pockets—penlight, calculator, minirecorder—and into the tiny seething dark-ness under the grass.

The noise abated, the plane vanished, and we collected ourselves, the six of us, with shouts and laughter. We'd come among the shel-tering trees for cover. I believe we were probably in error here, because a near miss might have toppled a few and crushed us.

We drove over to the village. People with small flashlights in their hands wandered up and down the road in the dark among the shacks, exclaiming and weeping and trying to put together a picture for themselves of what had happened.

Nothing had happened. Nobody had been hurt. The pilot had missed the village and hit a large hill without even any rubber trees to suffer for his efforts.

Everybody had a few beers and celebrated, and when we got back to the guest house it was completely dark. Someone, after the plane had gone, had managed to douse the big lamps, and now all of Greater Liberia stood under the moonlight.

The two young men at the checkpoint said rockets had damaged our temporary home. They now had orders to let no one approach and wouldn't let us through, although Max Willie recognized them and called them both by name.

The guard said, "No one can enter at this time."

Max said, "Michael, don't be an ass, man—this American journalist is living at the guest house."

The guard shook his head. "We have our orders, sir."

"He pretends he doesn't know us!" Max said.

"This man is a personal friend of the President," Augustus said. "Do you want me to get the President and he can have a talk with you?"

"Sir," the man said.

"All right. Let's go get the President!" Max said.

"Sir, please, please—"

"Turn it around, we're going to the President now, turn the car around."

"All right!" the guard said. "No problem, please proceed."

The guest house hadn't been hit directly. On one end of the building several windows had burst. Leading us around with a flashlight, Joseph Baba showed us the blast craters out on the lawn. He picked up the fragments of rockets and held them in his gigantic hands and laughed happily. "My room is a mess of glass. Good thing I was downstairs having a beer."

We wandered along the hallway in the damaged wing, kicking through shards of debris intelligently. "What happened to the tall lights?" Max asked.

"The guards shot them out," Joseph said. "Sebo and I insisted. Crying like a couple of babies. They had to do it to shut us up. We made an embarrassing spectacle."

"Let's go over to the radio station," Max said.

"I loathe rocketry!" Joseph Baba said as we left.

Joseph and Augustus stayed behind. Max and I went over in the jeep. The radio station's building lay directly across the spacious commons. We found lights on inside.

Upstairs we met two men seated beside the sound controls in rolling chairs with casters. One, if I remember right, was a colonel, who introduced the second as a major general—a grand figure in his crisp utilities, physically gigantic—both of them extremely drunk.

Max and the driver left me in the company of these two officers and went off to get news about my visit with the President.

We had nothing to talk about but the bombing. "Shall I tell you something?" the major general said. "I want to believe those are American planes." Both men swayed in their places with such pronounced disequilibrium they had to devote some effort to keep from rolling all around the place in their chairs.

"American planes? I don't see how that's possible."

"And why not?"

Why not? Because I didn't want them to kill me. I said, "I don't think the U.S. has any Alpha-jets. I've never even heard of an Alpha-jet before tonight"—hoping my ignorance would equate with innocence—"before about one hour ago."

"Then it was most certainly an American pilot. I'll grant it was very probably a Nigerian aircraft. But the Nigerians don't know how to fly at night. It was one of your CIA pilots."

The colonel leaned forward and stared at me and said, "The major general was educated at West Point."

"We're used to your goddamn meddling," the general said.

At that moment a very skinny young man in a white shirt and dress slacks came up the stairs and introduced himself to me as a subordinate of Max Willie, some kind of assistant around the radio station.

He looked sober. I could see that nothing fazed him, not bombings, not generals.

"I'd like to interview you," I told him.

"Of course. Perhaps we should step out into the evening air."

"You read me perfectly."

"General," the young man said, "with your permission, I'd like to fill our guest in on the situation."

"By all means, straighten this man out," the general said. To me he added: "I think later on I may have to arrest you."

"I don't know," I told him. "I think I might already be under arrest."

He said, "I have nothing but the deepest affection for your country. I spent a little time there in school."

"West Point," the colonel said.

"It's you meddling bastards from the Central Intelligence Agency I can't stand," the general explained.

"Will you excuse us now?" the young man asked. And took me out of there. We stood outside for a while and he spoke to me very articulately, I'd go so far as to say with a dazzling command of the English language, for about ten minutes. The troubled earth is dotted with these suave, impressive young people keeping a friendly contact with reality in its most hopeless places.

Very late that same night, Dr. Sebo looked me up in my room—a communication for me, he said. It turned out to be a satellite phone interview with the BBC, who probably never actually aired it, because I insisted all I could be sure of was that the night's destruction had come down from above. I couldn't identify the culprits. Nigerian bomber aircraft seemed a reasonable guess—but only a guess. Dr. Sebo listened to this, and I don't think he was happy. The NPRAG wanted word to get out to the world. Nigeria's hypocrisy must be unmasked. In the eyes of my hosts, propaganda was my purpose, but I thought it only a matter of time before even the sober ones suspected me of espionage.

After a week or so of half-acknowledged captivity, my status changed. Max Willie and Augustus Shaacks and two gunmen took me places. Who had granted the change I didn't know. I concentrated only on getting out of there. I was no longer the least bit interested in seeing President Charles Taylor. I had already waited for several hours in the night among a small battery of antiaircraft guns, assured the president was just yards away, but never seeing him; I had waited on a dirt road on a hot afternoon listening to a battle half a kilometer or so away, while, they told me, Charles Taylor directed his troops, and he would shortly send for me to view the defeated (but he must have lost, because he never sent for me); and I'd spent one night right up until dawn slinking from place to place around the rubber plantation, stopping and waiting and sending messages back and forth to the elusive President. That is, *I* sent messages to *him,* I sent Charles Taylor brief tearstained notes at each stop, thanking him for his incredible hospitality and regretting that I must leave his land prematurely, leave his land right now, because of pressing assignments elsewhere which I would complete before returning quite very soon to Liberia. In other words: *I coming back.* But I'd never yet seen Charles Taylor.

We traveled in style to these failed presidential rendezvous. Fine vehicles were everywhere, their owners were nowhere. To keep them moving involved dealing with the shortage of petrol. The search for gasoline might take hours. Eventually we'd buy some from somebody, always in an obscure place, an alley in the town of Kakata where the plantation roads met the highway, or from crazy-looking boys living under a bridge by a small river, or in a barroom, never at the gas stations, which were completely out of business, though families camped under their roofs, behind their broken plate-glass windows.

Propaganda was my purpose, but I wasn't helping. As we were friends now, I could joke with my escorts candidly and remind them, "You've lost the propaganda war." We just felt happy driving around, sticking our faces into the breeze like dogs.

Max and Augustus took me to Buchanan Port, the country's major harbor, which the Nigerians had bombed five days earlier. In the noon heat we stood and looked at the charred machinery and buildings and huge shipping canisters blackened and sculpted and spilling out tons of burning, stinking rubber from the Liberian Agriculture Company. Once it caught fire nothing could put it out, and all around us the material smoldered and hissed as if the destruction had brought it to life. Barrels of coffee beans had blown open and lent to the combustion. The Nigerian rockets had missed the 150-foot-tall loading crane they'd aimed for—they always missed. The damp sea breeze swirled around our heads while we traversed tall dunes of burnt coffee and rice from the Catholic Relief Services soaked with water and bulldozed aside. The air smelled like a café from one side of the dock, a car wreck from the other.

I stood around with my notebook while Max and Augustus watched me. I licked my penpoint, though I had never done that before. I wrote, "Oppressive heat."

Max and Augustus came to me early in the morning two days later. "Finally!" Max said. "Finally! Very good news! We're taking you to see the President."

"The president of what?"

Dr. Sebo said, "I'll be going along."

"Where are we going?"

"Bong Mine," Sebo said. "It's nineteen miles due east of Kakata. Charles Taylor has been directing an operation there against a small incursion."

We headed out through Kakata and onto a bush road and then to a bridge, where we spent most of the afternoon waiting only a few scant yards, I was assured, from the spot where President Taylor had his hands full trying to keep forces of a rival faction from overrunning his territory. We could hear the boom of mortars in the distance, like massive firecrackers in massive garbage cans. "He wears a Kevlar helmet and vest," Augustus said. "Yes," Sebo said, "I've seen him. He talks constantly on the radio telephone."

"Has he actually received my request to leave the country?"

"Of course. I certainly believe so," Max said.

After two or three hours we headed back to Kakata without having seen President Taylor, who I was utterly convinced by now had not even been born.

"Sir," our driver said to Max, "it's time for petrol."

For reasons that never became completely clear to me, I spent some hours that afternoon with Max sitting at a bent card table next to a blood-splashed police kiosk out front of the Virgin Disco—and with Francis Brewer, proprietor—observing the main highway through Kakata. We drank Fanta Cola and many beers and Max told me he'd forgotten to mention that Gbarnga, the capital of NPRAG territory, happened to be the sister city of Baltimore. Dr. Sebo came and went, Augustus came and went, the gasoline did not come.

Maybe the battle down the road wasn't going well. A hint of confusion entered the atmosphere. We sat and watched the general populace going up and down the street, up and down the street. Every last citizen was moving, you'd have thought.

Among the pedestrians were a lot of bush people. As I took note of this and of the number of gunmen suddenly all over the place, a dust-streaked guerrilla with a portable launcher on his shoulder and a rocket grenade dangling from his hand caught sight of me and came over to talk, saying his name was Rufus.

Rufus's black hair was powdered with red dust. His eyes looked unhealthy, jaundiced, and added to that they were crimson from the effect of whatever was also making his stare so unnerving and unfriendly. His gaze was steady, but his understanding of his purpose seemed to come and go.

Rufus said, "You know me."

"No, I don't think I do."

"Look again."

"I don't remember."

"Remember better."

"I can't," I said.

"Lofu."

"I wasn't there."

"Yes."

I asked Max and Gus if Rufus was high, and they laughed loud and long, as if it were so obviously true or so obviously false as to make the question hilarious.

After a while, a car cruising past caught his glance, and he turned and flagged it down and jumped in with a lot of other gunsels, and they peeled out down the road.

The voices on the street were a hubbub—louder and more rapid than just a few minutes before. People appeared in growing numbers on the road. The gunmen all around seemed completely unsupervised, roaring up and down the highway in pickups with the tops sawn off, the limbs of wounded and dead comrades dangling over the sides, the boys laughing and screaming. A man with a guitar on his back and a loaded rocket launcher on his shoulder pointed his weapon every which way, shadowing a weeping young woman down the street.

A feeling swept into the town like a palpable wind, a spirit of poisonous fear, it moved, I felt it, it was in one place and not another, it was coming, then it was all around. People thronged the road now, terrified, half-naked bush people carrying nothing with them, exhausted, finished, but still moving, energized by this thing that possessed them.

Sebo insisted we get in the jeep. "I don't like this," he said. He also was infected, I saw it in his eyes and the way he worked his lips. My own heart pounded, and I tasted something awful in my mouth—it had me too—the wind of change—both icy and hot.

An open carrier of gunmen pulled up beside our jeep. There wasn't any reason for them to stop here, and they were blocking our way, but they seemed unaware of us, celebrating madly, howling and laughing.

"I don't like this." Sebo glanced around us. "These boys are full."

I didn't know what he meant. I didn't want them to be full. None of them acknowledged us except for one wounded man who lay in the back of the carrier, with a bloody sweater wrapped around his head. He looked mischievous and quietly delighted and out of his senses. Clearly he thought he knew me from somewhere.

"Ah! This is the captain! I know him."

Sebo jumped out and went quickly to consult with the man and we were on our way.

We plowed slowly through the crowds in the streets, heading for the road to Firestone. Before we'd moved three blocks we heard Alpha-jets and rocket blasts and pulled beneath a widely spreading tree to wait for safety. The raid passed in minutes.

For the next couple of hours we toured the destruction, all of it, several places hit by the forty-millimeter warheads. One had struck a derelict gas station with a sign out front that said, DAY-OLD CHICKS WE SELL CHICKEN FEED. The rocket had descended through the roof just after a man named Joseph Koyio and his family had gathered under it for prayers. It blew out the walls and knocked down a shed fifty meters away, but Joseph's wife and children and brothers and so on, the whole family, twenty-one people in all, had been spared, probably because, as Joseph pointed out, they'd been praying. We spent some minutes gouging shrapnel out of the only item of furniture, a big stuffed vinyl chair.

The raid had been extensive. People had been killed or injured all over town and taken to the hospital, which I never actually visited. "It's something like a garage for expiring persons," Sebo said confidentially.

We waded through the rubble of a corrugated house that had been hit directly by four rockets: Two chopped through the grass and came up out of the floor, two tore through the roof, chasing people through the rooms, blasting holes and tearing polka dots in the walls with shrapnel and scattering hundreds of white pamphlets entitled "How to Know JESUS CHRIST" all over the ground. Bloody belongings scattered everywhere, and trails of blood in the grass as if slaughtered pigs had been dragged across the yard. A couple of dozen people from the neighborhood tagged me closely while I pretended to make some kind of examination and wrote in my notepad, "And I'm the idiot walking around with a pen and a pad and there's nothing, nothing, nothing I can do but this. They think these tears are sweat." I picked up one of the leaflets, which I have in my possession to this day. "My dear friend! Are you born again? Does God's Holy Spirit live within you?" The people crowded around me, explaining that these attacks were unprovoked, these victims were harmless families. "Look at how they have been killed! Look at where they died!" I stood there making notes, notes that said, "I'm standing here making notes in this book as if I have some business here. I'm making notes because they're looking at me. They're looking at me and I don't know what else to do."

The streets were less crowded as we drove out of town toward Firestone. "What happened?" I asked Sebo. "What made them all come running into town?"

"My God, I don't know. We'll have to find out . . ." But we never did.

Very early the next morning I ran into Joseph Baba downstairs under the awning at the Firestone guest house. He stood there flanked by two London-bought suitcases. Joseph Baba was quite a large man with deep black skin, a basso voice, spectacles with thick black rims. He looked like a foreign exchange graduate student. The whole time I'd been here, he'd had the good sense not to do anything at all except to soak up the air-conditioning and eat the food. I myself had sweated through the recent nights with my windows thrown open because I wanted to hear any approaching Alpha-jets. "Time to head home," Joseph told me.

"What? How?"

"A gang of legislators is going to Gbarnga to meet this fellow Gordon-Somers from the U.N. I've slipped in my own request for a car and I'll be heading farther on. To the border."

"I'm coming, too."

I ran upstairs and grabbed my pack and was just getting into a Nissan Patrol with Joseph and two gunmen when Augustus Shaacks came along with Max Willie, and they inserted themselves into my escape—but they didn't prevent it. They just delayed things an hour or so while we discussed the unintelligible pros and cons of everything on earth, and then they came along, too. Meanwhile Dr. Sebo had joined us and we had a full car heading toward the Ivorian border, but perhaps, now, not actually having the border as a stated destination, thanks to these new passengers, and their agendas . . .

We stopped at a small town halfway between Kakata and the border and ate some rice at a cafe. Nothing else, just rice. "Back to journalists' rations," Joseph Baba said.

Neither Max nor Augustus joined us. In fact they took the jeep and disappeared. I stood with Baba and Sebo outside the place for an hour or so, wondering what had happened.

Dr. Sebo said, "I'm sure they'll be back."

"They didn't mention where they were going?"

"They didn't even mention the name of this town," Dr. Sebo said.

"You're not familiar with the area?"

"I'm from Monrovia," he said. "I don't know anywhere else."

When Max and Augustus pulled up in the jeep, they had a rapid, nervous air about them, very uncharacteristic. "Come on now," Augustus said crisply. "We're taking you to see the President."

I can tell you I was dumbfounded—surprised that they could manage to surprise me.

As we drove through town nobody said a word. The feeling in the car was that something of great moment now transpired. We pulled to a stop in front of a garage where young boys lounged among scattered junk. Max Willie got out.

"What is it? Is the President hiding here?"

"We must give them our spare tire," the driver said. "You see," he said, "it's got a puncture."

We spent about thirty minutes on this project and then proceeded about ten miles farther down the highway and turned off onto a track through grassland and into, apparently, a plantation, a region of low banana plants, an ocean of them stretching off toward every horizon.

"I hope we don't have a flat out here," Joseph Baba said. "Those boys at the garage have our only spare."

"When it's fixed, we'll be as good as new," the driver said.

The track took us to lower elevations that might have meant a river somewhere ahead, and down in through a low elfin world of banana plants each about eleven feet tall. We'd come five kilometers or so off the highway when we found a place where the plants thinned out and dozens of men and boys, most of them just tiny children, camped among scattered vehicles, the smoke of their cook-fires hanging completely still in the dim uniform light.

"Yes," Dr. Sebo said. His tone was reverent. "This is the Small Boys' Unit."

"We are quite close now to the President," Augustus said.

"How do you know?"

"Because now we are with the Small Boys' Unit."

Sebo said, "Here he comes. This is the commander, I think."

A grown man, a man about forty, came forward now, led out from the recesses of the jungle by one of the small boys, who'd evidently fetched him to deal with us. Dr. Sebo shook the man's hand and introduced him to us: "This is the captain of the Small Boys' Unit."

"Well, Captain! They're certainly small," Joseph Baba agreed.

"Are they in training?"

"This is the personal bodyguard of the President," Dr. Sebo said. "If we've reached them, President Taylor can only be a few yards away."

That got us all peering diligently into the surrounding murk. But no President appeared from out of it.

I said, "His personal bodyguard? I don't get it."

"Don't you? These small boys are the soldiers Charles Taylor can trust implicitly, you see, because they love him as their father. These are all orphans who sought him out as their only parent. Many of these small boys witnessed the deaths of their entire families, they saw their mothers and fathers cut open from chin to crotch—or worse. Most of them walked here all alone, some of them as far as a hundred miles, to be with the President. They walked here barefoot. But you see them now—now they have shoes."

He waited for some comment. But I couldn't contribute to this conversation, because I had absolutely no idea what to say.

The captain asked, "Would you like to interview a prisoner of war?"

"A prisoner of war?"

"Yes, we have a prisoner of war here with us today, a Nigerian pilot."

"Was he shot down?"

"He infiltrated our border. He were walking in just from Ivory Coast, the area where these people come from."

I turned on my microcassette recorder. They led me around behind a large panel truck where several small boys surrounded a man on his knees with his face in the dirt. One of the small boys was stomping repeatedly on the man's head with the heel of his tennis-shod foot.

I said, "He had infiltrated? The border?—is that the—?"

"Yes."

"Come here!" The captain seemed to be speaking to the captive, although the man couldn't have moved on his own and was only being dragged toward us over the ground by a gang of small boys.

He wore only khaki pants torn off about his thighs. Both his shoulders were dislocated and his elbows pinned together behind him, wrapped with a black rubber strap that then looped around his neck to keep his head pulled far back. As a last gift, his trials had turned him completely permeable, so that the suffering just issued out of him and especially melted up toward us out of his eyes.

He said, "Save me, sah. Please, sah. I beg you."

I said, "When was he captured?" God help me. That is what I said.

His face and head were a mess of bloody knots and oozing lacerations, and some of his teeth had been knocked out and both lips split through. His legs were bound with a hemp rope. His left leg was swollen monstrously and appeared broken at the knee. All of him was swollen, his skin was shiny and yellowish, rupturing in places like a rind.

They raised him up by the strap around his neck to look at me. He said, "Save me, sah. Save me, sah."

"When—when was this man captured?"

"Please, sah."

The captain said to him, "Where you were arrested?"

"He's a pilot."

"Save me, sah."

"When you are arrested?"

"I was arrested at Maryland border."

"Maryland border?"

"Yes."

The captain said, "Where you are from? Nigeria?"

"Yes." He seemed weary with reviewing the particulars. He listed them out as if by rote: Yes, I'm a student, I'm not a pilot, I'm Nigerian, yes, I came from there . . .

"I'm a student in Britain, London—I work for Augustus Martin, Limited . . . got sacked. Because of events I couldn't continue my education again, I came back, I was, I came back to the country. So since then I been fighting to go back, so my girlfriend, who is a Liberian, who is in the U.S.—she went over the same time with me to overseas—she got into United States, I got into Britain.

"So when she heard of my problem, she said, she said—she sent me a ticket Lagos-London—Lagos ticket and a cash of four hundred fifty dollars to get my visa. But the British embassy couldn't give me a visa. They said I have to get a letter from my school. So I got my girl to do it, to try and get me a letter, but that was not possible, so she said I should come over to Monrovia where the visa is easy and they will assist us because she knew about the visa office. So as I didn't have the money to go by a flight to Monrovia, I started to go by flight to Abidjan and then come by road to the end of the border into, into Monrovia. So I was only following the directions I was given as I was coming—so—so, when I got into the border they arrested me. That is—"

The captain said: "You are a liar!"

"—that is true. That is true before God."

Naturally I've had occasion, in the intervening years, to remember this man. Sometimes he fills my memory. The way I remember him he bellows like a steer in the slaughterhouse, his agony is unbearable. And then, listening to the tape, I find it isn't true. On the tape his tone is measured and steady. His mind is focused, every bit of him is focused on getting himself across.

"Now, uh—"

"Excuse me, sah. I will do anything, I have told them anything for them to find the truth to save me cause I don't want to keep on living like this, if they let them shoot me, or let them leave me alive, and then—till every truth is verified. I will do anything, please."

"How, how long have you been –"

"I was arrested on Sunday. Since then I been in the custody of the general, he has taken me so many places, I have made statements, I have signed them, and then last night I was taken to the Kowa base where—all the places I've been taken to I've been —I've been undergoing different kind of tortures, and everything. So . . ."

"And you're a civilian?"

"Yes! I am a civilian! I live in Britain! I have my document in my bag with my ID card, everything to verify my story, so—I—please! Please save me!"

The captain, aware of the tape recorder, conducted his interrogation of the battered prisoner like a man-in-the-street radio interview. "Okay . . . Are you a civilian?"

"Yes! I am a civilian! I was repatriated—"

"—You are traveling in Liberia. Do you know there is a war here? Did your girlfriend advise you not to travel in here because of a war, or were you traveling with your girlfriend?"

"I was monitoring the war, so when they said the Monrovia capital is peaceful—there's no more war there, so I felt that there must be a way to get into Monrovia by hand, that there is route I have to follow so I can go by hand."—Did he mean "on foot?"—

"From which radio station," the captain said, his tone eliding now into that of a prosecuting attorney in a movie trial, "did you hear from them that there's no war in Monrovia?"

"I was watching the TV, so they said an announcement of the ceasefire on the Monrovia capital. So that's what made me to travel."

"Why you cannot travel by ship, because that is the easier—"

"I've never—I didn't know that, I've never traveled by ship, I didn't know—"

"—And what kind of student would say that he didn't know—look—don't tell me—"

"I'm not telling you lies!"

"I am a Canadian," the captain suddenly revealed to his prisoner. "I can show you my passport, everything, I'm from Saskatchewan. You don't tell me any student would say they didn't know from Abidjan to Monrovia. You can't tell me."

"I have never been to—"

"Either you tell me which are you lying—you are not a student."

"Look, I've never been to any West African countries before—"

"You were not born in Africa?"

"I was born in Nigeria."

"So? You have no school in Nigeria?"

"Yes, I did my secondary school in—"

"You didn't take a geography of Africa in Nigeria?"

"I did in my—in my—in my—from high school days, yes—"

"Yeah? Well then how can you tell me you didn't know—"

"Please, sah," the prisoner said to me. "Please, sah, help me, sah, whatever any cost, just to verify the truth, sah, please—"

The captain grabbed his ear. "How can you tell me that you didn't know from Abidjan to Monrovia about a ship?"

"About a ship? You see, since I came back from London, see, to tell you the truth, I've never been following the war or—or knowing what actual—I was so desperate to get back to London. And that's why I can say I was stupid. I didn't check very well."

I held out toward his lips the microcassette tape recorder. "Can you state your name for the—?" There's no sense evading an admission that I was completely out of my depth here.

"My name is Benjamin Ugwu. "

"Spell it?"

"U, G—G is for God—W, U."

A small boy said, "The man lying!"

"No—I'm not lying."

Dr. Sebo stepped in. He didn't like this man. And I could see he was angry with me, too, for interfering. "Didn't you tell your interrogators this morning that you are a pilot?"

"They put me on that type of tortures and say that whatever I'm saying they don't believe me, that unless if I say I'm a pilot, that I came here to bombard, then that's when they set me free. I was doing everything to see that I don't die, I'll be free, or to go under anything they say, I will do. So that was the only thing—but the statements I have made before—signed and everything, when they arrested me— is before God the truth."

At this point I made a bizarre gesture. Around my neck on a chain I wore my photo ID card from *The New Yorker*. I took it off and hung it around Ugwu's neck, loudly and clearly saying his name and saying my name and the name of the magazine and the name of the United States of America: that the magic from these names would stand around him against his misfortunes.

Dr. Sebo was stung by this, attacked by this. "I don't think that is a good idea at all. No, no, no," Sebo said.

I addressed the captain and the multitude of small boys. "When I get back and make my report in the American press—I have to tell you, this is going to be considered atrocious behavior. This man's captors will answer to the United States." I tried to deliver these words in a mild, steady tone of voice that I suspect only made me sound cringing and apologetic.

Sebo kept control of himself but said most emphatically, "No. This cannot be. You must take this card off his neck. This is bad."

Bad. I didn't know bad for who. For Sebo? For me? It couldn't get any worse for Benjamin Ugwu. He'd broken down weeping. "Please, sah, all day they beat me, oh, how they beat me. Tell them please to kill me. Please. Shoot me, or let me go. I don't care if they shoot me. I don't care if they let me go."

Dr. Sebo spoke quietly with the captain in Creole. He came back to me and said, "Please, then. All right. This man is going to be all right, I have the captain's word on that. Just remove your credentials, and everything will be taken care of."

By now I was worried about what I'd done, afraid of my own fate in this place. And I behaved like a man afraid, stooping to remove my card from around Ugwu's neck while he wept.

The captain spoke, and a small boy stepped forward with a big knife. Straddling Ugwu's back he put his hand around the captive's forehead and forced the head even farther backward. I thought he was going to cut his throat. He sliced the black strapado pinning Ugwu's elbows to his neck. The prisoner fell forward, and the small boy cut the bonds around his legs.

"You are going to the hospital now and receive medical attention," the captain told Ugwu. While they arranged space for him in the bed of a pickup truck, I tried to look like I knew what I was doing, going around to the captain, to Sebo, to the innumerable voluble small boys, claiming power to monitor this situation from afar. I don't know whether they believed me.

They put Benjamin Ugwu unbound in the bed of the truck and took him away. What has become of him I have no idea.

For a while afterward we stood around discussing his case.

Nobody seemed to believe the young man's story. I said that when I got home I would call Charles Taylor's American attorney and lodge some kind of protest and write an article which, if it had a happy ending for Benjamin, would help Charles Taylor in the propaganda war. I didn't know what else I could do, except to mention it also to the President himself. "Will we actually be seeing Charles Taylor in our current lifetimes?" I asked Sebo.

"Yes. The captain says we can go now."

"Go where?"

"Go here. To the President. Here."

At this point even more small boys surrounded us, also a lot of gunmen I hadn't noticed before. The captain led us all out of the dell along a path that turned steeply uphill, and within a hundred paces we were trudging up a bare knoll, and then up stone steps toward the back end of a minor mansion standing under a dark cloudscape and looking over the endless sea of banana plants.

We passed over a flagstone patio perhaps half the area of a football field where gunmen, a couple of dozen or more, lounged around an empty swimming pool.

President Taylor waited in a deck chair with his legs stretched out, and he wore a blue-gray jogging suit accented, I believe is the term, with vermilion piping along the seams of the pants and around the crew neck and the cuffs of the long-sleeved sweatshirt. Mrs. Taylor sat beside him similarly posed, wearing a brilliant dashiki. Mrs. Taylor was a large plain friendly woman who absented herself as soon as the introductions were made and we were seated. I put my recorder on the low glass table between us. Joseph Baba sat with us, Dr. Sebo also, but I asked all the questions, and the President did almost all the talking.

Because I didn't know what I was doing and turned the device toward the wind, the recording is almost unintelligible. To the best of my perishing recollection, this is what he told us:

"I started," the President said, "with a shotgun and three rifles and a few dozen men behind me. The first garrison we came to put up no resistance, they ran without a fight. My dear, they thought we had a multitude. It was dark, it was night, and they just assumed.

Their guilt and their corruption magnified their enemies in their sight. Now we had arms to take the next garrison. General Varney and Prince Johnson, seasoned military men, lifelong soldiers, joined our cause. Of course with many of the troops under them. Suddenly we'd become formidable!

"We camped a few dozen miles from Monrovia and fell to arguing about strategy. Colonel Varney and Prince Johnson elected to move in, to take the city. They surrounded the presidential mansion and began shelling here and there randomly and stupidly. It looked like our group would have to move against them. But your American ambassador to the Ivory Coast came to see me in the middle of the night with a bunch from the CIA. Oh yes. They just appeared at our perimeter suddenly from the darkness, out of thin air.

"What your ambassador told me was that if I waited, if I didn't plunge the capital into a bloody battle, the U.S. would back me 100 percent. They and the West African peacekeepers would quickly take care of Prince Johnson, and I would be installed as President of Liberia. So I waited in the bush until the rains started and it was too late to move. Meanwhile Prince Johnson killed the President and the city was divided among the peacekeepers and Johnson's forces, and the U.S. suddenly backed Sawyer as an interim president of Liberia. They lied to me. Why did they do that?

"Prince Johnson? I've heard he's in Libya, I've heard he's a prisoner in Nigeria, I've heard he was killed. Nobody knows. Colonel Varney is with me now. Yes, my dear! I made him a general and he came back to my side!

"Yes. The U.S. is believed universally to be pulling strings, almost Godlike. I'm not a child, my dear. I realize it's a myth. But I tell you now that in the middle of the night CIA people appeared at the perimeter of our encampment—they materialized out of nowhere, like ghosts. The CIA works in mysterious ways. Your government must have approved of our insurrection at first, or how could it have survived? How could any of us have survived? Why would they have allowed me, personally, to go on living?

"I wouldn't even be in this country today if not for the CIA. My escape from the American jail in Boston—I think they must have arranged that. One night I was told that the gate to my cell wouldn't be locked. That I could walk anywhere. I walked out of jail, down the steps, out into America. Nobody stopped me. I came home to Liberia. What was I in jail for? My dear, I don't remember. It was nothing . . .

"Yes, sure, I lived ten years in the U.S. Then I was jailed until the CIA sent me home. The CIA probably had me jailed to begin with."

The President went on to describe his solutions for Liberia: a nationwide referendum on who should rule; a withdrawal of the peacekeeping forces; an ambassador from the U.S. with experience of West Africa and a true understanding of its people. Throughout this interview his manner was relaxed and friendly, except when he described how he'd been deceived by the U.S. government, and then he seemed truly baffled, truly hurt. I asked him about Benjamin Ugwu. He spoke with the captain of the Small Boys' Unit and assured me all was well with the prisoner. He served us drinks and held forth some more and then most graciously dismissed us.

My assignment in Liberia was over. As far as I could see at the time and as far as I can see now, I accomplished nothing.

When we got back to the small boys' encampment we learned that the men of our car had been conserving themselves in the interval, they'd done nothing, in other words, and before we could go anywhere we still had to deal with the jeep's flat spare tire. It was done in this way: The men drove off to town, and we waited with the small boys for a couple of hours or so until the car returned and the men told us the tire was ready to be fixed, although not yet fixed. We then drove to the garage where the men who fixed things waited for us, and after we arrived they commenced; they pried the tire loose from the rim with a crowbar and pulled out the inner tube and patched it, replaced the tube in the tire and the tire on the rim, blew it up with a foot pump, and off we went into the dusk.

"They waste your time," Joseph Baba said.

By now Joseph, Augustus, and I were the only passengers. We traveled with a driver and one gunman. Max Willie and Dr. Sebo had stayed at the President's quarters to wait for a staff car going back to Firestone.

As we rode toward the border I checked the tapes I'd just made and discovered that on a couple of them I'd got nothing but the sound of the wind across the plantation. The sound of the wind across Liberia, across the camp of the Small Boy's Unit. On one tape I found the voice of Charles Taylor. On another the carefully reasoning voice of Benjamin Ugwu.

We reached the fragmented eastern portion of the highway and bumped along through a muggy night under a waning yellow moon. The road was almost deserted at this hour, but occasionally we caught sight of two or three shafts of headlights way ahead: vehicles also going east. Our driver and our gunman discussed this in low tones; I couldn't make out what they said.

At one point it appeared the other vehicles had turned around and stopped on a rise. We gained steadily and came on them, two troop carriers and a jeep, and a crowd of dark silhouettes with guns blocking the road. One approached—a young guerrilla scratching his bare chest with the barrel of his rifle. Our driver switched on our dome lamp.

"Stand by now for General—" the gunman ordered.

The driver sighed.

"Ah, God," Joseph Baba said.

"Who did he say?" I asked. "I didn't hear."

"I don't know. He's staggering drunk," Joseph said as the general ambled over to the car between two of his men. This was not a general we'd already met. This was a general entirely new to us. The general spotted me right away and bawled at his escorts, and they lugged him over to where he could lean about halfway through my open window to introduce himself and acquaint me with his admiration for my country, with his hope, "most decided and strongly profound at this particular moment," that our two countries— "our pair of sister nations," he called them, "might march harmoniously toward a goal of mutual friendship that will be both decidedly mutual and profoundly . . . profoundly mutual . . . and decidedly eternal . . ."

We could hardly breathe in the damp windless night, the stench of rotting vegetation and flowers, the general's liquor-breath, the car crowded around by silent youths not clear at all about what's being said, but understanding that something transpires and they want to be near it, something momentous and yet completely irrelevant to them. Many others had draped themselves motionless in the back of the troop carrier, the sweat on them glistening in our headlights. Great! One more tosspot General Grant! His speech grew tender, inspired, became a love song under the melting banana moon. To keep from slipping away and down onto the ground, he folded his arms on my windowsill and sort of jammed his head sideways against the ceiling of the car. He only gurgled now, and two of his men stepped forward to grip him around the waist, but only to hold him there so he could continue.

At this point our driver intervened, saying, "Please! You two men! We must go! You two men!"

"On with your convoy!" the general said as the men drew him back. "On with your convoy! And carry our message to your—carry once again your message, your message, your message," he said.

We got into the border camp at Loguatuo not long before midnight. I gave Augustus Shaacks two hundred dollars and we parted there, on the Liberian side. He would come along to Danané early tomorrow, perhaps find us at our lodgings and say good-bye again before we left for Abidjan.

Joseph said, "On to better realms!"

Since the day I'd met him nearly three weeks earlier, Joseph Baba had really done nothing to attract attention to himself, done nothing at all, as far as I could see, other than to keep his sense of humor. I didn't know anything about him except that he'd come from Ghana and resided in London and had ended up here at the end of this journey with me.

We walked together across the patchwork footbridge into Côte d'Ivoire. While the sleepy guard at the Ivorian border station turned our passports this way and that in his hands and held them up toward the lamp, we woke a driver sleeping there in his cab who said he'd take us on into Danané. But the guard held onto my passport. Joseph got his documents back, but the guard only flipped through mine over and over and spoke in French about the telephone.

"Why won't he give me back the passport?"

"The soldiers will be coming to take you. I think that's what he meant to say."

"Soldiers?" I said. "What soldiers?"

The guard spoke again, and Joseph said, "What did he say? I couldn't make it out. He said 'gendarmes' I think."

"You don't speak French?"

"No. What about you?"

"He said soldiers again, that's all I know. Soldats? Pourquoi soldats? Pourquoi gendarmes?"

"Something about detaining you," Joseph guessed after the guard had spoken again. Two or three others had turned out from their quarters off among the shanties, and now they all conferred over my passport with the first guard.

"Shit," I told Joseph. "You better just get going."

"No, I don't mind. I'll stay and see they put you right."

We stood around looking at the guard while he operated his telephone. He didn't seem particularly excited about any of this. From that I tried to take comfort. None of the other guards, who now appeared actually to be *guarding* us, knew any more English than we did French.

"I urge you again, Joseph, and I'm not kidding—take the cab and get out of town."

"Well, I don't mind. In any case, so late at night there won't be transport past Danané."

The soldiers came in a giant troop lorry with a diesel engine that could be heard from very far off, approaching through the dark. I climbed aboard beside the driver. Joseph sat on a bench under the tarp in back with one other man. There were only two of them, and two of us. The truck could have carried dozens.

"Avez-vous Anglais?"

"A small bit," the driver said.

"Where are we going?"

"I'm order to go to the police station in Danané."

"The police station? Why?"

"I don't know why."

"Well, I don't know either."

And really, I had no idea. For days I'd been so focused on getting out of Liberia that I'd forgotten how I'd circumvented the Commissaire de Police in Danané; but he hadn't forgotten me.

"You're an officer?" I said.

"No. Just a corporal."

"Corporal," I said. "Save me."

He stayed silent a while and finally said, "I don't know. It's nothing here. Don't worry."

The whole town of Danané was dark as we came into it. Cattle sleeping in the street had to get up and move for us. The entryway to the police station was dark, too, when we pulled up in front of it. "Is it closed?" I asked in hope.

"No," the corporal said. "We'll go there."

"Please. Corporal. Save me."

"If I can help," he said. "But I don't think so."

He took me into the station and spoke in French with the night man, who sat behind the high counter in a purple uniform. Joseph followed us in. The other soldier stayed in the truck. Immediately on turning us over to the desk, the corporal left. For a while the man in purple didn't say a word, but just examined the bulky telephone on the counter in front of him. We waited in the blinking shadow of a fan that turned in the ceiling, giving a grunt each revolution. After three or four minutes the man took hold of the receiver and began very cautiously dealing with the telephone and had a short conversation in French.

He put the phone away from him and said nothing more. Joseph and I kept quiet out of meekness and doubt. After we'd spent twenty or so minutes without a word passing between us, the Commissaire de Police came in with a dapper old gentleman who turned out to be the Mayor of Danané.

The Mayor and the Commissaire started questioning me in

French. I couldn't understand what was being said. "Je ne parle pas français," I told them. The Commissaire, an imposing man with huge brown eyes I took under the circumstances to be full of hate, got angry. "Il peut parler français! Il parle français!" he told the Mayor.

"Je ne comprends pas," I insisted. The Commissaire made a noise of disgust. "Non! Non! Non!" I said.

The Mayor spoke to the night man in purple, who got on the telephone again. I kept an eye on Joseph Baba, standing there beside us at the front desk. By his silence I took it that I should keep silent, too.

Now it became evident we were waiting for something to happen, or for someone to come. Meanwhile the Commissaire spoke a long time to the Mayor, who listened sadly. From his gestures I gathered the Commissaire described our interview in his office some three weeks back, when I'd tried to bribe him and he'd slapped my passport shut and shoved it back at me.

Within a half hour or so a man came in and spoke deferentially in French to the Mayor and the Commissaire, and then greeted Joseph and me in English. He began to translate.

The Commissaire and the Mayor focused, at this point, on the question of the twenty-dollar bribe I'd put into my passport and handed to the Commissaire during our first interview. They had to ask me over and over, because I pretended now to have lost my English, too, and in my panic to think of something to say other than the truth, I very nearly didn't have to pretend. Had I offered money? Had I handed over an American bill of currency? Had I done such a thing? The fan whirled overhead and the lips moved in the ebony and mahogany faces, the voices got louder and angrier as the same question came again and again, until suddenly I told them yes, I'd handed over some money: only because I'd wanted to make a long-distance call to the U.S. embassy in Abidjan—I'd only been offering to pay the toll for the call.

Silence. By the glances among them, I sensed I'd told the right lie.

And how, the Mayor asked through the translator, did the Commissaire react to this offer?

I showed them the two palms of my hands. I brought them together emphatically and shook my head in contempt and disgust, just as I'd seen the Commissaire do while talking only moments ago with the Mayor. "He refused to take it. He absolutely refused and gave it back to me instantly."

The Commissaire's attitude changed magnificently. He didn't look at me, he kept his eyes on the face of his superior, but plainly he saw that the descending hand of fate had missed him.

Next they took my statement. The Commissaire and I went down the dark hallway to his office with the translator, who sat beside me across the desk from the Commissaire. They got out pens and papers and started a long, long interview.

I didn't care what I said. I didn't think there was very much to help me or hurt me in whatever I might tell them. Everything lay in their hands and beyond my power.

Certainly I hadn't forgotten: I had a small fortune in U.S. hundreds folded into tiny strips and secreted in the waistline of my pants. It was too late for bribes. The Commissaire adjusted the large pad of lined white paper on the desk before him and asked me about my purpose and my activities in his country. I told them everything I could remember.

I gave them everyone's name and explained what each one had done without any understanding that these simple acts the Liberians had performed on my behalf were condemnable. No, not these simple acts, but the names themselves condemned them, nothing more than their own names, because in much of the world nothing at all can actually be permitted, and simply to make your existence known is to demand punishment. But none of this occurred to me. I was angry and I wanted to make them work, writing down lots and lots of details, names and dates and places, my every move from the moment I stepped off the plane in Abidjan until I crossed the border three days later. In this way I betrayed every last person who had helped me.

After an hour or so I was done. The Commissaire escorted me out to the anteroom, where Joseph Baba napped sitting upright on the bench. For a while I napped beside him, and then the night man took me back into the Commissaire's office. The translator was still with him. They'd brought in Augustus Shaacks.

He accused me with his eyes. I was speechless. How had they managed to make Augustus Shaacks appear in this room? I thought it was some voodoo trick with ghosts. He didn't seem to have been harmed. He was standing up on his own power with his hands bound behind his back.

To Augustus the translator said: "The Commissaire say do you know this man? Did you guide this man across our border into Liberia in violation of statute law?"

Augustus was outraged. "I never took him across the border! Never!"

"Well?" the translator said to me. "Did this man Augustus Shaacks guide you into Liberia in violation of statute law?"

"I'm sorry, no, no, no," I said, understanding now what a horrific blunder I'd made, the latest of many, many blunders. "He merely accompanied me around town to assist me. Here in Danané. He didn't cross the border with me. I crossed the border alone. If I gave any other impression, it was false."

The Commissaire understood. He nodded. The translator turned Augustus around. The Commissaire leaned over the desk and unlocked the handcuffs. Augustus left quickly by the rear door out into the yard and I never saw him again.

I went back and sat on the bench. The Commissaire, I realized, had done me a favor. I'd backed his denial that he'd taken a bribe from me, and in return he'd prompted me to retract part of my statement and get my guide released.

I pondered this. I now determined that the Commissaire was demonstrating that I should lie. That I should have lied from the start. That the only proper thing I'd done all night was to lie.

Our translator came along and told us we could go, but I wouldn't get my passport back until my statement was ready for review. Nothing more would happen until daylight.

It was well past 4:00 A.M. The hostels were closed. Joseph and I lay on our packs under a vendor's awning, which we shared with a herdsman and his wife. At dawn we woke to the commotion of a goat chasing a dog away from her kid. We went inside the station and sat in the anteroom, where the same desk officer presided. Behind him ran three rows of lockers made of wood and chicken wire for prisoner's belongings—nearly empty, but the jail seemed full mainly of Liberians being arrested and released capriciously on a nonstop basis as the morning wore on and the town came to life.

Petty officials arrived for work, and the place echoed with the squawking of wooden chairs on the floor. The green shutters in the offices stayed open to the light and air—when someone went in or out they left the rusty metal door open until a breeze slammed it shut. Around 10:00 A.M. a new desk officer came on. As an experiment, I asked him for my passport. He actually took it from a drawer and looked at it, and I held my breath. He didn't give it back. He said I had to wait for the Commissaire, who was at home, asleep, as might be expected.

I hoped I wouldn't go into the cell. It had a thick wooden door with a dozen one-inch air holes punched in it—like a woodshed door, nothing more—and two metal bolts across it. It must have been hot in there—the prisoners were dripping wet with sweat when they came out, blinking and squinting because the cell was lightless. None of them wore anything more than a pair of shorts. All were men. Each came out looking as if nothing much concerned him. A boy in green shorts came out and was taken into one of the offices by a cop in khaki—later a second cop went into the same office and I saw the boy in there on his knees on the floor beside the desk. His interrogator ignored him, took care of some paperwork, his face blank.

The Commissaire arrived about eleven, and I was brought to his office again. He rubbed his face and stared at me a while. I could see that I disgusted him, also that he pitied me. He said the report of my activities would be typed in triplicate and I would be asked to sign all three copies.

I realized I didn't know this man's name. I asked him, but he refused to tell me. He shook his head. "You won't tell me your name?" I said. He just shook his head.

The Commissaire took me back into the anteroom, where a dozen half-naked Liberian men now stood in a line with their hands bound behind them. I recognized Lincoln Smythe among them. They all stared at me with sorrow and rage as I passed by.

Joseph and I sat in the yard beneath an acacia next to a trash pile and ate bananas we bought from a vendor.

I told Joseph I didn't think the Liberians would be held for very long. I rehearsed for him the details of how the Commissaire had helped me get Augustus released. It comforted me to go over it all several times.

"This is a hard country. It's a hard country. It's a hard land," Joseph said, "Ah, it's a hard country," his voice deep and kind like God's.

I'd come to this place and I was not whole enough or real enough to accept its terms. "Save me," it says and you want to. "Shoot me" it begs and you think, wouldn't that just be the best and quickest thing? I'd given a statement in English which would be presented to me in French and which I was supposed to sign without any idea what it said. Everyone I'd dealt with, and everyone *they* had dealt with, had been arrested. The Commissaire de Police wouldn't speak his own name.

We watched orange-headed lizards about half the size of squirrels playing in the red dirt and hopping through the trash piles. A banana peel flying out the window missed the trash.

"Nice shot."

"He's starting a new pile," Joseph said.

A white van carrying four white men stopped out front of the station. They were Americans, missionaries, Southern Baptists with Southern accents.

"It won't take but a minute, Bob," I heard one say.

I approached the one called Bob, who waited alone by the van while the other three had gone inside. I introduced myself and told him I was a confused American and I didn't know how much trouble I was in and I didn't know what to do. In tears I beseeched him to talk to God about this.

Bob was about thirty, tall and thin, not at all impressed by my emotion, having seen, I was sure, many people in much more horrible circumstances. He took me around the corner of the building, out of sight of anyone else, and stood close to me and bowed his head and said, "Lord, this is Denis, a stranger and a sojourner and your very own child, your child in need of guidance, your child in need of strength. Help him to find what to do now. Lord we thank you for your providence, your guidance, and your sacrifice, all this we do in Jesus' name amen." Green lizards crawled over our feet while he prayed. Red-headed lizards ran by on two legs like Martians excited to be landed on our world. I wept, I snuffled. I was right to call myself confused.

For a while I held out, demanding to talk to the U.S. embassy, but nobody called the embassy, and anyway I'd visited several countries, never gotten any help from our officials, and had long ago ceased expecting it; and at the end of the day I signed the unintelligible statement. The young man who'd typed it handed me the original and two carbon copies, the last of which was too faint to read in any language. I thought this would be my copy, but I got no copy at all. However, the Commissaire gave me back my passport, and I was released. It was too late to find transport out of town. Joseph and I went to a hotel to get some rest before leaving the next morning.

Halfway through our supper, policemen came and arrested us again, both of us. They took us to the station, where this time both our passports were confiscated by the Commissaire himself, who explained that he'd been instructed to contact the Minister of Communication in Abidjan concerning our case.

"Our case?" I said. "This only concerns me. Mr. Baba is just standing by as a friend."

The Commissaire explained sadly and wearily that, as journalists, Joseph and I both needed official documents from the Ministry of Communication in Abidjan. We would have to provide letters from the magazines we worked for. These would be faxed to the ministry, and perhaps permission to act as journalists in Côte d'Ivoire wouldn't be too long in coming back.

The New Yorker had provided me with such a letter, but from the *Talking Drum* Joseph had nothing. Without comment the Commissaire took what we could give him.

We spent the night at the hotel we'd found, quite a good one by local standards. At supper Joseph told me it was a very bad thing the Ivorians had taken his Ghanaian passport. The U.K. had granted him a special visa and status as a political refugee, because the Ghanaian authorities wanted him. Some years before, as a young Air Force officer, Joseph had participated in a plot against the regime. The plot had been exposed and the plotters sentenced to death. Joseph had escaped with his life. Should these Ivorians decide to get him off their hands by deporting him directly to Ghana, that would be the end of him.

The next morning, having faxed my credentials to the Ministry of Communication, the Commissaire returned our passports and let us go. Apparently he'd done us the favor of failing to mention Joseph to the ministry. We thanked him profusely, giddily, while backing rapidly out the door and into the street.

We collected our packs at the hotel and headed down the road walking. Any bus, any car for hire that passed, we'd get aboard. Right now we only wanted to be moving away from here.

Before we'd reached the outskirts of Danané, two policemen riding together on one small motorbike cut us off and demanded our passports and told us we were under arrest and took us back to the center of town.

This time we bypassed the police station and went instead to the offices of the prefecture in another building, somewhat more modern and presentable than the station, in a part of town we hadn't visited. Our policemen ushered us into the offices of the Prefect himself, a small elderly man who, at this moment, presided over a gathering of ten or so people, every one of whom I recognized. Here were the Commissaire, and the boy who'd erroneously stamped my passport my first morning here, and the various officers who'd manned the desk during our visits to the station, and the man who'd done all the translating. Here were the Mayor and the four policemen who'd arrested us, counting the two who'd just escorted us in, who seemed to be expected to participate in what was about to happen, which seemed the sort of thing, while its precise nature was cloudy to me, that would begin with a speech.

The Prefect spoke. The translator translated:

"A new regulation will now be enacted among the people of our prefecture—"

As he delivered his remarks, the Prefect moved from one to the other of those present, and as he singled each one out for attention, that one's eyes boiled in his head and he withered discernibly, became sick in his features . . . A swift contamination had set out from my transgression, and everyone was at fault now, not just me. I'd broken the only rule, and in breaking the only rule I came to learn it: that when questioned by officials I must never speak of actual facts. I must traffic only in fictions. These fictions will be judged according to their usefulness to the interrogators in the very short term. The interrogators just have to have something to transmit when they, in turn, will be questioned, something that exonerates them from blame and allows them to fade from the sight of their superiors. Something they can give over and then get out—

"Never again shall any journalist, or person of foreign origination, be permitted unofficially to cross our border with the nation of Liberia.

"Never again shall any official of our prefecture put any kind of such stamp in any foreign passport to allow such passage, unless and until our regulations are satisfied in full, including and most especially our new regulation. To wit:

"All journalists appearing in this prefecture shall present themselves immediately to the Commissaire de Police, who will transmit knowledge of their presence most immediately to the Mayor and to the Prefect. Said journalists shall present to the Commissaire, the Mayor, and the Prefect, each one of them a legible copy of their credentials from the news organization by which they are employed to be working in this prefecture.

"Gentlemen: You will now indicate your understanding of this regulation by signing it in my presence."

While Joseph and I sat side by side in chairs, like a small audience, the officials present formed a line, and each approached the desk in his turn, took the pen from the Prefect's assistant, signed his name, handed back the pen, and made way for the next signer. When all were done, the Prefect raised the document before his face and examined it carefully. He handed it to his assistant and said something that wasn't translated. The assistant bore it away to another part of the building. We waited in utter silence. In five minutes' time the assistant returned with multiple copies of the document and handed them out to everybody but me and Joseph.

"And now, dear sirs," the Prefect said to us through his translator, "you will please present to me the documentation from your respective news organizations, and your obligations to our prefecture will be complete."

I handed over to the assistant a copy of my letter from *The New Yorker.*

"Please excuse me," Joseph said, looking rapidly between the Prefect and the translator, "but I'm sorry to tell you I haven't got such a letter."

A great sadness descended onto the room, a terrible mute depression of palpable weight. For a long time nobody said a word.

After some moments the Prefect said to me in English, "Thank you, Mr. Denis Johnson of *The New Yorker* magazine. We have in our possession your documentation. You are dismissed."

"I'm very grateful, Your Excellency," I said, my heart ramming around inside me, "and I wish to apologize for this inconvenience caused by my ignorance—"

"You are dismissed. Thank you."

"—and by a lack of respect for your institutions which resulted, please believe me, only from a childish haste to accomplish my mission within the deadline set for me by my employer. Mr. Baba and I will now go."

"You are dismissed."

Joseph said, "And we're both dismissed?"

The Prefect spoke briefly, reverting to French.

"Most unfortunately," the translator translated, "you, sir, Mr.

Baba, must remain in detention until such time as your documentary obligations are fulfilled."

The cops took us back to the station and gave me back my passport and sat Joseph down on the bench again in the anteroom.

"Oh my God, Joseph," I said.

"It's a hard country," Joseph told me. "They waste your time." I have to say, he didn't seem particularly put out.

"I'll wait around for you. Maybe—"

"I can't get through to *Talking Drum* while the telephone strike is on. The best thing you can do is get back to civilization and make some calls for me, get the magazine to send a fax."

I was immensely happy that he suggested I leave. I'd been willing to stay only because I realized I'd hate myself later for going. But I wanted to leave, nothing more.

Neither the Commissaire nor the Prefect would reveal the numbers of their fax machines, a policy which, though utterly incomprehensible, might have been expected.

"Oh well," Joseph said. "At some point along the way, see if you can get through to the compound in Liberia. Maybe a message delivered overland from the NPRAG would do the trick. They can put together some kind of credential package for me."

I gave Joseph four of my one-hundred-dollar bills. I hoped he'd be able to bribe his way out of this. We shook hands and I left him standing there in front of the prefecture's offices.

I hired the first car I could find. The driver had to spin the steering wheel several times completely around in order to change the car's direction just a little. We made it only a half-dozen miles out of town before the car broke down. I paid him and got out and hailed a passenger van. I took the van to the next town and hired a car that took me directly to the airport in Abidjan. When I got to Paris I tried to make calls from there on Joseph's behalf, but without success, because the hour was late. I called the States and put my wife to work making calls to the compound at Harbel, and to London.

On the plane out of Orly in Paris, the woman sitting beside me turned to me and said, "My hand is going to fall off."

Do you think I blinked at that? No, I didn't. It was a little bit longer before I blinked at anything.

On the tray-table before her she had a stack of cards and envelopes. She'd been busy writing and addressing Christmas cards the whole flight.

If nothing went too wrong, I'd get home to my family just in time to wake up with them on Christmas morning. I'd been gone hardly longer than three weeks.

When I got back to the States, I joined them in North Idaho for the rest of Christmas break. Snow covered the mountains.

Why did I go to Liberia? What was I thinking, why did I do it, why? I don't know. I don't know.

I called my editor at *The New Yorker* and told him I'd gotten nothing for him. I said I was keeping what was left of the magazine's expense money and they could come after me and try and get it if they wanted. I hoped they'd try.

I was no help at all to Joseph Baba. I never got through by phone to the NPRAG at Harbel. I had the wrong number. My wife spent hours on the phone to London, but the only *Talking Drum* magazine she could locate claimed never to have heard of any Joseph Baba. He must have been a spy.

I called Charles Taylor's stateside attorney in Washington, D.C., and told him I was writing a tremendous article that would pivot around the fate of Benjamin Ugwu, and he should check on Mr. Ugwu's condition and make sure he was released. I never heard one way or the other.

All through the Christmas break and for some days after I returned to Iowa City, I called Joseph Baba's London phone number frequently, and eventually got through to him. He'd spent ten days in Danané as punishment, I'm tempted to believe, for his kindness to me.

DENIS JOHNSON is the author of *Already Dead*, *Jesus' Son*, *Resuscitation of a Hanged Man*, *Fiskadoro*, *The Stars at Noon*, and *Angels*. His poetry has been collected in the volume *The Throne of the Third Heaven of the Nations Millennium General Assembly*. He is the recipient of a Lannan Fellowship and a Whiting Writer's Award, among many other awards for his work. He lives in Northern Idaho.